The warrior merchants

The warrior merchants:
Textiles, trade, and territory in south India

MATTISON MINES
Department of Anthropology, University of California, Santa Barbara

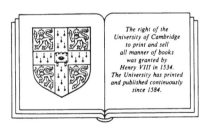

The right of the
University of Cambridge
to print and sell
all manner of books
was granted by
Henry VIII in 1534.
The University has printed
and published continuously
since 1584.

CAMBRIDGE UNIVERSITY PRESS

Cambridge
London   New York   New Rochelle
Sydney   Melbourne

CAMBRIDGE UNIVERSITY PRESS
Cambridge, New York, Melbourne, Madrid, Cape Town, Singapore, São Paulo, Delhi

Cambridge University Press
The Edinburgh Building, Cambridge CB2 8RU, UK

Published in the United States of America by Cambridge University Press, New York

www.cambridge.org
Information on this title: www.cambridge.org/9780521105019

First published 1984
This digitally printed version 2009

A catalogue record for this publication is available from the British Library

Library of Congress Cataloguing in Publication data
Mines, Mattison, 1941–
The warrior merchants.
Bibliography: p.
Includes index.
1. Kaikōlar. 2. India, South – Economic conditions.
3. India, South – Social conditions. I. Title.
DS432.K17M56 1984   306'.09548   84-5899

ISBN 978-0-521-26714-4 hardback
ISBN 978-0-521-10501-9 paperback

For Morris E. Opler and C. Natesan

Contents

Preface   *page* ix
Maps   xii

1. Introduction   1
2. The Kaikkoolars of Tamilnadu   11
3. The Kaikkoolars and the iDangkai (left-hand) and
   valangkai (right-hand) castes   33
4. Kaikkoolar beliefs and the order of their social world   51
5. The naaDu system   73
6. The caste association: the Senguntha Mahaajana Sangam   99
7. Caste, politics, and the handloom weavers' cooperative
   movement: 1935–1971   121
8. Interpreting the Kaikkoolars today: models of caste,
   weaving, and the state   143

References   164
Glossary   169
Index   173

Preface

What do we learn about south Indian society by studying weavers? South Indian society has been for millennia a commercial society in which textile production and trade have played a prominent role. Yet the images that India conjures up in the minds of scholars are rarely of artisan production and trade; rather, India is perceived as a rural society characterized by provincial villages and interdependent castes organized by agrarian production. These images ignore the weavers who even today form the second largest sector of the south Indian economy. They also largely ignore the interplay between these different sectors of the economy and the south Indian and colonial states that benefited from them. The image of Indian society that emerges is highly local.

The study of the Kaikkoolar weavers in Tamilnadu reveals that this provincial image of Indian society is misleading. The Kaikkoolars have been organized for centuries into supralocal organizations and have been engaged in commercial, often international, trade. As such they have been both a source of wealth for states and, at times, an independent power with which to reckon. In medieval times, they maintained armies not only to protect their warehouses and caravans but also to plunder the agrarian sector. Until the mid-1920s, weavers engaged in constant competition with the dominant agriculturists for status and for control of their regions. Only occasionally were they able to rival the agriculturists' power, but for centuries they maintained a separate locality-segmented confederacy called the seventy-two *naaDu* and a distinct ritual and status identity in the context of the symbolic division of Tamil society into right-hand and left-hand sections. Both systems have left a legacy of their former importance in the character and shape of modern Tamil society. Much of the Kaikkoolar's naaDu sys-

ix

tem still survives in the Salem District. These council territories are one of several corporations used by the Kaikkoolars to organize their affairs in south Indian polities and to act as institutional bases for caste leaders.

The Kaikkoolars are one of the major weaver castes of south India. The description of their identity and organization requires us to modify our anthropological image of Indian society. This account presents evidence that the Kaikkoolars are integrated differently from the interdependent agriculturists, in part because of the political and economic importance of textiles. Although at the local level weavers and other artisan-merchants appear to have an indistinct status that reflects their separation from agrarian castes, they have impressive supralocal organizations, which they use to administer their relations in trade and to structure their affairs with polities.

I owe many thanks to many people and institutions that helped me in researching and writing this book. The American Institute of Indian Studies funded my research among the weavers during 1978–1979. My gratitude to the institute is not only for research funds, but also for the considerable hospitality its officers extended to my family and me during our stay in India. Special thanks must also go to the members of the staffs of the Department of Anthropology and the Social Process Research Institute at the University of California, Santa Barbara: to Paul Heuston, who drew the maps, and to Rose Mucci, Doris Phinney, Roxann Rowsey, and Deborah McGrath, who prepared the manuscript on a word processor. I thank them for their patience and skill. I also wish to thank Jeffery Serena, who assisted in editing the manuscript. A special note of appreciation is due to the people who read and commented on the manuscript in its earlier versions. Morris E. Opler, Pauline Kolenda, Donald E. Brown, Elvin Hatch, Eugene Irschick, Albert Spaulding, and Arjun Appadurai all devoted many hours to these tasks. The book was enriched and improved by their efforts. Finally, I wish to express my special appreciation to C. Gourishankar, whose photograph graces the dust jacket.

To my Indian friends and informants, my debts are legion. To all of them I offer my deeply felt thanks and appreciation for their assistance, information, hospitality, and friendship. Especially important to my research were my colleagues at the University of Madras: Professor D. Sundaram of the Sociology Department who always showed an interest in my work, Professor N. Subba Reddy of the Anthropology Department, and Professor C. Balasubramaniam of the Tamil Department. I also wish to thank Dr. Partap C. Aggarwal, critic and friend—I need a good critic now and then—Suddesh Aggarwal, friend and superb cook, and C. Natesan. A Tamil scholar in his own right, Natesan has over the years been my guide through the complexity of Tamil society and a special friend. His wisdom has helped me innumerable times.

M. Natarajan sacrificed his own time on many occasions and created marvelous contacts for me. B. Shaktivel was my compatriot and alter ego as my research assistant. In Akkamapettai my many-time host was C. Manikam and his family; in Erode I owe a special note of thanks to R. Lakshmanan and A. Muthuswamy; in Trichengode I especially wish to thank Kasiviswanthan. To all of these people and to more than those I name here: I thank you for innumerable kindness, your friendship, and your enthusiastic assistance in my work.

Finally, with special affection, I thank my wife, Barbara, who in a thousand ways made field work possible, and my daughter, Laurel, who when asked what she thought of Madras City, replied: "it's neat—just like Los Angeles."

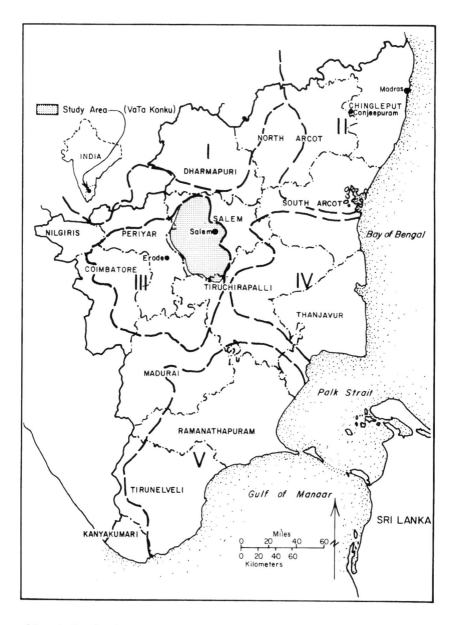

Map 1. Tamilnadu State. The traditional microregions of south India are: I. Kar MaNDalam; II. Tondai MaNDalam; III. Konku MaNDalam; IV Chola MaNDalam; V. Pandiya MaNDalam.

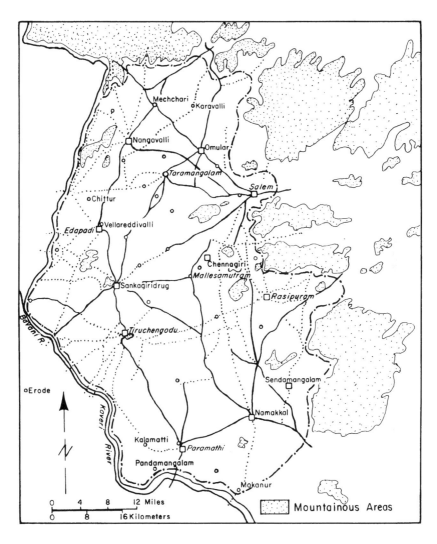

Map 2. Fair Towns, Kasbas, and periodic markets 1750–1800. VaTa Konku and the location of the Seven-City Territory (EeRuurunaaDu). Seven-City Territory council towns are italicized. (Adapted from Murton 1979:23–24.)

1 Introduction

India is an ancient civilization and consequently immensely complex. Jumbled into India's present is a medley of traditions and contrasts with which Indians appear to be eminently comfortable. As an anthropologist working in south India, I have often felt that our accounts of contemporary Indian society fail to convey a sense of this fascinating complexity of myth, history, beliefs, and a heritage of state organizations, or even to convey a full sense of the manner in which castes are integrated into the state societies in which they have existed for thousands of years. This book is about the complexity of south India. How do all these elements – caste, history, beliefs, and state organizations – fit together?

This study is oriented by four questions. First, *what do we learn about south Indian society by studying artisan-merchants?* Most studies of south Indian society focus on agriculturists and their dependent castes. In so doing, they tacitly ignore the artisan-merchants, who form the second largest sector of the Indian economy, or treat them as anomalous actors in an agrarian-based world. This book presupposes the importance of the artisan-merchant castes in understanding south India's complexity, and focuses on one such community, the Kaikkoolars, who are an ancient weaver-merchant caste living today predominantly in Tamilnadu State.

How is our image of south Indian society altered when we take a regional perspective? Most anthropological studies of India focus on highly localized village communities. I worked not in a single locality but within a number of localities in a traditional area of south India. This study is an examination, therefore, of weaver-merchants in the context of the organization of a region.

What role have state/local relations played in the organization of south

Indian society? I have found that weaver-merchants change their organization in response to changes in the state that affect regional administration. They do so in order to conduct the supralocal affairs that are an important aspect of weaving, itinerant trade, and state administration. Significantly, the organizations of weaver-merchants reflect their integral roles in the fragile kingdoms of the past and the bureaucracies of the present.

How does the study of artisan-merchants modify models of Indian caste society? Anthropological models of Indian society are usually based primarily on the behavior of agriculturists and their dependents, and seem unable to account for the behavior of castes whose organization is in many ways independent of the agrarian-based system. Integrating these castes into our models requires that we rework our understanding of Indian society.

Nearly all caste persons in India can relate tales of their castes' past greatness. In south India, many speak of their service to great kings and generals; they point to ancient eulogies of kings and courts and sometimes castes. Those with a warrior heritage relate with relish stories of their courage and sacrifice, loyalty and fierceness. They tell of their honors and titles, of their caste gods and sponsorship of major *pujas* (religious rites), and sometimes of their control of temples and temple offices. The traveler in south India encounters fortlike temples in which ancient inscriptions have been cut, telling of donations and endowments and of the persons and villages that offered them. There are references to kings and to the special rights granted to castes. One observes the symbols of bordering kingly states cut into the rock of medieval temple pavilions. Clearly, Indians give eminence to their temples and kings, to their own pivotal roles in states, and to their antiquity and heritage.

The complexity of contemporary Indian society is enhanced by its contrasts. Folk beliefs contrast with the traditions of Brahmanical Hinduism; fierce, small gods with benevolent high gods; and blood sacrifice with vegetarian customs. There are kingly caste traditions of dominance based on control of land and armies. These kingly traditions, which emphasize conquest and human sacrifice, contrast sharply with the Brahmanical castes' traditions that maintain priestly superiority, emotional restraint, vegetarianism, and priestly functions. Yet other castes mix elements of these schemes and stress autonomy and comparability in status to the highest ranking of the kingly and priestly castes. There are also the contrasting heritages of past kingly states, colonialism, and contemporary democracy. Forts and ruins spot the south Indian countryside, and fortlike temples mark communities and larger social domains. There are epigraphs that speak of great mercantile associations and of artisan and mercantile armies. Land control and commerce intermingle in the realms of former kingdoms and form an intriguing potpourri in contemporary south India. What imprint does this legacy of kingly states, of myth and history, and of agrarian-based dominance and warrior mercantilism have on the organization of contemporary society?

Indigenous Indian social theory holds that Indian society is organized around agriculture and a Brahmanical interpretation of the social order. Accepting this theory, anthropologists argue that landowning castes integrate the society politically and economically through their employment of dependent non-Brahmans, and ritually through their adherence to a hierarchical interpretation of society that ranks castes by degrees of ritual purity. In south India, the secularly powerful Brahmans provide the ideological basis of this order through their ritual acts as priests when, in the course of ritual performances, they symbolically reinforce this interdependent caste hierarchy. Together, Brahman and non-Brahman landowning castes and their dependent service castes form an integrated, hierarchical, locality-delimited caste system. Landowners command an array of economic and ritual services from the castes of their community. Carpenters, blacksmiths, potters, priests, barbers, washermen, and agricultural laborers all perform services in exchange for a share of agricultural production. Service castes are ranked subordinately to castes to which they render services, whereas other castes rank above those they can command.

But not all Indians participate in this integrated, interdependent social order. Artisans and merchants are frequently independent of the landowners' control, although they engage in production and trade aimed at servicing agricultural villages and indeed may live in these villages. However, many live in cities and towns that function as hubs of local and regional trade networks, serving a local rural area. Indigenous social theory is largely silent about these castes. Although the artisan-merchant castes are not as numerous as the populace integrated by agriculture, their economic and social significance has at times rivaled that of the agriculturists. The artisan-merchants are the producers of textiles, gold ornaments, and sculpture. They also include castes that produce blacksmith and leather goods. Together these castes draw around them an array of service castes such as barbers, washermen, traders, untouchables, and even some landowners. Among these, some serve and others ally themselves with the artisan-merchants to gain support in their opposition to more powerful agriculturists. Together these castes form a loosely integrated system of castes that roughly mirrors the system of their agriculture-based counterparts, but without the latter's characteristic interdependence. The importance of this dichotomy among the castes in south India was regularized ritually and socially by the formal conceptual separation of the two categories of castes. The agriculture-based castes were designated the "right-hand castes"; the artisan-merchants and their allies were called the "left-hand castes." These castes worshiped separately, lived separately, and took different symbolic insignia as signs of their identity. They were often rivals in the pursuit of status and power.

The left-hand castes are important for several reasons. Their economic behavior has generated a separate source of wealth, and so a power base separate from that of the agriculturists. They have been more mobile, less tied to a specific locality, and through their trade networks they have helped to link the settlements of agriculturists. They have also provided the wealth and commodities important to foreign trade. Not only have they produced and traded products essential to local inhabitants, but they have also proved to be a source of revenue for polities, and political leaders have sought to control them. Their trade networks distribute goods to rural areas and act as channels through which local products are traded up and out of a region. In ancient times, some of the left-hand castes maintained armies to protect their trade and formed large associations to administer their interests (Hall 1980). Unlike the agriculturists, their associations involved supralocal organization in order to administer interlocal relationships that arose from their itinerant trade. The left-hand castes' organization and economic independence made these castes a locus of political power rivaling that of the agriculturists. The importance of the left-hand castes is reflected in their rivalry for status with the right-hand castes and in the special ritual status they were accorded by Brahmans and kings in the historic past.

Clearly, a description of Indian society that ignored this important sector of society, the artisan-merchants, would be incomplete. Yet on the whole, accounts of artisan-merchants do not form a part of the image of Indian society projected by anthropologists.

Anthropological descriptions of India portray it as a land of agricultural villages in which traditional urban society is "basically similar to village society" (Mandelbaum 1970, vol. 1:9-10; see also Pocock 1960; Lynch 1967; Marriott 1968; Dumont 1970b:224). With four-fifths of India's population living in villages, it is only natural that anthropologists have focused their field studies on village life, or occasionally on particular castes or rural-urban relationships. In the images of society that emerge, caste organization and kinship are the basic components, and control of land is the basis of power relationships within the village locality and the source of traditional urban dominance. "Land is the most important possession, the only recognized wealth, and it is also closely linked with power over men" (Dumont 1970b:156).

Politically dominant castes control land and the services of other castes. This control determines the patterns of interdependence among castes and local caste ranking. Caste as a hierarchical system is limited to a single village or a few linked villages (Kolenda 1978:40-41). Localism and the self-sufficiency associated with it produce "a *tendency* for regions to close in on themselves, a tendency sufficient to differentiate the regional systems, but not sufficient to shelter them from external influences and upheavals" (Dumont 1970b:156).

The image of Indian society that emerges is provincial. The impact of state organization is described as remote and only indirectly felt in the countryside. The significance of commerce and mercantilism is given little consideration. Localism, an agrarian-based economy, and the political and economic interdependence of the people living in these small village worlds prevail. Each caste within a locality is recognized as having a traditional occupation and a ritual status that reflects its place in the local social system.

The localism of this small world is also reflected in the fundamental organizational role of kinship. Each subcaste of a locality is an endogamous descent group. The descent organizations of the locale's dominant caste and its other high-ranking castes form the basis of local organization and the local judicial-political organization (Mandelbaum 1970, vol. 1:273-293; Fox 1971; Beck 1972; Kolenda 1978). Descent organization is seen to form the basis of ties with higher levels of political organization in some parts of northern India (Fox 1971), but in south India kinship seems to organize only narrowly delimited territories (Beck 1972:78ff). This means that for most villagers, ties with states are indirect and are administered through the kinship organization of a localized segment of a dominant landholding caste.

Although reports of Indian society stress its village orientation, it has long been recognized that the village is not a social isolate. Ethnographers depict the integration of villages into regions as occurring both in the past and in the present through a variety of extensions that also bring to regions the influences of the greater civilization (Marriott 1955; Opler 1956; Mandelbaum 1970, vols. 1 and 2). Markets, traveling plays, priests, pilgrimages, the extensions of kinship, newspapers, schools, films, radio, and various systems of travel increasingly make involvement and integration the norm. In addition, taxation, elections, public administration, and the police make the presence of government a commonplace in the twentieth century. Despite these extensions of village awareness of the greater civilization, however, the basic ingredients of the social order and the ideology that supports them are demonstrated to be resistant to change (Dumont 1970b:223-224). Caste and kinship remain basic, and concerns of ranking and interdependence associated with local caste dominance characterize caste relationships. All are features of localism.

Because social change in the twentieth century involves the formation of caste associations and the development of state and national ties that transcend localities, modern change is commonly described as something new that has little meaning for or impact on the lives of villagers until they leave their localities and become involved in modern urban life. Although modern cities still exhibit elements of localism in their migrant sections and traditional residential areas (Fox 1970; Rowe 1973; Beck and Joy 1979; Joy and Beck 1979); they are also the centers of supralocal extensions and associations. Regional, national, and international corporations abound. Economic diversity and industrialization offer alternative sources of income to residents, and weaken caste dominance and the caste interdependence that integrates local systems of village ranking. Nonetheless, Indian society is depicted as resistant to change (Pocock 1960; Ames 1973; Khare 1973). India's population is still largely rural, and most of the urban population adheres to traditional values and social forms. Only a small westernized elite may be seen as deviating from this conservatism (Kolenda 1978:141-143); cities, industries, and the state have, with but few exceptions, adapted to this conservative traditionalism (Dumont 1970b:223-224). Localism prevails.

If anthropologists were to use a regional perspective, as opposed to this locality-oriented one, would this portrayal of Indian society be significantly altered? As a student of south Indian society, I am often made aware of differences between northern and southern India that suggest the two regions are organized differently. True, caste and kinship are fundamental ingredients of social organization, and agriculture and caste dominance produce similarly integrated systems of localized caste ranking in both regions. But there are also major differences that come into relief only when a regional rather than a local perspective is taken.

The first difference between the two regions involves marriage patterns (Kolenda 1968). Marriage ties are more localized in the South than in the North, and suggest that marriage alliances and descent may not be as important in the South for integrating an area as they are in the North. Second, major temple complexes are a common feature of the south Indian region and appear to exist in greater numbers than in the North, suggesting that they play a different role in south India. Except for studies of pilgrimages (Obeyesekere 1974), the importance of these temples to south Indian social organization is rarely analyzed carefully by anthropologists (however, see Beck 1972; Appadurai and Breckenridge 1976; Appadurai 1981). Third, whereas agricultural dominance is associated with castes claiming a kingly mode for behavior (*Kshatriyas*), and Kshatriya dominance (*Kshatriya raj*) is characteristic of political organization in villages and locales in north India, Kshatriyas and Kshatriya raj are absent in the South. Instead, south Indian society until recently was characterized by three different features: the secular and ritual supremacy of Brahmans, who have legitimized the social order and provided its ideology; the organization of the region into *naaDus* (territories administered by caste councils) dominated usually by an area's preeminent agriculturists; and the division of non-Brahmans into contrasting left-hand and right-hand sections. All three characterizing features of south Indian society were closely associated with each other and with the uses of temples, and they were an integral part of the segmentary organization of south Indian states.

What was the nature of this regional social organization? How were these three social forms interrelated, and what importance did temple use and state polities have in determining the development of south Indian social organization? Previous studies have focused on the supremacy of Brahmans in south India (Miller 1954; Gough 1955, 1956, 1960; Harper 1964; Beteille 1965; Mencher and Goldberg 1967; Appadurai 1981) or on dominant agriculturists (Epstein 1962; Beck 1972; Barnett 1973), but except for the work of the historian Hall (1980), who described trade in the age of the Cholas, almost nothing has been written about the social integration of the artisan-merchants into the region, nor has there been much consideration of the social organization of the region or its characterizing features (Beck 1979; Murton 1979; Stein 1980; Pfaffenberger 1982).

I offer a regional analysis in this book. I concentrate largely on the organization of the region in Tamilnadu known indigenously as *VaTa Konku* (northern *KonkunaaDu*), which extends north and west of the Kaveri River to Salem City in what is today Salem District (Map 1). My social focus is the Tamil caste of handloom weavers, the Sengunthar Mudaliyars, who are also known by their ancient name, *Kaikkoolar*. Tamilnadu State is historically well known for its handloom textiles, and VaTa Konku is the location of a number of weaving centers in a district that is today still an important locus of this trade. The Kaikkoolars, who speak Tamil, and the *Thevanga Chettiar,* who speak Telugu, together represent over 60 percent of the total weaving population of Tamilnadu State. The Kaikkoolars are a caste that formerly belonged to the left-hand section of castes.

The VaTa Konku region is part of the larger KonkunaaDu region, one of the five macroregions of the pre-British Tamil-speaking area. This is both a "naively given" and an "instituted" region (Saberwal 1971:83 following Schwartzberg 1967). It is "naively given" in that it is an indigenously recognized territory; it is an instituted region insofar as its territorial limits explicitly define the boundaries of certain features of local organization and administration. The geography of VaTa Konku still reflects the location of native administrative towns from the pre-British eighteenth century. These towns are nodes in the region's networks of textile trade in which Salem City has played the role of regional market center or *entrepot*. Among the Kaikkoolars the region is known as the *EeRuurunaaDu*, the "Seven-City Territory." These seven towns and their hinterland areas together form a hierarchy of caste councils that administers interlocal affairs. The region stretching from Taramangalam in the north to Trichengode in the south also forms an interlinked network of major temples, which in conjunction with the EeRuurunaaDu defines the Kaikkoolars' membership and territory. VaTa Konku is a region, therefore, that exhibits its own structure even today when it is overlain by contemporary state organization.

One might ask why I have chosen to study weavers; what have they to do with the integration of south Indian society? The answer is complex. Beck (1972, 1979) has depicted, in two useful and intriguing studies, the integration of the KonkunaaDu region in terms of agriculturists, who formerly belonged to the right-hand section of castes. In her work, she contrasts the two sections of castes as, on the one hand, incorporating interdependent agriculturists and service castes (the right hand) and, on the other hand, as including independent artisans and merchants (the left hand) who were to a degree free from the control of agriculturists. Agriculture formed the greater part of the economy, and control of agricultural resources gave the dominant castes power over the castes that were economically dependent on them. Next to agriculture, commerce formed the largest sector of the economy, and within commerce textile production and trade was most prominent. Artisan-merchant castes were nondominant, but their occupations and mobility gave them autonomy from dominant agriculturists. Landholders adhered to a kingly model of caste behavior in accord with their political dominance, and the artisan-merchants adhered to a priestly model that depicted them as independent and Brahmanical in behavior.

The right-hand castes, according to Beck, were organized into naaDus (territories) controlled by dominant agriculturists. NaaDus were kin-based political organizations with a strong locality bias created by the dominant caste's ties to land. By contrast, the left-hand castes lacked local political organizations and important kin organizations beyond the level of the lineage, and they were characterized by the mobility and social separation encouraged by their occupation as itinerant traders. In Beck's view, therefore, dominant agriculturists are the source of the area's social integration, which can be understood as a product of the economic control of the main source of production, land.

However, there are no studies focusing on castes formerly of the left-hand section. Consequently, we know little about the left-hand category and the manner of its integration into society. In her analysis, Beck seems to follow Dumont in believing that there is no separate normative status for merchants. They must either be subordinated to dominant agriculturists or assume a priestly, Brahmanical mode of behavior.

One can say that just as [in Hindu ideology] religion . . . encompasses politics, so politics encompasses economics within itself. The difference is that the politico-economic domain is separated, named, in a subordinate position as against religion, whilst economics remains undifferentiated within politics. Indeed one can study kingship in the Hindu texts. . . . But if we go one step further and raise the question of the merchant, the normative texts are silent. (Dumont 1970b:165)

Although the "normative [Hindu] texts are silent" about the question of the merchant in south India, epigraphs do reveal much about merchants in history (Hall 1980). Indeed, merchants seem not always to have been encompassed by agricultural dominance, but rather to have been assigned frequently to the left-hand section of society, where they established a dominance of their own. Clearly, south Indians once had an idea about the place of merchants. If we are to understand this place, we must first know the nature of the right-hand/left-hand division.

What is the place of artisans and merchants in the organization of the Konku region? Are they relegated to positions of subordination, inferiority, and marginality – to the left side – as their moiety identity suggests, or are they, like agriculturists, an integral but separate part of the political economy of south Indian states? Perhaps they are integrated differently or occupy a different social space, again as their left-hand designation might alternatively imply.

In this book, I argue that the Kaikkoolars as artisan-merchants are integrated differently and once occupied a separate social space. By studying weavers, we can determine how an important sector of the society and economy is integrated into the region, what role the three features of south Indian society have played in the weavers' organization, and what their place in the political economy of local states has been.

This book is also about change, for south India, despite its centuries of cultural continuity, has evolved and developed throughout its history, and in the twentieth century the society in its broadest sense has been transformed. The three characterizing features of south Indian society have either disappeared or have been considerably altered and weakened since the 1920s. The Kaikkoolars today show a complexity of traditions and behavior that are understandable and explainable only in the context of their history and relationships with their region. If they are studied without regard to these factors, they appear ambiguous in their status and mixed in their traditions. However, if a historical and regional perspective is taken, this confusion disappears.

Historically, the Kaikkoolars' caste organization has been determined by the political organization of their region. As states have come and gone, the political economy of the region has changed, and the Kaikkoolars have responded by reorganizing their caste to serve them better in their relations with the state and its regional administration. This is as true of their efforts in the twentieth century as it was in the past. Twentieth-century reorganization has involved the creation of new institutions, but the impetus for these changes has been the same. It is erroneous to depict change in the twentieth century as being different from change in previous centuries. I argue in this book, therefore, that state-hinterland relationships today and in the past have had considerable importance in determining caste organization.

Another conclusion of this book is that the importance of commerce and the textile industry in south Indian social history has been overlooked. Next to agriculture, the textile industry has been and still is the largest sector of the economy. This has given textile production and trade an important place in south Indian society that is reflected not only in the wealth this industry produces and the desire of governments to control it, but also in the central symbolic role of textiles in Hindu ritual and worship. It is this acknowledged importance of the textile industry, and of artisan-merchants in general, that is reflected in the division of south India into left-hand and right-hand castes.

2 The Kaikkoolars of Tamilnadu

Listen to the voice of attack, its might as hard to oppose as Death, Brahmans! It has nothing to do with *dharma* [caste duty] . . . since it is concerned with gain.

(Hart 1975a:52)

The Kaikkoolars are a large, widely dispersed caste in Tamilnadu State, south India.[1] They are weavers by occupation and warriors by ancient heritage. They are proud of this heritage and relate with relish tales of fierce caste heroes; annually, they celebrate their mythical defeat of the evil giant Suurabatman. Their most important caste hero, OTTakkuutar, a famous medieval Tamil poet, typifies this warlike and sometimes cruel character of the caste. Kaikkoolar tradition says that he once demanded that 1,008 sons of the caste be sacrificed as a condition for writing a set of poems laudatory to the Kaikkoolars. He is often depicted as writing his poems while sitting on a throne made from the heads of the sacrificed.

OTTakkuutar is a literary figure, one of Tamil's greatest poets, but he exhibits none of the attributes of Brahmans, the caste traditionally associated with letters and learning. He is a bard. Nor is OTTakkuutar's caste Brahmanical. The power of the Kaikkoolars' bellicose past permeates the caste's self-image, but their tradition is not that of kings or chiefs, the category traditionally associated with war. Their tradition depicts the loyal army men who fought in the armies of kingly gods and in those of the ancient Chola Kingdom. In later times it stresses their fierce independence. The Kaikkoolars do not command other castes to serve them, as kings and local chiefs once did and as dominant landowning castes may still try to do, nor are they commanded. In a society characterized at its inner core by priestly Brahmans and kingly agriculturists who command the services of their dependents,

[1] In this chapter and throughout the book, ethnographic field research provides the primary source of information unless historic sources are cited. This information was collected among the Kaikkoolars in 1978-1979, primarily in the northern region of KonkunaaDu in the modern districts of Salem and Periyar and in Madras City.

the Kaikkoolars occupy a third sector of society, that of merchants and independent artisans. These castes form the outer core of Tamil society (Stein 1980:250).

The Kaikkoolars' artisan tradition is ancient. The earliest epigraphic mention of the caste dates from the eleventh century, a time of great flux in south Indian society. This was a period of urban growth and the development of the great south Indian temple complexes in which Brahmans legitimized the rights and honors of castes. We know little of the Kaikkoolars of this time, except that they were handloom weavers and textile merchants, and they maintained armies to guard their caravans and warehouses and perhaps also to plunder villages upon occasion (Stein 1975:75; Hall 1980:154, 193).

South India in this ancient time was spotted with nucleated settlements inhabited by agriculturists and their dependents, and with *Brahmadeyas,* or Brahman villages, inhabited by Brahmans and their non-Brahman dependents. Between these settlements were hostile areas inhabited by warlike tribes. Often these hostile peoples lived in the hills and mountains that mark the western margin of what is Tamilnadu today. The hill people were greatly feared by the settled Hindus for their fierceness in war and by what Hindus saw as their personal disorder in worship. In ancient times, one of the main Tamil gods was Murugan, a hunter who lived in the hills and possessed women and girls (Hart 1975b:28-29). Twentieth-century Kaikkoolar spirituality retains many of the features of his early worship; in their worship of small gods, some supplicants drink intoxicants, perform frenzied dances, and when possessed foretell the future.

Itinerant traders, including Kaikkoolars of the eleventh and twelfth centuries, maintained armies for protection as they traveled between nucleated settlements. There must have been several kinds of textile merchants even at this time in history, for textiles have been an important item of trade in this part of India from at least the first century A.D. From the eleventh century, south Indian cottons formed an important item of trade with much of Southeast Asia, with China, and with the western Asian and Mediterranean worlds (Hall 1980:162-184; Gittinger 1982). In earlier times, Tamil merchants conducted trade as far east as China (Indian Standard, December 10, 1967) and had trade contacts as far west as Greece and Rome. Numerous caches of Roman and Greek coins have been found in Tamilnadu, dating from the first to the third century A.D., and there are early Tamil references to Greeks (Schwartzberg 1978).

We do not know the extent of the Kaikkoolars' involvement in this trade, but they may have acted as suppliers if not as merchants. One ancient epigraph, which mentions Kaikkoolar armies, suggests that they were centrally involved in Ceylon in one of the great mercantile associations of Tamil country, the *Ayyavole 500,* during the twelfth century (Stein 1975). Within south India itself, it is safe to assume that some members of the caste were engaged in merchandising textiles, transporting them among localities by bullock-loads and headloads, and participating in the cycle of weekly markets held in villages. This trade explains their need for armies. Early European travelers described the pattern of indigenous trade that is still practiced by Kaikkoolars in much the same manner (Buchanan 1807, vol. II).

Textiles are important in south India not only for their common uses, but also as luxury goods, as important gifts given at rites of passage, and as formal gift payments for ritual services. They are also given as gifts to gods, temples, priests, and, prior to the 1930s, to the *deeva-daasis,* women dedicated to temples and symbolically married to the temple god. Textiles, therefore, have long been an important source of wealth in trade and an important symbolic item in gift giving and ritual. Their manufacturers, the Kaikkoolars, are a relatively high-ranking caste who rival in status the main agriculturist caste, the *VeL-LaaLas,* with whom they are often juxtaposed in temple offices and in status rivalry in the Salem and Coimbatore districts.

Kaikkoolars and the left-hand and right-hand sections of south India

The Kaikkoolars emerged at a time when there were at least three loci of military power within south Indian kingly states. There was the king, who was the most potent locus of military power; the high-ranking agricultural castes, primarily the Brahmans and VeLLaaLas; and the armed merchants and artisans. Among the artisans, the Kaikkoolars alone appear to have maintained armies and to have been warriors (Arokiaswami 1956:272-273, 284-290), almost certainly as a by-product of their involvement in itinerant trade.

Because the Kaikkoolars are, to this day, primarily handloom weavers and itinerant merchants who sell their goods in urban and country bazaars, they lack the primary attachment to the land of the agriculturist castes: the Brahmans, the non-Brahman landowners and their dependents, and the kings, all of whom are directly dependent on agriculture. For these castes, agriculture forms the economic base on which their political power rests. In contrast, the Kaikkoolars make goods to sell or trade; or are petty businessmen, usually in entrepreneurial fields associated with the textile industry; or follow other occupations that set them apart from agriculturists. Thus, Buchanan commented that around Salem none of the weavers cultivated land (1807, vol. II:265). There, he wrote, "The *Coicular* are weavers, writers, or accomptants, schoolmasters, and physicians" (1807, vol. II:266).

Kaikkoolars thus exhibit an independence from other castes that is a product of their economic behavior, and that contrasts dramatically to the interdependent land- and locality-attached castes: the agriculturists and those that serve them. These castes are units in a system of interdependence that characterizes this section of society. David (1974) depicts these types of castes as following a "bound-mode" of caste ranking. They are bound by their interdependent service and exchange transactions, and they are ranked by their ability to command services or to be commanded. The Kaikkoolars and other traders exhibit a "nonbound mode" of ranking. They are not bound by transactions, and they neither command nor are commanded. As self-sufficient artisan-traders, their intercaste relationships are characteristically independent. In medieval times, they were members of supralocally organized trading corporations known from inscriptions as the *manigraamam*, the *nagaram*, and the Ayyavole 500 (Arokiaswami 1956:287-290; Hall 1980). They formed regional organizations and were a distinctive source of power in the political economy of their age.

In medieval times (eleventh to thirteenth centuries), this economic dualism was manifested at the village level as a social dichotomy between the interdependent agricultural castes and the more independent and mobile artisan-merchant castes. This was symbolically represented in Tamil culture as a bifurcation of society into right-hand (*valangkai*) and left-hand (*iDangkai*) sections (Arokiaswami 1956; Beck 1972; Appadurai 1974; Stein 1980). The main agriculturist castes and their interdependent service castes were members of the right-hand section; the artisans, itinerant merchants, and lesser agriculturists were members of the left-hand section. This division of society, dating from pre-Chola times (pre-tenth century), has continued in some form down through the centuries. Even today, when the distinction is only a fading memory, something of the dichotomy persists in intercaste relationships, beliefs and models for behavior, local residential and temple organization, caste administration, and the contrasting customs of castes.

In some areas of Tamilnadu, the distinction between right-hand and left-hand castes had disappeared by the end of the nineteenth century. In others, however, such as the region of Erode (Map 1), men in their seventies still remember vividly rural-based conflict between the two sections, especially between the Kaikkoolars and the right-hand agriculturists, the Gounders. They speak of villages where the dichotomy is still the basis of alliances and disputes. Today these disputes are related primarily to temple worship and ritual, and involve Kaikkoolar use of temples and their right to specific ritual honors. The disputes concern dominance and symbolic denotations of relative rank. The continuing legacy of the old division of society is to be found in the status rivalry between Kaikkoolars and Gounders, the continued separation of their residential areas, the existence of separate temples used by the two castes, and their separate caste administrations.

The social status of Kaikkoolars today

In a social world in which relative rank is critical for determining the nature of caste interaction, the Kaikkoolars' rank seems markedly ambiguous. Moffatt (1979:72) expresses this ambiguity clearly in his assessment of the position of Kaikkoolars in a village near Madras City. He refers to them by their alternative name, *Sengunthar Mudaliyars:*

The Sengunthar Mudaliyars are . . . not directly connected to the land and their overall economic position in Endavur is not strong. Despite its relatively high rank, the caste in no way shares in the dominance of the village; its only potential effect on village-level politics is in the sheer number of votes its members can bring to village-level elections. Nor has it any strong vertical relations by which it can enforce authority over the Harijans; there are no Harijans in *paNNaiyaL* [traditional subordinate labor tie with a member of a dominant caste] tied-labor relations to members of the Sengunthar Mudaliyar caste.

The social position of the Kaikkoolars is similar throughout Tamilnadu. They are a numerically strong community, but because they lack ties with an array of dependent castes, their social position is ill defined. They claim a relatively high non-Brahman status similar to that of the Gounder VeLLaaLas, but there is a slightly reluctant acceptance of it by others. This status stems from their economic and social independence from the authority and dominance of agricultural castes. However, their relative poverty and lack of dominance taint their status with ambivalence.

The Kaikkoolars' status is ambivalent in several other respects. Customary Kaikkoolar behavior includes the worship of family gods (*kuladeevam*) with blood sacrifices of chickens, goats, and pigs, all of which are eaten, at least by some Kaikkoolars. They are not only nonvegetarians but also pork eaters. Pork is considered by most to be the food only of untouchables. This means that by Brahmanical standards the Kaikkoolars are of low rank. Yet the Kaikkoolars closely identify with Shiva and Saivism, with its stress on vegetarianism. Kaikkoolar *teesikars* (non-Brahman priests) at the temples of Murugan are vegetarians. Indeed, many Kaikkoolars are strict vegetarians. As a whole, the caste accepts vegetarianism as a higher principle than nonvegetarianism, but because they believe that their small gods demand sacrifices and that these gods directly affect their well-being, most members of the caste continue to perform blood sacrifices and to eat meat (Heesterman 1973; Mines 1982). The conflict between the two customs causes them some discomfort.

There are other indications of the Kaikkoolars' ambivalent ritual status. Low-status indicators include a past tradition of dedicating their daughters as deeva-daasis to Shiva temples, a custom associated with prostitution and disavowed by many Kaikkoolars as early as the late eighteenth century (Buchanan 1807, vol. II:266). Similarly, Frykenberg's (1977) report of the nineteenth-century dispute between Kaikkoolars and VeLLaaLas in Tinnevelly suggests that Kaikkoolars were regarded as having low, even untouchable status. By contrast, Stein (1968:87) infers a ritually clean but low status for the Kaikkoolars in Tiruchirapalli some 600 to 900 years ago, when they had "the ritually pregnant task of offering coconut to the deity" at the Srirangam temple (a Vishnavite temple; to this day, a small number of Kaikkoolars are Vishnavites). There, as we have already come to expect, they were juxtaposed to the dominant landowning caste, the VeLLaaLas. A VeLLaaLa held the office of temple accountant (*kooyil kanakkan*). However, at about the same time (twelfth and thirteenth centuries) in KonkunaaDu (Salem-Coimbatore), the Gounder VeLLaaLas and the Kaikkoolars were the two main warrior castes and seem to have been closely associated in rank (Arokiaswami 1956:273-274). Evidently, the status of Kaikkoolars varied from locality to locality in ancient times.

In the twentieth century, Kaikkoolars similarly have followed ritual practices suggesting ambivalent status. On the one hand, Kaikkoolars build Saivite temples presided over by Brahmans and used by high, clean castes, behavior that suggests high, ritually clean status. The temple at the Kumaragiri mountain outside Ammapettai in Salem City is one such temple. Kaikkoolars administer it and employ a Brahman priest to preside over prayers. The temple is regularly visited by persons of high caste status. But on the other hand, the Kaikkoolars' worship of small gods involves blood sacrifices, the use of intoxicants and cigars, and spirit possession. These practices are similar to those that characterized the worship of Murugan in early times, and are today generally thought to be typical of low castes.

Kaikkoolar caste organization

Another indicator of relatively high status for the Kaikkoolars is the caste's statewide system of councils known as the 72 naaDus. Low-caste interaction and administration are characteristically localized and limited. By contrast, the 72 naaDu system is impressively regional. The naaDu system is a territorially defined set of judicial and administrative councils ordered in a pyramidal hierarchy of increasing authority and territorial jurisdiction. The system forms the basis of a statewide caste organization. It is old, parts of it probably dating from the twelfth century (Stein 1980:138), and is viewed by Kaikkoolars as an important ingredient of their heritage. The system today is more important to Kaikkoolars as a membership-defining, goodwill-creating, and prestige-making association than as an actual administrative network. It underscores the caste's claim to a regional identity and an independent status. The council offices are vested with prestige and sumptuary rights to turbans and other signs of office. Council officers have the right to move in processions with music, to use torches in these processions even during daylight, and to use flags. They had the right to use deeva-daasi attendants before the latter were outlawed. Council meetings are regal and follow a formal courtly etiquette.

Although the judicial-administrative aspects of the councils have been on the wane throughout the twentieth century, much of the hierarchy remains and is considered symbolically important as an ideal statement of caste organization and regulation. The Conjeepuram Council, called the *MahaanaaDu,* forms the apex of the system. Prior to the late 1920s, this council, with its hereditary head, the *aaNDavar,* was the ultimate authority in caste affairs, backing its decisions with the sanction of outcasting. Below the Conjeepuram MahaanaaDu are four *thisainaaDus,* councils with jurisdiction over Kaikkoolars residing within the subregions, or localities, that divide the Tamil-speaking region. The thisainaaDus have jurisdiction over town and village *panchayats* located within their territories. Below them are the panchayats of particular sublocalities, individual towns, and villages. These are clustered under a head council, *meeLuur naaDu* (western town council), a subcouncil, *kiiRuur naaDu* (eastern town council), and the satellite councils of their immediately surrounding areas. Within a particular residential area the councils are known as *paavaDi naaDus,* because they meet on the weavers' common land where each morning their warps (*paavu*) are stretched as the weavers prepare them for their looms. Each successive level of the system has greater jurisdiction and authority than the levels below it, and cases that cannot be settled locally are appealed to the next higher level.

Today the naaDu system is seen by Kaikkoolars as having once united the caste as a single uniform, centrally administered community. But this contemporary image is misleading, since a careful look at what remains of the system suggests that it was a locality-segmented network of caste councils with more symbolic and ritual unity than real administrative unity and power. The key to understanding the articulation of the system is locality segmentation. The higher levels of the naaDu hierarchy of councils have increasing prestige and authority over the lower councils, but lack sanctions to enforce compliance other than the threat of outcasting. This threat can be enacted only with the consensus of the communities involved.

Prior to the twentieth century, customs among the different Kaik-koolar communities varied significantly from one locality to another. For example, some communities were vegetarians but most were not, marriage was locality endogamous, and some Kaikkoolars allowed widow remarriage whereas others did not. Dress styles varied, as did marriage practices and other customs. Consequently, the naaDu councils had to administer according to local custom, and the higher councils required that a case or item of business be presented from below in order for them to take action. Before a higher council would hear a case involving lower councils, it required the disputants to agree to abide by the higher council's decision on pain of their caste localities being outcaste. If this happened, a lower council area would be at a disadvantage in interlocality disputes. At the same time, the higher council could not be arbitrary in making decisions because it lacked power to enforce them. In the face of widespread opposition, it had to make decisions that took into account local customs and interests in order to achieve compliance. Consequently, decisions were made on the basis of customary rule and followed local opinion.

The naaDu system, therefore, did not create caste uniformity. It linked independent caste segments in a ritual-judicial confederacy with a bottom-to-top administrative orientation more than a top-to-bottom one. This confederacy seems to have been important for maintaining an atmosphere of good will among the weavers of member localities and for establishing means for negotiating terms of exchange. These functions were and still are important features of supralocal textile trade.

Textile trade and Kaikkoolar caste organization

Several important characteristics of weaver-textile entrepreneurial activity shed light on the nature of the Kaikkoolars' naaDu system. First, weavers living in concentrated settlements need to market their textiles beyond their own locality. Handloom weaving in Tamilnadu is a full-time occupation, and weavers outproduce local demand. Furthermore, weaver localities specialize in producing particular textiles, necessitating extralocal marketing. This is an old pattern of production in the Tamil region that has continued into modern times. In 1948 and today, Ammapettai in Salem is known for coarse-count *saris* and *dhotis;*

Chennimalai is known for bedcovers and furnishings; and Conjeepuram for silk saris. Salem ranks second to Conjeepuram in silk production. Trichengode is known for the production of coarse varieties of saris, Coimbatore and Madurai for fine-count saris, and Bhavani for carpets. North Arcot and Chingleput are known for *lungis* (a sarong-like garment), and Madras once was famous for handkerchief production (Naidu 1948:6). Clearly, different weaving centers produce for dispersed markets.

Buchanan also comments on the indigenous system of moving goods (1807, vol. II:180-191 and elsewhere). Cotton was shipped to weaver centers, and fabric was shipped to markets on bullock back. Buchanan mentions Ammapettai, Erode, Salem, Rasipuram, and other towns as lively participants in this trade (Buchanan vol. II:191; 263-264). Locality specialization has changed over time – old fabrics and designs have been replaced by new ones – but specialization continues.

The concentration of weavers in particular homogeneous residential localities and their product specializations, therefore, require some system of marketing. Murton (1979:24) has shown that in the eighteenth century, northern KonkunaaDu was laced by textile trade and market networks that linked the administrative towns of the region. Although naaDu organization is undoubtedly older, these trade networks seem to be the source of the system's structure in northern KonkunaaDu, the Seven-City Territory, because the towns of the precolonial administration and the present-day member towns of the territory correspond closely. Murton (1979:25) also implies that the Kaikkoolar naaDus administered the textile trade of the region. The early confusion of the British about naaDus and the role of their leaders stems from their misinterpretation of this administration. The British thought weaver naaDus were guilds and their officers guild heads. In reality, the officers of the naaDus settled disputes, and appear to have thought themselves to be their localities' rightful brokers, regulating interlocality trade. However, they administered only what passed through the system. They had no control over production.

Second, some weavers are textile merchants or brokers, and others are engaged in various aspects of the business end of textile production, including masterweaving, marketing yarn, and yarn dyeing, printing, and sizing. Masterweavers are loom owners who hire poorer weavers to produce their cloth. They either work for wholesalers or do their own marketing. This characterization is as true today as it has been for centuries (Stein 1980). Similarly, Arasaratnam's references to such traders in the mid-eighteenth century, and Buchanan's remark about the weavers and merchants of Ammapettai and his description of masterweavers (Buchanan 1807, vol. II:239, 240, 264), all point to the mercantile involvement of Kaikkoolars. Certainly, not all weavers were interlocality traders, but a fair number were if the behavior of Kaikkoolars today is any indication, and if Buchanan's descriptions of the lively textile trade in 1800 in Salem and Coimbatore are to be given credence.

Several kinds of Kaikkoolar textile merchants exist today in the Salem region. Even in a small village such as Akkamapettai, located outside of Salem, there are three main types of retail merchants: itinerant, "head-load" textile merchants; "bullock-cart" textile merchants; and bazaar-located, petty textile shopkeepers. "Head-load" and "bullock-cart" refer both to the mode of transportation used and to the size of the business these merchants traditionally had as itinerant traders. Today, buses are the standard method of transportation. With their textiles tied into bundles for easy transportation, the head-load and bullock-cart merchants follow a weekly cycle of bazaars located in the surrounding towns and villages. Conducting what are known as *santhai,* or bazaar, cloth businesses, Kaikkoolar merchants typically sell textiles five days of the week, purchase new supplies from wholesalers located in a nearby town on the sixth day, and rest on the seventh. The third type of retail textile merchant, the shopkeeper, sells from his shop located in the nearby town of Sankagiridrug. These three types of merchants are commonly also textile manufacturers; members of their families weave at home.

Spotted throughout the countryside are towns or cities such as Erode and Salem, which act as wholesale textile centers. On particular market days of the month, textile merchants from near and far make purchases and place their orders. These orders are relayed to masterweavers, who farm them out to weavers located in surrounding centers. Akkamapettai Village, for example, as one such center, is tied to the Erode market by its weavers' commitments to Erode's masterweavers. Trichengode and Chennimalai are other production centers supplying Erode's market in this manner. A network of interlocal economic ties is the result. From precolonial times until about 1970, Salem played a similar entrepot role as a major regional market center, and to this day Ammapettai and Salem are large centers of handloom production and trade. In this system of trade, textiles pass down to agricultural villages through the santhai system and up to external markets through masterweavers, purchasing agents, and wholesalers located at the entrepots.

In Akkamapettai there are two additional types of weaver-merchants: masterweavers who supply their own inputs and sell their goods wholesale on the open market, often through an agent located in Erode's wholesale textile bazaar; and masterweavers who own several looms but work on contract for wholesale agents. These latter master-weavers may themselves work on contract with suppliers or exporters located elsewhere in India, typically in Bombay or Delhi. Any of these masterweavers and traders may be Kaikkoolars. In addition to production and marketing-related enterprises in Salem and Erode, there is a range of financial enterprises designed to meet the needs of the textile business. These include banks, in which Kaikkoolars do not figure prominently, as well as more informal businesses. Among the latter are the enterprises of moneylenders, who deal in a variety of secured loans, usually involving pawned goods; petty lenders, who take textiles in pawn; and petty yarn buyers and sellers, who buy and sell small amounts of thread, often involving only a few *pice* per transaction.

It is apparent that Kaikkoolars have been and are involved in a great variety of enterprises related to textile marketing and manufacture. The naaDu system plays a central role in this complexity. First, it provides a means of integrating and organizing a locality-segmented population well enough to enable it to deal with interlocality trade and the disputes that may result. Second, it mediates trade between localities. Third, it provides the Kaikkoolars with their territorial identity and supralocal sodality organization.

Today the naaDus do not involve themselves in business disputes, which are handled in the courts, but they do mediate certain kinds of interlocality disputes concerning naaDu jurisdiction; they are concerned with preserving appropriate rules of council procedure, with maintaining the hierarchical structure of naaDu jurisdiction, and with solving more conventional problems related to marriage and custom. Disputes that cannot be settled locally or that involve more than one locality are referred to higher levels in the naaDu pyramid. Thus, the naaDu system continues to have the framework necessary to organize and regulate trade relations, even if today it no longer does so.

The Kaikkoolars' caste association

In the 1920s and 1930s, the segmentary nature of the naaDu system and its reliance on local custom to provide the authority for administration were thought by a new elite then rising within the caste to encourage an archaic provincialism no longer suited to the times. The political arena of Madras Presidency had been changing since the 1870s and government was being centralized in Madras City (Baker 1976; Washbrook 1976). Political-economic dictates were creating conditions that called for statewide caste organizations that represented a caste's unified interests to the centralized bureaucracy. In addition, Indians were being given opportunities for greater involvement in local government, and statewide caste associations were being formed to press the British for the castes' particular interests. Among the Kaikkoolars, the new elite sought to transcend the segmented naaDu system by organizing an association, the *Senguntha Mahaajana Sangam,* which sought to establish the caste as a single, united community. This new leadership did not seek to displace the naaDu system but rather to create a new organizational structure that would enable the caste as a unit to take advantage of the changing political situation.

They saw several advantages in forming the association (hereafter Sangam). First, as a numerically small elite, the new leadership advocated interlocal marriage, in part because it would enable them to form advantageous marriages. Interlocal marriage was also encouraged because it symbolized the breakdown of locality segmentation and the reorganization of the caste into a single unit. In the new Sangam organization, locality was superseded by the ideology of caste homogeneity. This formed the basis for the second advantage of caste reorganization: The Sangam, representing a homogeneous regional community, could effectively lobby the state for benefits, whereas a heterogeneous community of diverse interests could not. Third, a Sangam that gained the support of its members would give its leaders a vehicle to disseminate their ideas about how caste custom should be changed, and how caste economic and social disabilities could be overcome. Caste codes for behavior were to be homogeneous and were designed to benefit the whole community. This involved a dramatic reversal of the usual form of caste administration. Customary rule was out; a loose form of executive administration was in. Although the naaDu system continued to exist and is even today considered an important vehicle for elder statesmanship within the caste, the Sangam was the more influential system of caste organization during the period from its inception in 1927 until about 1960. However, the Sangam bore the seeds of its own eventual decline.

The handloom weavers' production cooperative system and Kaikkoolar caste organization

Two factors weakened the Sangam system of organization and led to its eclipse. First, the Sangam derived its power from the supposed homogeneity of caste interests. As an inevitable result of economic and political diversification, this fiction of homogeneity could no longer be maintained, and the Sangam lost its effectiveness and its power. Second, the Sangam acted as a pressure group, with no natural institutional ties to the region's political structure or economy. Kaikkoolar members of the Sangam were textile producers, but the

Sangam was not a weavers' organization per se, and although Kaikkoolars were supporters of Indian independence, the Sangam's membership did not remain politically homogeneous. Consequently, when in the 1940s the handloom weavers' cooperative movement gained momentum in Madras State, it was not long before it formed a new and more easily manipulated institutional framework that gave the Kaikkoolar leadership direct access to economic benefits and political influence.

The weavers' cooperative system had precisely the elements the Sangam lacked to give leaders real power. First, it offered economic rewards to Kaikkoolars who joined the movement. Second, after Independence it offered ruling parties a mechanism through which to distribute social welfare and from which to gain political support in return. The primary cooperative societies, therefore, were grass-roots institutions that provided Kaikkoolars with an institutional framework within which to exercise their leadership as brokers for the mutual benefit of local weavers and the dominant political parties at the state level. But the cooperative structure was more than just a useful institutional tool. It became the medium for organizing the caste in the modern political arena, and it provided new roles for caste leaders as political and economic brokers. It also provided a way to attract Kaikkoolar support and unite followers under local leaders through their shared interests in handloom weaving. The cooperative replaced the naaDu system and the Sangam as the primary organizational structure of caste leadership.

There is nothing inherently caste based about the cooperative system, for although the Kaikkoolars are one of the largest weaving communities in Tamilnadu, they are only one of several. Further, the weaving occupation is potentially open to all, and in the 1970s it attracted persons from a wide range of castes. In recent years, Kaikkoolars have lost their control of the statewide system because of this absence of a natural link between caste and weaving cooperatives. As a result, there is no longer a structural basis for Kaikkoolar leadership, or the unity of interests that would make appeals to caste consciousness an effective basis for leadership. Self-interests are now too divided. Economic and political diversity has gone so far that at a time when caste is the only basis for appeal, it can no longer be used. The caste, therefore, has evolved in the twentieth century through a series of organizational transformations: from regionally linked, locality-based segmentation (naaDus), to homogeneous association (Sangam), to cooperative-based and politically supported production societies (weavers' production cooperatives), to self-interest-oriented, economically and politically diversified associations (for example, private textile producers' associations, powerloom owners' societies, textile-sizing associations, exporter associations, diverse political party organizations, and a variety of handloom protectionist organizations).

The legacy of locality: the Kaikkoolar subdivisions of KonkunaaDu

I have so far presented a general developmental picture of the organization of Kaikkoolars in south India. This picture conveys a broad sense of the way Kaikkoolars structure their identity. It can be drawn more sharply by examining the organization of Kaikkoolars in the specific locality where I conducted fieldwork, northern KonkunaaDu (VaTa Konku). This locality corresponds roughly to the area the Kaikkoolars call the "Seven-City Territory" (EeRuurunaaDu), and includes the hinterland city of Salem. Erode is located just beyond the Bavani River to the southwest.

Salem and Erode are located some 35 miles apart and 200 to 250 miles south-southwest of Madras City (see Map 1). Salem is in the contemporary Salem District and Erode is in Periyar District, although both are part of the more ancient territorial division of KonkunaaDu, or Konku Mandalam, which incorporates much of both of these modern districts. KonkunaaDu is one of the five traditional political regions, or naaDus, into which modern Tamilnadu State was once divided. KonkunaaDu is itself traditionally divided into twenty-four or twenty-five subregions, which I call "localities" (also known as naaDus), which are themselves further subdivided. The region between Taramangalam and Salem City to the north and Trichengode City to the south belongs to one such traditional administrative locality (thisainaaDu, "territory of jurisdiction"), known to Kaikkoolars as the EeRuurunaaDu (Map 2). Erode, although only a short distance from Trichengode, belongs to a different subregion, the AkkarainaaDu. The Bavani River roughly separates the two localities. Kaikkoolars, therefore, are traditionally locality segmented. The major division of Kaikkoolars living in the region of Salem and Erode corresponds to this territorial subdivision.

Kaikkoolars who originate from the Erode side of the Bavani River are called *Konku Kaikkoolars* or *Periyataali Kaikkoolars,* referring to the large size of the *taali* worn by their women (the taali is an ornament indicating marriage worn at the neck). Salem Kaikkoolars call themselves *Cinnataali* (small taali) Kaikkoolars or, more rarely *SaamikaTTi Kaikkoolars,* referring to the now-defunct custom of wearing a Shiva *lingam* (an icon of the god Shiva) tied to the arm. Cinnataali and Periyataali Kaikkoolars use three main distinguishing customs to demarcate the social boundary between them. The first is the difference in the size of taalis. The second is that widow remarriage and divorce are proscribed among the Periyataalis but not among the Cinnataalis. The third is that Periyataali widows wear white saris, whereas Cinnataalis allow widows to wear colored saris as other women do. Because of this latter custom, Periyataalis are sometimes called *VeLLai* (white) *Kaikkoolars.* Cinnataalis say that Periyataali customs are borrowed from the landowning Konku Gounders, who dominate the region around Erode. The Periyataalis consider their customs superior to those of the Cinnataalis. Prior to the formation of the caste Sangam, inhabitants of the two sections did not intermarry.

In social terms, the Periyataali-Cinnataali distinction represents the extreme of a geographic gradation of cultural differences between Salem City in the north and Erode in the southern part of the northern Konku area. Three features of this gradation are outstanding. First, as one moves from Salem toward Erode, the heritage of competition between the Kaikkoolars and the main agricultural caste of the region, the Gounders, increases in intensity. Second, Kaikkoolars who originate from just south of the Bavani River display key customs that duplicate Gounder behavior. North of the Bavani River, however, Kaikkoolar and Gounder customs are distinct from each other. Third, the old distinction that once divided castes into right-hand and left-hand sections is almost unkown in the Salem area. This suggests that the distinction has had little meaning in the living memory of informants. However, as one moves south toward Erode, elder informants remember the distinction with a vividness that underscores the importance of the moiety well into the 1920s. These gradations of customs and behavior suggest the reality of the southern border of VaTa Konku and the social distinctions of the VaTa Konku locality: the focus of this study. Periyataali Kaikkoolars in the Erode region are themselves divided into two divisions, the VeLLai Kaikoolars and the *Rattukaarar* (carpet makers) *Kaikkoolars,* sometimes also called *Rendukaarar* because they weave with warps composed of double threads. Many of the latter group, originally from the region of Chennimalai Town near Erode, have migrated in large numbers to Erode, where they are now considered a wealthy mercantile community. Rattukaarars consider themselves superior to other subdivisions.

Among the Cinnataali Kaikkoolars, those from Trichengode consider themselves superior to Salem Kaikkoolars, as do those from Taramangalam. Trichengode and Taramangalam are located at the extremes of the Seven-City Territory, the EeRuurunaaDu, and are the location of large, ancient temples; they are also the location of the two main councils of the Kaikkoolar caste in the locality. The presence of these councils is an element in their claim to higher status compared with Salem and other residential communities of Kaikkoolars in the Seven-City Territory. These two towns may have been marketing centers in pre-British times, selling wholesale textiles produced by weavers living in their hinterlands. Today Erode and Salem have taken over these important entrepot functions.

There are three reasons for suggesting that Trichengode and Taramangalam were entrepots. First, the presence of large temples is historically associated with artisan and mercantile activities. Temple funds were sometimes used to finance trade. Second, temples were and are used by Kaikkoolars as council centers in their naaDu system. They also used these temples to integrate their trade network. Third, Trichengode is called the thisainaaDu, and Taramangalam is considered its counterpart. *Thisai* means "direction" as well as "jurisdiction," and in Chola times was part of the title of an association of itinerant traders, *thisaiyaayirattainnurruvar,* "the five hundred merchants of the thousand directions" (Hall 1980:141). It is possible that these two localities were once connected with these ancient traders. The temples of the two towns date from these early times. Conceivably, thisainaaDu may once have meant "entrepot." This conjecture remains to be proved, of course.

Within Salem City, Kaikkoolars from the borough of Ammapettai consider themselves superior to those from Shevapet or Salem boroughs. Ammapettai's Kaikkoolars are predominantly migrants from Venandur and Attiyampatti, although today the population is becoming increasingly heterogeneous. Each of these areas was endogamous before the 1930s, indicating, as many Sengunthars still point out, that identity is closely associated with sublocality.

Kaikkoolars of different sublocalities or localities make comparative claims of superiority relative to each other, but taken together their assertions do not appear to compose any unitary system of ranking. The system of naaDus is, however, pyramidally ranked in terms of increasing ritual and administrative authority. Since this system is locality linked, it may once have formed the basis of a ranking of caste segments. Ceremonial recognition of this ranking is still expressed at the locality level when the member councils of the Seven-City Territory hold their annual meeting in Trichengode. At that meeting, the officers of each council receive honors in order of their council's rank.

Another feature of the locality-based segmentation of the Kaikkoolars is their worship of family gods (kuladeevam) at shrines located near their places of origin. When caste members migrate, their connections with their ancestral locality are kept alive by the need to worship these deities at their ancestral villages. Although members of several castes may worship at these regionally known small gods' shrines, Kaikkoolars believe that only Kaikkoolars who are related in some ill-defined way (this vague sense of kinship is sometimes expressed as *vakaiyaraa,* or kindreds) worship at the same kuladeevam shrine. Kuladeevam worship is dictated by the need of a closely related kin group to preserve its well-being or that of one of its members.

It is clear that Kaikkoolar identity is complexly segmented. The caste is divided into endogamous groups associated with named residential centers. Subdivisions are also differentiated by key customary differences; the subdivisions are organized by the naaDu structure with its associated temples, and kin groups are linked to ancestral locations by kuladeevam worship.

Kaikkoolars from the Salem-Erode region recognize a number of other subdivisions of the caste from outside their locality, which they characterize by references to cultural heritage or to customary distinctions usually associated with locality. They recognize a group that prohibits the use of saliva when tying warps; a group that uses alcohol in worship; a group that once required young men to wear beards until marriage; a small number of Vishnavites; and locality groups such as the vegetarian Conjeepuram Kaikkoolars. Vegetarianism is a choice of personal preference among Kaikkoolars, and most observe meatless days as part of their worship of Shiva and Murugan. Only a few localities are vegetarian by code. Yet another recognized subdivision is the TalaikooDa Kaikkoolars from KoorainaaDu, in Tanjore. They are called TalaikooDa ("head refusers"), because it is said that in ancient times they refused to sacrifice the heads of their first sons to the caste hero-poet, OTTakkuutar, and have been stigmatized ever since. The key to understanding the Kaikkoolars' differentiation into groups, along the lines noted here, is their perception of different localities as being customarily distinct. To reiterate the major point of this discussion: Prior to the 1930s, locality provided the primary basis of caste segmentation and localities were endogamous. Locality endogamy is no longer the code, but in the Salem-Erode region the Periyataali-Cinnataali distinction is still recognized.

In the Seven-City Territory there is a third group – the *Moolakkaarans* – who claim to be Sengunthars. A description of the Kaikkoolars would be incomplete without a discussion of the Moolakkaarans, not only because they claim Kaikkoolar ancestry and sometimes marry Kaikkoolars, but also because the Kaikkoolars have waged a long campaign to deny the Moolakkaarans membership in their caste. An examination of Moolakkaarans is also warranted because their origin as deeva-daasis clarifies what was once a central feature of Kaikkoolar ritual behavior and status. The examination also reveals an aspect of the ritual juxtaposition of Kaikkoolars and VeLLaaLas.

Prior to the 1920s, it was common for the larger Saivite temples in south India to have attendant women, the deeva-daasis, who in their youth had been dedicated to the temple and symbolically married to the god. The main castes that dedicated their daughters were the right-hand VeLLaaLas and the left-hand Kaikkoolars; the resulting two sections of daasis served their separate moieties, the temples, and the attending Brahmans (Thurston 1909, vol. II:127-128). Some temples had several hundred daasis.

In the Salem-Erode region, the town of Chennimalai is well known for once having had a large number of daasis. Buchanan (1807, vol. II:285) comments in some detail on their presence in Chennimalai nearly two hundred years ago. Kaikkoolars still describe the town as the location of many daasi descendants.

Daasis attached to temples performed a number of services. They were part of the retinue that would greet a visiting official at the edge of town, and so were one of the many signs of honor he might be accorded (Buchanan 1807, vol. II:267). They would then travel in procession into town. Similarly, they were one of the marks of honor accorded the head of the Kaikkoolars' regionwide naaDu system; daasis accompanied him in procession, fanning him and dancing. They also attended the temple and its processions, dancing for the god.

In particular ways, the south Indian temple is a symbolic representation of the kingly court, with its emphasis on redistribution (Hart 1975b:14, 34; Appadurai and Breckenridge 1976:190) at the cosmic level. This is an important point, because "In ancient Tamil society, the king was the central embodiment of the sacred powers that had to be present and under control for the proper functioning of society" (Hart 1975b:13). In time, the qualities of a king came to be associated with those of a god, and the words "that meant king in ancient Tamil now denote God . . . while Kooyil ('king's house' or 'palace') now means temple" (Hart 1975b:13). The king commands loyalties, imposes taxes, and forms alliances, just as the god does. Sacrifices are made as offerings to the god, who symbolically partakes of them. A portion of the offering is kept by the Brahmans, and a portion is distributed by them to the worshipers in an order and manner indicating the status of the supplicants. Daasis were sacrifices, in a manner parallel to other types of offerings made to temple gods. Brahmans took some of them as concubines; of the remainder, many became concubines of prominent men of the community and some became prostitutes.

The right to dedicate women as daasis, I am told, was considered an honor, a sacrifice to the god of one's own blood. But the dedication also involved a marriage, and in south India a marriage establishes an enduring alliance between the wife giver and the receiver. The symbolic value of the tradition to the rival Kaikkoolars and VeLLaaLas is clear: Daasis were used to mark status and honor and to create an alliance between each daasi and the temple, which in turn reflected honor upon the family and caste, even if this honor was the humble one of the supplicant. By the 1920s, however, when the institution was outlawed, its public image emphasized the immoral aspects of the system: concubinage and prostitution. By this time, both castes had disavowed the custom and denied any connection with the descendants of daasis. But the connection persists, and the infamy of illicit sexuality attributed to the custom continues and is attributed to the descendants of daasis.

Although daasis were dedicated by Kaikkoolars, their children lacked clear membership in the Kaikkoolar caste because they were the offspring of mixed unions. Their pedigree was not pure. The offspring of daasis had several options. Some became daasis; some male children were trained to become dance masters and were known as *Nattuvans*. But most arranged marriages among themselves and became musicians and drummers who accompanied the daasis' dances. They became known as Moolakkaarans (drummers). Today the Kaikkoolars claim that Moolakkaarans form a separate caste, but Moolakkaarans say that they are Kaikkoolars.

One of the purposes of the first regionwide meeting of the Kaikkoolars' caste Sangam in 1927 was to separate the Kaikkoolars as true Sengunthars from the Moolakkaarans. Nonetheless, despite efforts to keep the two groups separate, there is little that behaviorally distinguishes the two communities, and intermarriages do occur, Kaikkoolars say, when the true Moolakkaaran origins of one party go undetected. Kaikkoolars say that Moolakkaarans are never handloom weavers, but many are textile merchants, and the community as a whole is thought to be wealthy in the Salem-Erode region. Kaikkoolars say, with a touch of cynicism, that this attribute alone provides enough of a motivation for some members of their caste to form marriage alliances. When these marriages occur today no social ostracism takes place, although Kaikkoolars fear that Moolakkaaran women may not be appropriately circumspect in their behavior.

In summary, the Kaikkoolars of the Salem-Erode region are divided into two main subdivisions, the Periyataalis and the Cinnataalis, with an important satellite community, the Moolakkaarans, representing a separate division. The caste is further segmented on the basis of locality and custom within these subdivisions. The 72 naaDu system of organization corresponds to this segmented order. At the lowest level, paavaDi naaDu councils are associated with villages; the thisainaaDu is associated with the locality; and finally, the mahaanaaDu is associated with the region.

Caste, supralocality, and relations between locality and state

It has been customary for anthropologists to describe caste organization at the supralocality level as consisting of a noncorporate identity composed of a shared "occupational specialty, name, and subculture (including myths, deities, history), [and] closely-similar rank for constituent sub-castes" (Kolenda 1978:19). Caste at this level is perceived as more ideological than organizational or interactional. Regionwide caste associations formed in the twentieth century have been described as new organizational forms associated with modern urbanism. They are said to have little importance to castes as they exist in villages. Thus Hardgrave (1970:48), referring to this level of organization, argues that the "caste category [his term for supralocal caste] . . . is fundamentally urban" and has no relevance to villagers within the caste community except insofar as they are taking part in a shift to urbanism. Accordingly, the usual view of regionwide caste identity is one of a noncorporate, largely ideological identity with no organizational structure. Alternatively, if such a structure exists, it is described as something that has been recently added as an adjustment to urbanization.

This characterization may be accurate for the agricultural castes and their interdependent castes today; however, it is historically inaccurate. In the twelfth century, cultivators in south India organized themselves into supra-regional assemblies known as *cittirameeli-periyanaaDu*. These were created, according to Hall (1980:31, 203), by agriculturists to protect their autonomy from royal Chola penetration. These periyanaaDu survived into the eighteenth century (Hall 1980:205). A period of political parochialism occurred during colonial rule (Washbrook 1976; Baker 1976:1-39). Nonetheless, supralocal agrarian caste organizations do persist to the present (Beck 1972:68ff), although today the political importance of such groups seems to be long gone. One must note, therefore, that supralocal agrarian caste organizations, if not regionwide structures, have existed for centuries. Hardgrave's generalization about caste categories is also untrue of itinerant traders and artisans, who have had supralocal organizations at least since the twelfth or thirteenth century (Stein 1980:138, 227). Following the colonial period, the political insignificance of these systems and the village or "place" focus of anthropological research accounts for supralocal caste organizations being overlooked by anthropologists.

The simultaneous existence of the Kaikkoolars' locality and supralocality structures reveal two levels of caste organization. Before the twentieth century, locality defined the caste's endogamous units and the arena of intense interaction; this was the level of leadership constituencies. Even persons holding office at higher levels of organization were first and foremost local leaders. In contrast to this localism, the naaDu system and later the Sangam and the cooperatives constitute hierarchical networks of supralocal administration. These corporations are the caste's and its leaders' main organizational responses to the requirements of trade and to the need for interaction with state-level organizations. At this level, a two-way interaction between state and caste is evident.

Caste leaders base their strength on their local influence and on their ties with state-level offices and political leaders. Kaikkoolar caste, therefore, has an important organizational dimension that enables it to coordinate effectively a widely dispersed network of locality-based caste segments. This allows members in one area to trade and otherwise interact with other segments in different localities, with a means of administering identity, ranking, trade agreements, and interaction with polities and with a means of settling disputes that may arise. These organizations also form a variety of hierarchical channels of communication through which state and locality interact.

In this context, it is illuminating to emphasize two ways in which Kaikkoolar caste organization may be seen as a form of ethnicity. First, one of the important features of ethnicity is group boundary flexibility, which under some circumstances allows for situational identity switching (Brunner 1974; Nagata 1974; Mines 1975). The Kaikkoolars engage in such identity switching by manipulating their organizational identity. Thus, for example, the endogamous group has been variously defined by Kaikkoolars; it may be sublocal, local, regional, or selectively supralocal, and it may or may not allow intermarriage with Moolakkaarans. The endogamous group is defined by whether a person chooses to adhere to a locality definition of marriageability, the Sangam definition that all Kaikkoolars are marriageable, the view that Moolakkaarans are or are not Kaikkoolars, and if they are not, which "Kaikkoolar" localities are not suitable for marriage because of a past tradition of deeva-daasi residence.

Second, ethnic identity generally is used for political and economic ends in plural societies. In these societies, ethnicity provides identity and a reason for organizing people in order to present their interests at multiplex levels of political organization. Kaikkoolars have used their supralocal identity and organization in this manner for centuries. Their regional organization is not a result of twentieth-century urbanism. As conditions in the state have changed, the Kaikkoolars have added new types of organization. This means that at the supralocal level, caste members and caste leaders today have several forms of organization at their disposal that can be used for political and economic purposes.

Accordingly, Kaikkoolar caste organization at the supralocal level has a dynamism and flexibility that have not been described in caste studies. At this level, the caste is defined as much by its changing interaction with state organizations as it is by any inherent quality of casteism.

The picture of caste that emerges from the description of the Kaikkoolars in this book is different from the one usually presented in the anthropological literature. Mayer (1960:44-47), Pocock (1962:85-87), Beck (1970, 1972, 1979), Heesterman (1973), and David (1974) are concerned with understanding the ethnographic and theoretical place of groups of castes such as the Kaikkoolars, which are outside or marginal to the core of hierarchically interrelated castes. But there is little awareness of the significance of these castes, which David (1974:56) calls the "nonbound mode," to our understanding of Indian society in general. This is perhaps because at first they do not appear to be an imposing sector of society. They have the modest distinction of being clumped together in the middle ranks, within which their relative status is commonly described as unclear, or where they are said to be "not distinctly ranked" (David 1974:46).

We have seen, however, that the Kaikkoolars' local status ambiguity contrasts to the clarity of their supralocal organization. This is where their significance to anthropology lies. They are a caste whose organization reflects their regional political-economic interests. Since in India most anthropological works have focused on agriculturists whose primary political-economic interests are local, it is easy to understand how the significance of artisan-merchants has been missed. But that these castes have been important to Indians is apparent, because society in the south was until recently divided into right-hand and left-hand sections.

3 The Kaikkoolars and the iDangkai (left-hand) and valangkai (right-hand) castes

"We will jointly assert our rights" . . . only those "who display the *birudas* [plug of a lute] of horn, bugle and parasol shall belong to our class. Those who have to recognize us now and hereafter in public must do so from our distinguishing symbols – the feather of the crane and the loose-hanging hair. The horn and the conch-shell shall also be sounded in front of us and the bugle blown according to the fashion obtaining among the 'iDangkai' left-handed people."

> (Thirteenth century inscription listing the symbols marking Kammalar [goldsmiths, bronze workers, blacksmiths, stone carvers, carpenters] identity found in KonkunaaDu [Arokiaswami 1956:275-276])

The left-hand/right-hand distinction has disappeared in the Salem-Erode region of Tamilnadu. People in their late thirties remember hearing about the sections in their childhood, but they are vague concerning the meaning of the division. Older Kaikkoolars in their late seventies living in Erode, however, recall the division vividly. They relate tales of heated conflict and murder, and quarrels between the moieties over their respective rights in festivals and the uses of temples in surrounding villages. Piecing this information together, it is apparent that the left-hand/right-hand distinction was an integral part of status reckoning in the Salem-Erode region as late as the 1920s, but that by the 1940s the distinction was rapidly fading, and by the late 1970s only a few people were still aware of it. The disappearance of the distinction corresponds to the increasing Indian participation in local government that culminated in Indian independence in 1947. This correspondence is more than coincidental.

The left-hand/right-hand distinction was in part a symbolic way (Appadurai 1974) of incorporating the two differently integrated systems of castes – the nonbound-mode and the bound-mode castes – into a single cohesive social order. This cohesion was supplied neither by the

33

precolonial, indigenous, segmented states nor by the British in colonial times (Stein 1975:76; 1980:484). The indigenous states had attempted to define the relations among the castes of the two divisions by designating separate social domains for them. Later, when disputes arose, the British frequently followed the same course. Castes of the two divisions were awarded different emblems of identity, including the right to carry torches and flags, wear particular styles of dress, build certain kinds of houses, wear hair in specific ways, display special emblems, and hold certain temple offices. Right-hand and left-hand castes maintained separate ritual identities. At major temples they maintained separate resthouses, called *maNDapam*. Each section had its own deeva-daasis. And when disputes arose between castes of the two divisions, they were separated residentially and ritually to prevent rioting and bloodshed.

The left-hand/right-hand categories were appellations that carried no general rights common to a whole category; they were not corporate groups. In the contexts of temple worship and naaDu organization, however, they divided the south Indian social cosmos into two parts and established separate social arenas within which castes made claims to particular social statuses, defined the dimensions and nature of their religious-political domains, and displayed their distinctive ritual statuses. The separate domains of the two sections were symbolically marked during temple pujas and in the redistributive functions of temples that gave recognition to the separate statuses of castes of the two divisions (Appadurai and Breckenridge 1976). Territorial domains were established when caste segments jointly sponsored major temple pujas. This action defined these caste segments as a territorial confederation, a naaDu. Caste status was marked during pujas by symbolic acts, such as the manner in which caste members were treated by Brahman priests. In addition, castes of each section were prohibited from entering the residential streets of the other section during ritual processions.

Spatially and ritually, therefore, the two sections were separated; caste identities, naaDu territories, and statuses were marked by their temple worship. Temples, rituals, and naaDus were the institutions in which left-hand/right-hand distinctions were utilized and given expression. Brahmans administered or legitimated the signs and symbols of the moiety, and in this manner enacted the Hindu ideology of a bifurcated south Indian social order.

In 1870 the British began a process of administrative centralization that shifted the locus of governmental decision making and power from the districts to Madras City and Fort St. George, the seat of colonial government in the Presidency (Washbrook 1976; Baker 1976:1-39).

This process began a social transformation of Tamil society that reached a critical point of metamorphosis in the late teens and 1920s, when the British introduced dyarchy (Irschick 1969:55-135). The level of social integration shifted from local domains defined by district administration, magnates with large landholdings, and the temple networks and naaDus of the higher-ranked non-Brahman castes to the regional level, where statewide and nationwide political parties were the primary integrating institutions. The shift was from locality-based, magnate politics and from segmentary organization and caste sodalities to emergent populist regional political parties and a democratized state.

When centralization diminished the importance of temples and naaDus as the main institutions defining native political organization, the left-hand/right-hand distinction lost its institutional base and its symbolic value. The shift to democracy was gradual; although it began as early as the 1870s, the change in governmental form was not fully implemented until Independence. Consequently, the central role of naaDus, temples, and temple Brahmans as administrators of integration in Tamil politics did not end abruptly, but gradually waned throughout this period. NaaDu temples today continue to be important arenas where the ritual statuses of worshipers are defined, but they have lost their importance as one of the society's primary political institutions because the naaDu domains defined by the temples no longer have political value.

In the early years after the introduction of dyarchy, the Kaikkoolars stopped using Brahman priests in their life crisis ceremonies and began building temples in which their caste fellows acted as priests (teesikars). Today they say that their purpose was to weaken the Brahmans' power to define their ritual and social position and to circumvent Brahman refusals to give them the honors they wanted. In these new temples, Kaikkoolars could publicly display a superordinate status through the honors they received. Kaikkoolars were able to do this primarily at the sublocality level, where they were numerically strong. Given their diminished economic and political importance, the Kaikkoolars used the temples primarily to define their status and to integrate their locality-segmented identity. Brahmans continued to preside at locality and regional temples, but Kaikkoolars benefited at these temples both from the unity provided by their joint sponsorship of pujas and from their prominent role as worshipers. Twentieth-century non-Brahmanism was made possible in part by the process of centralization and by the consequent weakening of the political and economic roles of temples and temple Brahmans. The weakening of Brahman roles and the diminished importance of temples as integrators of caste segments represented major changes in the nature of south Indian society and caste organization.

The origins of the right-hand/left-hand division

It is historically impossible at this time to reconstruct the origins of the right-hand/left-hand division. It has been suggested by Stein that the system may originally have developed as a way of conceptually incorporating into society non-Brahmans whose social status was ambiguous "given the commitment . . . [to] Brahmanical ideology by the Pallava period" (Stein 1980:207-208). Subsequently, during the Chola period of expansion, the division provided a mechanism for tribal absorption and a means of conceptualizing the opposition between peasant leaders and artisans and merchants (Beck 1972; Appadurai 1974; Stein 1980:208).

This latter opposition is one that Meillasoux (1973) has argued is a critical feature in the historical development of India's political economy of stratification. He argues that what we now call castes developed as class oppositions. Basic among these oppositions was one between rulers and priests closely associated with the agrarian sector and an emergent artisan-merchant sector. This dichotomy is ancient in India, and the right-hand/left-hand division embodies something of this class dichotomy observed by Meillasoux. But caution is warranted, since even in these early times, what Meillasoux would have us see as homogeneous class interests were crosscut by many castes, each with its own distinctive political-economic interests. Thus, there were in Chola times weavers of several castes, merchants of several types and castes, and artisans of diverse sorts. Each of these, as far as we can tell, sought its own status and identity, and may well have administered its own affairs.

Judging by the use of the division in the Middle Ages (eleventh through thirteenth centuries), right-hand/left-hand moiety identity provided a conceptual framework for incorporating castes and their dependents that were engaged in different modes of production, had different power bases, and competed for status and influence within weakly centralized kingdoms. Within these kingdoms, commercialism became an increasingly important source of wealth and liquidity for kingly treasures (Hall 1980).

Initially, artisan-merchant groups and activities were under the control of agriculturists (Hall 1980). But as trade developed in the Chola age, these artisan-merchants became increasingly distinctive both in how they were represented in kingly policy and in the growth of their own power. Throughout much of the Chola period, kings seemed to have used temples as a way of financing commerce and as a means of controlling the artisan-merchants. Temple endowments, including gold, were sometimes put under the control of merchants or lent to them in the form of gold for investment in production and trade (Hall 1980:76ff). Weaving was carefully and thoroughly taxed (Hall 1980:58). And as itinerant trade grew in importance, artisan-merchant organizations moved away from the authority of agriculturists' organizations (naaDus) and began making their tax settlements directly with Chola revenue officials (Hall 1980:81). They also formed their own military units (Hall 1980:81) and sought status parity with the leading agrarian castes (Stein 1980:138). In other words, the artisan-merchants became a political and economic force unto themselves that sought separation from agriculturist control. The core character of the right-hand/left-hand division had taken form.

The Kaikkoolars and the legacy of the left-hand/right-hand distinction

The legacy of the left-hand/right-hand distinction is still apparent in the social organization of the Salem-Erode region, and it is easy to misinterpret the status and behavior of Kaikkoolars if this legacy is disregarded. By examining the remnants of the system, one can reconstruct the social division of right-hand and left-hand castes. This is a useful enterprise for two reasons. First, awareness of the nature of the division helps to clarify otherwise confusing aspects of Kaikkoolar behavior. Second, it allows social scientists and historians to gain a better understanding of the basis of the left-hand/right-hand distinction. Beck (1970, 1972) sees the contrast as one between castes following distinctive modes of economic behavior. She argues that the distinction is between locality-based agriculturists and mobile artisan-merchants. The influence of this distinction on Indian caste behavior has been recognized by others, at least in general outline (Mayer 1960; Pocock 1962; Heesterman 1973; and David 1974). But Beck also argues that the right-hand castes followed a kingly model for behavior, whereas the left-hand castes were basically priestly. Heesterman (1973) supports this kingly/priestly generalization of the two moieties.

There are problems with this generalization. First, some agriculturists are distinguished as former members of the left hand, and some merchants and artisans as former members of the right. Second, Kaikkoolars, like most left-hand castes, do not espouse priestly behavior (Mines 1982); their behavior is mixed.

Appadurai (1974) offers another explanation: The distinction serves the primarily symbolic function of creating the image of a single social body divided, like the human body, into right-hand and left-hand sides. The division creates an image of social unity that polities of the time could not establish, while providing a framework for organizing conflict as the natural opposition of juxtaposed social segments. Stein (1980:480ff) suggests that a combination of Beck's and Appadurai's hypotheses provides a more complete explanation, which is that the division combines a symbolic integrative function and a natural economic division between agriculturists and mobile artisan-merchants (see also Meillasoux 1973:92). This is an assessment with which my findings generally agree.

It is necessary, however, to clarify the mechanism by which this symbolic integration was achieved, in order to show that temples and naaDus were the institutions within which left-hand/right-hand distinctions were maintained, and to demonstrate that left-hand castes were neither priestly nor necessarily artisan-merchants. They were castes that followed a third model of caste behavior, one that replicated in many of its features aspects of both priestly and kingly caste behavior, but not the organizational form of castes following either of these models. The upper left-hand castes formed regional sodalities that competed at local levels with dominant agriculturists, while drawing on the strengths of their supralocal organization and largely artisan-mercantile occupations. The lower-level, left-hand castes were service castes that served either higher left-hand castes or, in some cases, right-hand castes. Because temples and rituals defined caste status and caste domains, these were often the focus of disputes between the divisions.

Temples and disputes: the last sixty years

In Ammapettai, a ward of Salem City, the Kaikkoolars have built for their own use a Murugan temple, the Sengunthar Subramaniyan Kooyil. Murugan is an important Saivite god in south India, and is special to the Kaikkoolars because they identify their ancestral origins with him. He is their caste god. The Kaikkoolars control the temple's administration and festivals, and Kaikkoolar priests preside over worship within it.

By contrast, there is on a nearby hillock, Kumaragiri, another Murugan temple built by a locally famous Kaikkoolar *sannyaasi* (religious mendicant). This temple has a Brahman priest, and members of several different castes visit there. The Kaikkoolars neither control this temple nor are its exclusive users.

The Sengunthar Maariyammaa Kooyil in Ammapettai is an important temple exclusively controlled by the Kaikkoolars. Maariyammaa, the goddess of smallpox, is a central figure in Tamilian ceremonial life. Every residential community has such a temple. What is unusual about Ammapettai is that it has two. The other is called the Palapatarai Maariyammaa Kooyil – the "multicaste Maariyammaa temple" – where, in contrast to the Kaikkoolars' temple, persons from several castes worship. Each Maariyammaa temple and its surrounding temple streets (*maaDa viiti*) demarcate a separate congregation. Usually, when temples are located so close together, it indicates that the congregation of one is an excluded, untouchable community and is replicating the ritual behavior of the purer castes that use the other temple (Moffatt 1979).

The story surrounding the Sengunthar Maariyammaa temple suggests a different reason for the separation. Kaikkoolars relate a hazy history of how they once worshiped at the multicaste temples when Ammapettai was only a few households strong, but when they tried to gain control of the temple, they were denied the right. The Kaikkoolars withdrew and subsequently built their own temple. This tale indicates that the Kaikkoolars were denied control of the original temple but were not excluded from worshiping in it, as untouchables were.

In Kolanalli, a village near Erode, there are two Pillaiyar temples. One is restricted to the landowning VeLLaaLa Gounders and their dependents, and the other is attended by Kaikkoolars. The story surrounding this duplication is one of a series of disputes between Kaikkoolars and the village Gounders that began during Taipuusam (a festival for Lord Murugan). During the celebration, Gounders attempted to deny the Kaikkoolars temple entry. In retaliation the Kaikkoolars, armed with sticks, prevented a Gounder wedding party from gaining access to the village Pillaiyar temple. All weddings must begin with a visit by the groom to this temple. Moderate Kaikkoolar leaders, hoping to prevent bloodshed, admonished their fellows for this bellicose act. The informant who told me of this dispute went on to say that in the time when the dispute took place, the Gounders were much more powerful than the poor Kaikkoolars, and as a result of Gounder attacks, many persons, including himself, moved to the city of Erode, which was to become an important textile production and marketing center. Subsequently, a judge from Erode, a Sengunthar Mudaliyar, ruled that Kaikkoolars had a right to enter the Murugan temple. The Gounders responded by building their own Pillaiyar temple. Today when Kaikkoolars celebrate Taipuusam, the Gounders of the village still do not attend, although they are invited. The two castes remain ritually separate, although there is no longer enmity between them.

In Akkamapettai, a village located twenty-four miles south of Salem City, a dispute between the VeLLaaLa Gounders and the Kaikkoolars prevented the annual celebration of Maariyammaa over a period of several years in the mid-1950s. During the festival, Kaikkoolars sang a song about brave Sengunthars who killed VeLLaaLas in battle. The village VeLLaaLa Gounders took offense at this statement of Kaikkoolar bravery and Gounder defeat and demanded that the Kaikkoolars give up the song. For three years the VeLLaaLa Gounders prevented the joint celebration, until finally a compromise was reached that allowed both castes to save face. The Kaikkoolars were to give up their song during the joint festival but could continue to sing it during another celebration, the Muttukumaarasaami festival. This celebration was held at the Kaikkoolar-controlled Murugan temple located on the Kaikkoolars' *paavaDi* (warp-stretching) grounds.

Social status and the legacy of the right-hand/left-hand social division

What explains the duplication of temples and this ritual separation of Kaikkoolars? Given the behavioral evidence, it might be concluded that the Kaikkoolars were once a low-ranking caste, perhaps even an untouchable caste, that has managed to achieve a higher status in the twentieth century than it formerly held. If so, what we are observing are the remnants of their former status. Certainly there is other evidence that suggests an earlier low status; for example, Kaikkoolars are meat eaters and blood sacrificers, some of whom even today sacrifice pigs to their family deities (kuladeevam). They are avid worshipers of small gods, have a reputation for drinking intoxicants, and engage in black magic. Some caste members are regularly possessed by local deities. These are all non-Brahmanical traits that mark them as having a relatively low status. This assessment seems to be supported by Frykenberg (1977), who notes that in mid-nineteenth-century Tinnevelli, bloody riots broke out when Kaikkoolars attempted to take a funeral procession through the residential area of the VeLLaaLa. Violence is what might be expected if an upwardly mobile, untouchable caste attempted to proceed through an upper-caste residential area from which they were ritually excluded.

In fact, however, the Kaikkoolars are neither former untouchables nor a particularly low caste compared to other non-Brahmans. What explains the ritual separation of Kaikkoolars is that from Chola times (the eleventh century) until about sixty years ago, Tamil society was divided into right-hand and left-hand moieties. The left-hand section ritually and socially replicated many of the features of the right-hand section. This left-hand replication was more a copying of the general symbolic substance of the right-hand caste system than a duplication of its organizational form. From an organizational perspective, it appears that the right-hand castes were primarily tied to agriculture and locality, and together formed an integrated, interdependent social order administered through the dominant and chiefly agricultural castes. Mobile artisan and merchant castes formed the core of the left-hand section. These latter castes were only indirectly tied to agricultural production. Consequently, they were economically distinctive, and the economic base of their political relations was distinctive, too. They were not readily dependent on the dominant agriculturists. In addition, there were some nondominant agriculturists who sought the protection of the higher left-hand castes by establishing alliances with them. Each of the higher left-hand castes was incorporated through its own chiefly administrative organizations. These organizations were composed of interlocally allied caste segments organized as administrative sodalities. The Kaikkoolars called their system the "72 naaDus."

The castes of the two moieties formed roughly equal hierarchies in which paired castes from opposite moieties made parallel status claims. Three general types of evidence support this image of left-hand castes as economically, ritually, socially, and politically separated from their right-hand counterparts. First, the economic behavior of the two sections was different. Although some left-hand castes were agriculturists, most of them did not cultivate land. Buchanan (1807, vol. II:265), for example, was impressed that Kaikkoolars in the Coimbatore area did not cultivate even the land they rented; they hired others to farm for them. The *Padaiyaachi,* who are left-hand agriculturists allied to the Kaikkoolars in the Erode area, were an exception. But their affiliation was a result of their search for an alliance to help them in their conflict with the more powerful Gounders of the area, according to Kaikkoolars.

Second, although the left-hand section carried the stigma of inferiority to the right-hand section, as its name suggests, castes of the two divisions locally vied with each other for equal or superior ritual status, which was partially expressed and validated by the acquisition of temple offices and honors, and by the right to display particular signs of identity and status such as caste flags. Basically, the clean castes of the left-hand section sought to replicate the dominant right-hand castes' pomp and involvement in temple and ritual. This replication included the now-outlawed deeva-daasi system. In return for their offerings given to temples, the clean left-hand castes sought from Brahmans a public display of honors. These were expressed by the manner in which Brahmans redistributed the offerings of puja sponsors to worshipers, and by the signs of status and pomp the left-hand castes were able to exhibit as their exclusive right during the course of major temple celebrations or during caste rituals. Third, both the higher left-hand castes such as the Kaikkoolars and *Kammalars* and the higher right-hand castes such as the VeLLaLas maintained their own supralocal caste organizations (naaDus), which provided the structure for self-regulation. A naaDu also united its caste on a regional level as a corporate group that sponsored annual pujas at important locality and regional temples. In this manner, a caste's naaDu system was geographically defined by its temple's location.

This vying for mirror symbolic status and for signs of pomp and honor by the left-hand section has an ancient history in Tamilnadu. According to Stein (1980:252), the growth of cities in the twelfth century was associated with the development of the Vedic temple complex that still characterizes south Indian religious geography today. Artisan-merchant groups including Kaikkoolars found a new basis of power in the developing towns, where they were more clearly separated from the core of land-linked relations of the agrarian village (Stein 1980:250). Support of the temples provided a means of demonstrating symbolically their trade-related wealth. Temples also provided financing for production and trade (Hall 1980:82-86). Temple endowments, which included land, gold, and special tax considerations, were sometimes controlled by mercantile organizations (nagarams) in medieval times, and gold was lent to weavers and merchants to finance their enterprises. Consequently, control of temples was extremely important politically and economically. Kings, chiefs, artisan-merchants, and agriculturists sought to control them (Hall 1981).

The jointly sponsored temple puja was also a primary way of symbolically underscoring a sense of interlocal ties among caste segments. For merchants and artisans, a large puja must have offered opportunities to exchange gossip and establish or reinforce economic and political alliances. Tamil-speaking Muslim merchants use similar occasions for such purposes today (Mines 1975).

In the temples, the artisan-merchants received symbolic honors that expressed the status to which they aspired. Even today, the landowners in agrarian-dominated villages try to monopolize these symbolic honors (Pfaffenberger 1980:203, 205).

In the twelfth century, artisan-traders in Kongu and elsewhere appeared to have strived for and attained status parity with the local peasant folk among whom they lived. (Stein 1980:138)

. . . during the twelfth century merchant and artisan groups began to separate themselves from the constraints of Brahman and peasant rural control. This process of separation, in the Coromandel plains at least, was accompanied by new status claims by merchants and artisans, as noticed . . . in temple honours sought and gained by these [left-hand] groups. Essentially, the growing importance of urban places was dependent upon the increasingly vigorous trade throughout the Macro region resulting from the wealth and stability of the agrarian integration of the previous two centuries. Settlements with substantial numbers of merchants and artisans rose to new importance. (Stein 1980:252)

It was in the twelfth century that Kammalars (the *Aachaari* artisans) claimed Brahman status (Arokiaswami 1956:277). It is in this period also (twelfth to thirteenth century) that Kaikoolar claims to warrior status originate: "Expressions like *'Kaikolaperumpadai,' 'Valperra Kaikolar,' 'Velaikarar'* (trusted soldiers) of the *'Valangkai'* [right-hand] are often found in Chola inscriptions of the times" (Arokiaswami 1959:273). At this time, Kaikkoolars were associated with the right-hand moiety, according to Arokiaswami (Arokiaswami 1956:273), but subsequently they became linked with the left-hand section, perhaps as their rivalry with the dominant VeLLaaLa Gounders deepened. The VeLLaala Gounders of Konku were the other warrior caste of this region, so the competitive relationship between Kaikkoolars and VeL-LaaLa Gounders is a natural outgrowth of their duplicate status.

The social mobility described by Stein is consistent with what we know today about how caste groups in India go about changing their social positions (Marriott 1968). Once a significant change in economic position is achieved, an effort is made to end the dependence on the agrarian castes; finally, ritual substantiation of the new social status is sought. The artisan-merchant castes could not dominate in the agrarian villages, where even today they lack the interdependent ties upon which the landowners' dominance is based. But in the new urban centers, they removed themselves from that context. They formed what Stein (1980:25) calls the urban "outer-core," the left-hand side, to the rural "inner-core," the right-hand side, of the south Indian social order. Society was agrarian centered, but the artisan-merchants also formed an economic locus of wealth. In medieval times, the right-hand castes were located in the nucleated agrarian centers spotted throughout the plains areas of the region. The hostile lands separating these nuclear areas were bridged by members of the left-hand section: itinerant traders such as the Kaikkoolars (Stein 1975:75).

During Chola times (eleventh to thirteenth centuries), itinerant traders, apparently including the Kaikkoolars, belonged to great trade organizations such as the Ayyavole 500 and the MaNigraamam (Stein 1965:56, 58) and had considerable military and political power. These traders traveled with armed escorts. "The military pretensions of these organizations can be seen in inscriptions which boast of their bravery, their sharp swords, and their honors as 'sons of warriors' " (Stein 1965:58-59). This warrior tradition is still a crucial aspect of the Kaikkoolars' self-image today. The ancient historic demand for symbolic parity with the dominant agrarian castes, therefore, must be seen in the context of the political and economic power that the itinerant traders were able to wield. One can speculate that in KonkunaaDu, whose hills and mountains harbored dangerous tribals that preyed on settled nuclear areas (Stein 1965:58-59), it was necessary that itinerant traders travel well armed.

The decline of the Cholas in the thirteenth century led to the decline of the great trade organizations and to the weakening of the military and political power of itinerant traders. Nuclear agrarian centers surrounded by hostile, tribal-controlled lands were replaced in the succeeding Vijayanagar period (A.D. 1350-1650) by military fiefdoms. The result was a more localized trade and apparently a decline in the military independence of itinerant traders.

The tendency toward more localized trade as a reflection of more localized warrior power and the desire to maximize control over all resources did not eliminate the older diffuse trade network, but it limited the commodities in such trade to such essentials as salt, iron and horses and such luxuries as fine textiles and precious stones. (Stein 1965:58)

By the seventeenth century, the great trade organizations had disappeared and the Tamil artisan-merchant groups were weak.

Nonetheless, Kaikkoolars as artisan-traders continued to have an economic base and an organization network (their naaDu system) that were only tangentially tied to agriculture. This political-economic separation continued to form the basis of their claim to ritual-symbolic honors equal to but separate from those of the dominant agrarian caste, the VeLLaaLas.

Other high-ranking left-hand castes such as the Kammalars (Aachaaris) and *Beri Chettiars* (Thurston 1909, vols. I and III:108-110) seem to have been organized much like the Kaikkoolars, forming regionwide sodalities free from the control of right-hand castes. The Kammalars, for example, were organized under a caste head, called *Urumaa Kattaradu,* who was elected by representatives of the caste's five divisions (Thurston 1909, vol. III:108-109). This system of organization probably dated from Vijayanagar times. In other words, over a period of several hundred years, Kammalars, Kaikkoolars, and some Chettiars maintained their own regionwide networks.

The economic power base of the left-hand section was urban, so much so that Appadurai (1974) sees the function of the right-hand/left-hand moiety in the colonial period as a predominantly symbolic and conceptual attempt to regulate urban-based disputes. Appadurai considers the moiety division a "root paradigm" of south Indian society (Turner 1974). It formed the basis of the south Indians' conceptualization of how the society was ordered, and created a sense of social unity resulting from the balanced antithesis of the two moieties.

Appadurai believes that the paradigm evolved from its early origins when it was used as a way of conceptualizing the entry of indigenous tribal peoples into caste society as members of the left-hand section. He sees conflicts from the seventeenth to the twentieth centuries as individual disputes between paired castes of the two sections and their supporting allies from other castes. Disputes never involved one division as a whole against the other. Kaikkoolars disputed with VeL-LaaLas and other weavers of the right-hand section (Appadurai 1974:241); Kaikkoolars sided with opponents of the *Balija* (right-hand) traders (Appadurai 1974:239); Baligas fought with Kammalars (Appadurai 1974:238), and so on. These disputes were concerned with the right to temple honors, the use of emblems such as caste flags, the right to use streets for ritual processions, and left-hand caste demands for equal rights within temples and the privilege of administering their own caste affairs. These disputes were extremely hard to settle without one section or the other having decisive power, and without a central authority with the strength to enforce a decision. As a consequence, disputes were settled less by adjudication than by defining the separate social and ritual domains of the disputants. Cities were divided into right-hand and left-hand domains (Buchanan 1807, vol. II:268), and the two sections were given separate rights.

Historical evidence supporting the "separate but equal" division of society includes the allocation of particular streets to the two sections for both residential and ritual purposes. Spatial separation is a common way of restricting interaction among castes in India. What makes the separation distinctive is that it was not used to isolate the ritually impure. On the contrary, separation was used to allow the existence of more or less equal categories of castes with their own internal status hierarchies:

A documentary award of 1652, allotting particular streets [of Madras] to the right and left sides, both for residence and ritual/festive purposes, seems to have been supported and defended by leaders of both sides. (Appadurai 1974:251)

Each faction [of the right and left sides] was expressly ordered [by the Rajan in Conjeepuram at the Kaamaakshi Amman temple] not to enter, with their marriage, funeral or festival processions, the streets allotted to the other [circa 1800]. (Appadurai 1974:239)

Both sections were declared equal to each other. On this account Coimbatore has been long divided into separate [right-hand and left-hand] quarters. In its own quarter, each party may perform its ceremonies in whatever manner it pleases; but it is not allowed to go into the adversary's quarters with any procession. (Buchanan 1807, vol. II:268)

Frykenberg's (1977) description of the dispute between the left-hand Kaikkoolars and the right-hand VeLLaaLas in mid-nineteenth-century

Tinnevelly depicts the transgression of such rules. Kaikkoolars attempted to take a funeral procession down a government road that ran through the VeLLaaLa residential section. Bloody riots resulted, and a number of people were killed.

Kaikkoolars in the Salem-Erode region still reside in homogeneous residential areas in cities such as Salem (Ammapettai, Salem City), Trichengode, and Erode, and in villages near precolonial administrative towns such as Akkammapettai Village, one mile from Sankagiri-drug. Kaikkoolars claim that they do so because their profession as weavers requires them to stretch their warps in the street and consequently to impede traffic. They live separately to avoid the conflicts this might cause. However, they also actively exclude others from their areas. This separation, however, is not restricted to maintenance of the spatial domain. It involves social and ritual segregation too, as the discussion of disputes and temple duplication presented earlier illustrates.

The now defunct deeva-daasi tradition reflects this duplication. As temple servants, daasis and their children performed a number of ritual services including washing the temple, dancing, taking part in processions, and performing music. According to my Kaikkoolar informants, the right to dedicate deeva-daasis was once considered a great honor and was a privilege to be defended. Thurston (1909, vol. II:127-128) notes that deeva-daasis were divided into right-hand and left-hand sections, and were recruited correspondingly from VeL-LaaLas (the right hand) and Kaikkoolars (the left hand). Daasis of the right would not perform music or dance in the homes of Kamma-lars (artisans) or other left-hand castes, the groups for whom the left-hand daasis performed. And although Thurston does not say so, daasis of the left-hand castes undoubtedly served primarily Brahmans and clean castes of their section of society.

In ritual status and in spatial domains, therefore, the right-hand and left-hand sections not only were separate but also mirrored one another. This mirroring was a feature of the left-hand castes' claim to status equal to that of specific right-hand castes; such claims were strongly expressed even in medieval times in south India (Stein 1980:250). Informants in KonkunaaDu told me that not only daasis but also service castes were and still are divided into those that served the left and those that served the right.

In the Erode region, barbers, who are important ritual functionaries in marriage, birth, and death, are divided into two sections. One section, the Konku barbers, serves the VeLLaaLa Gounders of the region (the Konku VeLLaaLas) and carries their utensils in a canvas bag. The *VeeTTuva* barbers serve the left-hand castes and carry their tools of trade in a leather bag (Arokiaswami 1959:269). Each Gounder land-holding group has its own household service families, including a barber, washerman, and drummer who work for the household (*kuDi*) and take part in its social functions. These castes perform personal services and have important ritual functions. In a parallel manner, both sections also once had their own untouchables: *Paraiyan* untouchables (drummers) are members of the right-hand section and are agricultural laborers, whereas *Maadeeri* untouchables (leather workers) are members of the left-hand section. Today, however, Maadeeris serve as the primary agricultural labor caste of the Konku VeLLaaLas in KonkunaaDu (Beck 1972:104, 108). This exception to the symmetry of the two divisions is perhaps an indication that moiety membership only imperfectly reflects economic alliances. The impoverished Maadeeris must work where work can be found.

Another example of ritual replication is that both VeLLaaLas and Kaikkoolars, as rival castes, are temple patrons and builders of high-god temples. Kaikkoolars claim credit for building the beautifully carved Kailaasanaatha temple in Taramangalam, which is one of the most important Saivite temples in the Salem-Erode locality. Pfaffenberger (1980:207) notes that the role of temple patron is one to which VeLLaaLas still wish to lay exclusive claim. Both castes are concerned with controlling and building temples because in this manner each can buttress its secular status with displays of wealth and religiosity, and with special temple offices, honors, and the support of Brahmans. Temple patronage is also important because joint sponsorship of pujas forms the symbolic basis of naaDu organization and political control of a local territory.

Taken as a whole, the left-hand section crudely replicates the caste statuses of the right-hand section. The left-hand Kammalans claim to be Brahmans, wear the sacred thread of the twice-born castes, and call themselves *Aachaaris*, as Brahmans do. Kaikkoolars claim a warrior heritage. At least two castes, Padaiyaachis and the VeeTTuva Gounders, compete with the dominant VeLLaaLa Gounders in the Erode region as lesser landowning castes and are loosely allied to the left-hand section. Both castes once paid to the Kaikkoolars a "tax" that was used to sponsor pujas until the mid-1920s. Below these are service castes, notably washermen, left-hand barbers, and potters. At the bottom of the left-hand hierarchy are the Maadeeris. Because these castes are to a great extent economically independent of each other, rather than interdependent as the right-hand castes are, their status claims are unsubstantiated by service and food transactions. Without these transactions to confirm their claims, the relative status of the higher left-hand castes is always ambiguous.

The replication of the right-hand social order by the left found expression in two other features of caste organization – the naaDu system and the duplication of temples – when competition between right-hand and left-hand castes was severe. Beck (1972:63) notes that the Konku region has been divided into twenty-four naaDus since ancient times. Although these divisions have little to do with the present-day administration of the region, the naaDus are "still prominently featured in folklore, caste organization [of the VeLLaaLa Gounders], and local ritual" (Beck 1972:65). Each naaDu has a leading Saivite temple that acts as its ritual center, as well as lesser temples in each of the naaDu. Beck (1972:74) sees this type of naaDu organization as exclusive to castes of the right-hand division, particularly the landholding castes: the Gounders and *Nadars*. In Konku the only other right-hand caste with a territorially based political organization is the *Udaiyaar* (potters), but its organization is distinctive (Beck 1972:72). Beck sees other right-hand castes, as tied to the landholding communities. As for the left-hand castes, she writes, "None of the socially high-ranking left-division subcastes has any territorially based organization at all" (1972:74).

In the Salem-Erode region of northern Konku, however, left-hand naaDus have existed for a long time (Buchanan 1807, vol. II:265). The Kaikkoolars' 72 naaDu system mirrors several features of the Gounders' system, with some differences. Similarities include the territorial structure of the system, the association of each naaDu seat with a temple, the functions of the naaDus as caste councils and organizers of ritual, and the councils' jurisdiction over certain castes of lesser rank.

A major difference is the greater extent of the Kaikkoolar system, which ranges from the village level through naaDus representing particular village clusters to the supralocal regional councils (thisainaaDu or periya naaDu) to the macroregional caste council (mahaanaaDu) located in Conjeepuram. Another difference is that Murugan temples rather than Saivite temples are most commonly associated with the Kaikkoolars' system. Finally, the Kaikkoolars' system is theoretically divided into four sections associated with the cardinal directions, rather than into a north-south grouping as in the VeLLaaLa system. These latter differences fit the distinctive economic behavior of the two communities. The marketing networks of the artisan-merchant Kaikkoolars are reflected in their supralocal territorial system, whereas the sedentary, agriculturist VeLLaaLas are associated with limited village localities. Their supralocal organizations have been destroyed by successive warrior kings and chiefs, who have sought to limit the power of local landowner castes since Chola times.

The Kaikkoolars' naaDu system in northern KonkunaaDu is independent of the VeLLaaLa system. Kaikkoolar naaDus once settled disputes among their caste fellows, as well as among washermen, potters, and barbers who were attached to their caste as dependents, and they collected taxes for ritual purposes. In some villages where Gounders controlled most interdependent relations, the Kaikkoolars' village naaDu was subordinate to that of the VeLLaaLas, and some disputes were settled by the local leader of the VeLLaaLa council, known as the *Uur Gounder*. This was the case in Akkammapettai Village until the 1950s. Nonetheless, on the whole, the Kaikkoolars' naaDu system appears to replicate the basic features of the VeLLaaLa system. It is territorial; each naaDu section is associated with a Saivite temple dedicated either to Shiva (VeLLaaLa) or Murugan (Kaikkoolar); the titles of naaDu officers are similar, if not identical (Chapter 5 and Beck 1972:69); and the council functions include settlement of disputes, administration of caste domains, and supralocality interaction.

The final expression of the left-hand castes' replication of the right-hand castes' social order is found in the duplication of temples described at the beginning of this chapter. Historically, it appears that even in medieval times, high-ranking left-hand castes sought and achieved equal status in temples. Thus, both VeLLaaLas and Kaikkoolars held important offices at the Srirangam temple in Tiruchirapalli during Chola times (Stein 1968:87), and artisan-merchants were able to achieve "status parity with the local peasant folk among whom they lived" (Stein 1980:138, 250-252), expressed in part in the temple honors they sought and achieved (Hall 1980).

In modern times, it appears that Kaikkoolars in the Salem-Erode region continue to seek status in temples equal to that of the landowning VeLLaaLa Gounders. This pursuit takes several forms. First, in some urban areas, right-hand and left-hand castes still maintain separate facilities. Thurston (1909, vol. III:118) reports that right-hand and left-hand castes had separate rest halls (maNDapam) in Conjeepuram. In Trichengode's Ardhanaariisvarar temple, the Kaikkoolars today still maintain their own maNDapam, which they use to house Kaikkoolars from visiting naaDu areas on the night of the caste-sponsored puja. Similarly, Kaikkoolars have built and operate their own Murugan and Maariyamman temples in Ammapettai and Salem City. Kaikkoolar priests officiate in these temples, as they do over household and life crisis ceremonies. As described earlier, Kaikkoolars have built temples in order to achieve the equal status they desire. In other words, Kaikkoolars use special separation, withdrawal, and duplication as a multifaceted method of achieving a status equal to that of the VeLLaaLas, their main competitors. After all, the right-hand/left-hand distinction may no longer be made, but the institutions and social separation that expressed this distinction continue to exist and are determinants of caste identity. Among the Kaikkoolars, the most important surviving institutions are temple domains and the naaDu system. But to understand them we must examine first their beliefs and then their caste organization.

4 Kaikkoolar beliefs and the order of their social world

Kaikkoolar beliefs reveal a mental blueprint of their relationships to the cosmos and to their social world. This world is composed of the relationships of men and kingly gods; kinfolk and fierce, meat-eating gods; ritual obligations and sacrifices; the redistribution of temple honors; and the bestowal of status and political office. Kaikkoolar beliefs reveal a duality in the universe. The exterior realm is the domain of kings and state; it incorporates depictions of regnal gods, relationships of redistributive exchange, and territoriality. It is concerned with honor, status, and political domain. The interior realm is the sphere of kinsmen and small gods. It is concerned with sickness and well-being, personal fortune and misfortune, and locality. Kaikkoolar beliefs are manifested in the form of stories, and in the ordered social uses of their beliefs. These are displayed in temple ritual, and are also evident in the uses of naaDu temples and in the signs and symbols of status and identity employed by the Kaikkoolars when they are engaged in temple and naaDu affairs. [1]

---

[1]Fox and Zagarell (1982) have argued that in Mesopotamia and south India, temples may have been used during the early period of state formation to remove production from lineage control. State temples had land, artisans, and persons tied to them who produced for the temple. A distinction is made, therefore, between kin-based and temple-based production. Intriguingly, the dichotomy of the Tamilian cosmos into interior (kin-based) and exterior (state-based) realms parallels this distinction proposed by Fox and Zagarell, as does the uses of great-god and small-god temples. However, the period of major temple development in Tamilnadu does not correspond to the origin of Indian states – far from it. It corresponds to a period of major commercialism, the medieval Chola period.

51

The exterior: kingly gods and territorial hierarchies

Hart has noted that "In early Tamil literature there is a dual focus: the king in *puram* or 'exterior' poems, which deal with life outside the family, and love between man and woman in *akam* or 'interior' poems, which deal with life seen from inside the family" (1975a:47). A similar distinction is made today by Kaikkoolars, who divide their sacred cosmos into two spheres. One is the sphere of small gods, who demand blood sacrifices and affect the individual's daily life. This sphere corresponds to the interior category of early poetry, because its gods are worshiped by kinsmen and are spoken of as family gods (kuladeevam). They affect the well-being of the family and its members. The second sphere is that of the great transcendental gods such as Shiva and Murugan. This sphere of great gods corresponds to the exterior category of Tamil poetry. Because these gods are kingly, their temples are their palaces, and their domains are the exchange networks created by temple endowments and the public redistribution of some of these endowments as honors to worshipers (Hart 1975b:13-14; Appadurai and Breckenridge 1976:191, 197-204; Stein 1980:465-466). The Kaikkoolars' territorial organization is associated with a hierarchy of temples dedicated to these great gods.

The meeting of the Seven-City Territory, the EeRuurunaaDu, which I witnessed in 1979, serves to illustrate the manner in which temples are still used by the Kaikkoolars to unite symbolically their community, which otherwise is highly segmented by sublocality, as a territorial unit. The meeting takes place in Trichengode during the annual Ardhanaariisvarar temple cart festival in the Tamil month of Vaikasi (May-June). This large, ancient temple draws pilgrims from all parts of Tamilnadu. The temple is famous not only for Ardhanaariisvarar, a combined embodiment of Shiva (male) and Shakti (female), but also for Murugan, known here as *Sengotuveelar*. Trichengode has a large, prosperous Kaikkoolar community. The EeRuurunaaDu headquarters, therefore, are located at an important Kaikkoolar population center, as well as at an important temple of Murugan and Shiva, the gods with whom Kaikkoolars identify their creation.

During this festival, the EeRuurunaaDu council meets in the town for the purpose, they say, of worshiping God. The meeting is attended by the officers of each village council in the Seven-City Territory, as well as by any villagers who wish to participate. In Chapter 5, I discuss in greater detail the multiplex nature of this meeting. Here I wish to focus on the role of the caste's puja in creating a sense of caste unity within the region.

The evening preceding the caste-sponsored puja, the village officers and representatives meet at the caste's meeting hall, a large maNDa-pam consisting of a roofed dais on which all of those attending can sit. Permission to sit on the dais, however, is granted only to representatives of villages that are in good standing within the EeRuurunaaDu. Communities outcaste during the previous year either come as petitioners seeking readmission or do not attend. The cases of supplicants are discussed, and the petitioners are admitted to the dais after agreeing to pay a symbolic fine. In this manner, the membership of the EeRuurunaaDu is clearly and publicly marked.

Once matters of admission have been settled, the head officers of the locality call a roll of member sublocalities. The representatives respond by indicating how many are present from their village and how much money their village is contributing to the collectively financed Ardhanaariisvarar puja the following morning. These actions again involve a public display of collective action, and each locality is perceived as a constituent of the greater caste corporation sponsoring the puja. This is further emphasized when all of those attending join in a formal procession to a nearby rest house, where representatives of the Taramangalam council and its constituents have been waiting.

A glance at Map 2 reveals that Taramangalam and Trichengode are at opposite ends of the Seven-City Territory. Both are locations of important ancient temples. Taramangalam's council is said to stand next in importance to that of Trichengode, so Taramangalam's special treatment is designed to acknowledge its rank and the territory it incorporates. When the procession reaches the Taramangalam rest house, the Trichengode council formally invites Taramangalam's representatives to join them, and the two groups return in procession to the EeRuurunaaDu rest house and dais. Taramangalam also contributes to the puja, and in this manner all Kaikkoolars of the Seven-City Territory are incorporated by their joint sponsorship of the worship.

The relationship of the Kaikkoolar community to the god of the temple is one of a subject people to their king. In drawing this conclusion, I follow Appadurai and Breckenridge's (1976) interpretation of south Indian temple worship. The puja establishes an exchange relationship between the kingly god and the Kaikkoolars of the Seven-City Territory. The Kaikkoolars give four things to the kingly gods, Shiva and Murugan: money, faith and devotion, service in the form of carrying out temple roles, and cloth. The cloth is given by Trichengode Kaikkoolars as it is periodically needed. The cloth decorates the huge, elaborate temple cart (*teer*) that carries the god when he is taken in procession through the streets of the community. In return, the temple Brahmans bestow temple honors on the caste by redistributing to the representatives the symbolic leavings of the god, including liquids (water, *ghee* or clarified butter, and milk), food (*prasaadam*), and sweets. As previously mentioned, officers of the constituent councils receive yellow turbans, and the caste is publicly listed as the sponsor of one of the pujas made to the god.

Kaikkoolar beliefs and sense of identity

The nature of the Kaikkoolars' relationship to Murugan and Shiva is clearly presented in a variety of myths and stories related by caste members and considered important expressions of Kaikkoolar identity. When Kaikkoolars in the northern KonkunaaDu locality speak of themselves, they invariably relate the same set of myths and describe certain key heroic figures. These myths and heroic figures describe the content of Kaikkoolar identity as an expression of their relationships and exchanges with Shiva and Murugan.

Kaikkoolars consider Murugan their caste god and Shiva their creator. Shiva is the chief deity of the Saivite sect of Hinduism and one of the high vegetarian gods of Hindu tradition. By contrast, Murugan is a local god associated with mountain tops, forests, and in ancient times with hunting. He has been incorporated into the Saivite tradition as a son of Shiva and brother of the elephant god, Ganapathi. Murugan is also vegetarian.

As a pre-Brahmanical god, Murugan is seen by Tamilians as the epitome of Tamil culture and heritage (Clothey 1978:2):

[T]he deity epitomizes the Tamilian's growing image of his own Tamil culture – its age, its persistence, its relative sovereignty in the face of accretions and modification from non-Tamil sources [typically associated with Brahmanicalism], and its vigorous and youthful potentiality. In short the Murugan cultus helps many Tamil adherents answer the question: "Who are we?"

When relating their caste's origin myth, Kaikkoolars say that Shiva's creation of Murugan frightened his consort, Parvati. Fleeing from Shiva, Parvati dropped nine jewels from her anklet. These took the form of nine beautiful women, whom Shiva impregnated with his gaze. Enraged with jealousy, Parvati cursed the nine women, so that the infants remained unborn for so long that they grew moustaches, a sign of their virility and their status as warriors. Eventually, Parvati relented and the nine original Kaikkoolar warriors (NavaviirarhaL) were born.

At the time of their birth, Shiva was plagued by an evil giant, Suurabatman, who was imprisoning gods. Shiva wished him destroyed and gave Murugan the task. Murugan enlisted the aid of a general, Viirabaahu, whose army was composed of the nine original Kaikkoolars. Together they pursued Suurabatman and repeatedly cut off his head, only to have him sprout another. Eventually, Suurabatman was down to his last head and hid by taking the form of a tree. But Murugan detected him and split him in two with his spear. From the two halves emerged a cock and a peacock, which Murugan took as his emblems along with his spear.

This battle is annually dramatized in Ammapettai Ward of Salem City following Deepavali. It is sponsored by the area's Murugan temple, the Sengunthar (Kaikkoolar) Subramaniyam Temple. Murugan is represented by his image carried on a palanquin, and nine Kaikkoolar youths dressed as the NavaviirarhaL wage their battle against Suurabatman, represented as an image with removable pottery heads. The battle is fought along the community's temple streets (*maaDa viiti*) until the evil giant is destroyed and the community has been circumambulated.

Kaikkoolars see their connection with Murugan as fundamental to their identity. They symbolize this tie with their caste flag and with their alternative name, "Sengunthar Mudaliyar." Sengunthar, they say, has the following meaning: *sen,* red; *kuntappadai,* spear; *ar,* people, and is an affirmation of their identity with Murugan, who is known as a red god. When answering the question "Who are we?", Kaikkoolars say that they are Murugan's people (see, for example, the caste memorium published for the 1976 Erode meeting). Their second name, "Mudaliyar," means "they who are first [given honors]." Their ancient occupational name is "Kaikkoolar" – *kai,* hand; *kool,* shuttle; *ar,* people – and their contemporary ritual title is "Sengunthar Mudaliyar."

When gods are seen as kings, their temples as palaces, and their domains as the networks created by redistributive exchange, the meaning of the Kaikkoolars' origin myth is readily apparent. The original nine Kaikkoolars gave their service as warriors to Murugan and Shiva, a service for which Shiva had created them. Their courage, loyalty, and fierceness as the gods' soldiers are character attributes emphasized by Kaikkoolars when describing themselves. They say that their ancestors also gave warrior service to the medieval Chola kings. In return, the Kaikkoolars received their identity as warriors, as the chosen offspring of Shiva, and as the brave soldiers of Murugan. They also received their caste flag and emblems, their title, and their social status as Dravidians and warriors who were an important part of the great Chola kingdom and the army of the gods.

Devotion and sacrifice

The Kaikkoolars' sense of their importance to Tamil culture is underscored by the stories surrounding their greatest caste hero, the twelfth-century OTTakkuutar, today considered one of Tamil's greatest poets. He bears the title *Kavisakkravarttin*, "king among poets." OTTakkuutar is famous among Kaikkoolars for a series of poems known as the *liTTiyeRabathu*. Kaikkoolars tell a story about how OTTakkuutar came to compose these poems. Poetry praising the *Vanniyar Kulashattriya* had been written by Kambar, another great Tamil poet, and Kaikkoolars were seeking a comparable eulogy of their caste. They approached OTTakkuutar, who was then the court poet of a Chola king, and demanded that he write a series of laudatory poems about the caste. At first OTTakkuutar rebuffed them because he thought the task was too self-serving. The community threatened to kill him if he continued to refuse, but still he was unwilling. The king valued the poet so much, however, that when the Kaikkoolars came to kill him, the king enclosed his own son in a bag and gave him as a substitute for OTTakkuutar. When the Kaikkoolars discovered whom they had bagged, they returned for OTTakkuutar. He than agreed to meet their demands, but for a price: Each Kaikkoolar family in the area was to sacrifice a son by decapitation, and from the heads a throne was to be constructed. Sitting on this throne, the poet composed the *liTTiyeRabathu* in devotion to Shiva and in praise of the Kaikkoolars. Shiva was so impressed by the beauty of the composition that he gave the decapitated bodies back their heads and lives.

Today Kaikkoolars consider the story macabre, but they also see OTTakkuutar as central to their identity. In Erode's Kaikkoolar marriage hall there is a large polychrome sculpture of the poet sitting on his throne of heads, whose faces look surprisingly delighted. A caste memorial published for a statewide meeting in 1976 includes a picture of this composition. And OTTakkuutar's story is one Kaikkoolars are quick to relate when they are talking about themselves. But Kaikkoolar pride is mixed, because the poet is a madman by modern standards and the Kaikkoolars' own role in the story seems to illustrate the evil consequences of overweening pride. However, this is not at all the meaning of the OTTakkuutar story.

Kaikkoolars are troubled by the features of the story that depict human sacrifice and cruelty. What is important to them is that through OTTakkuutar the caste is engaged in a redistributive exchange relationship with Shiva that marks them as a sodality especially favored by God. The caste gave Shiva their devotion through the sacrifice of their sons and through the unusual beauty of their devotional poetry. In return for this devotion, Shiva gave back the lives of the decapitated, an action bestowing great honor upon the Kaikkoolars and underscoring the importance of OTTakkuutar as a poet. The Kaikkoolars' collective action is similar to that of Abraham's in Judeo-Christian tradition. In this manner, OTTakkuutar's caste is also given a special place in Tamil culture, the sine qua non of which is its language and literature. Kaikkoolars, therefore, are not only great warriors and devotees of God (by which they mean collectively Shiva and Murugan), but also occupy a central place in Tamil literature.

It is worth recalling in this context that the section of Kaikkoolars that refused to give heads – the TalaikooDa Mudaliyars – was outcaste in part because it broke rank, but more importantly because its members refused to enter into the exchange that was to mark the caste as especially favored by Shiva. Joint worship defines the membership of supralocal caste sodalities. TalaikooDa refusal, therefore, was tantamount to a refusal to accept membership in the caste sodality.

Concerning the OTTakkuutar legend, Nilakanta Shastri (1966:377) writes: "popular imagination has trumped up wild legends which reflect no credit on their inventors or the poet." As a Brahman, Shastri interprets the story as reprehensible because it seems to eulogize human sacrifice. There is also no question that Kaikkoolars today deplore the violence in the stories surrounding OTTakkuutar, although they accept the details of the story as important to his drama. But OTTakkuutar's story is not the only one they relate that involves human sacrifice. At the Kailaasanaatha temple in Taramangalam, which they claim to have built in ancient times, there is a statue of a warrior with his sword held against the back of his neck. The story I was told by Kaikkoolars is that the figure represents a Kaikkoolar hero who is asked by Shiva to kill a lesser god. Shiva gives him the power to do so but swears him to secrecy about the manner of the killing. However, after accomplishing his task, the warrior is asked by another god how it was done. The soldier feels obliged to tell him but cannot do so without breaking his oath. The solution to his dilemma is to decapitate himself in the same manner as he had the god, thereby both keeping his oath and answering the question. Human sacrifice, therefore, may be seen as representing extreme devotion and loyalty to God. Arokiaswami (1956:300) notes that there are references from the twelfth and thirteenth centuries – the period of OTTakkuutar – indicating "that even human sacrifices in propitiation of deities were not uncommon in this region [KonkunaaDu]."

The story of a twentieth-century saint, Karuppanaswami, who lived in Ammapettai, Salem City, depicts similar devotion in modern times. Locally, Karuppanaswami is known as a Kaikkoolar sannyaasi who built a Murugan temple on Kumaragiri, a nearby mountain top. A householder in Ammapettai, Karuppanaswami had always been a deeply religious man. His Brahman guru one day dreamed that he was visited by Murugan, who asked that Karuppanaswami be offered to him as a sacrifice. The two men prepared for the event, but before it took place, the Brahman again dreamed that Murugan came to him and rescinded the request. Reprieved, Karuppanaswami devoted the rest of his life to Murugan.

Karuppanaswami went on frequent pilgrimages to the famous Murugan temple at PaRani. On one occasion while at PaRani, Karuppanaswami is said to have been visited in a dream by Murugan, who gave him a loin cloth, some rice, and a bowl (*tiruvooDu*) for begging. Murugan then told him that he had made two footsteps on Kumaragiri, and that Karuppanaswami should build a temple there for him.

Karuppanaswami became a vegetarian religious mendicant, giving up both his work and his ties with his family. He returned to Salem, where his first feat was to repair the broken axle of a huge temple cart at the Iswaran (Shiva) temple in Salem. He did this by begging money and employing laborers to repair the cart. According to my informants, this was a tremendous accomplishment and a clear demonstration of Karuppanaswami's religious power (*sakti*).

Karuppanaswami began building the Kumaragiri temple in 1919. Construction involved a huge flight of granite steps leading up the mountain to the temple, its adjacent kitchen, and a pilgrims' shelter. Again Karuppanaswami collected money for the project by begging. Elder informants recall him as a familiar sight with his beggar's bowl and an *annakaavaDi*, a pole with bowls on both ends, with which he carried offerings to the god. He distributed small savings banks (small clay containers, informants say) to local housewives and asked them to contribute one pice whenever they shopped for food. Temple construction was maintained by Karuppanaswami until he died, after which his followers continued the project. The temple was finally completed in 1959, twenty-four years after Karuppanaswami's death. People attribute the temple to Karuppanaswami and point to it as evidence of his great power as a *bhakta,* a devotee to God. He accomplished what even a rich man would have found difficult.

The stories told about Karuppanaswami reveal again the element of human sacrifice as a feature of unusual devotion to God. When Karuppanaswami's mother died, people say, he exposed her body on the mountain top for the birds and animals to eat. He placed a pot of water by her side so that the animals could quench their thirst after they feasted. Some believe it was at this time that the mountain received its sacred power. When his wife died she was similarly exposed, and then buried in a grave Karuppanaswami had prepared at the base of Kumaragiri. Karuppanaswami was also exposed on the mountain top when he died; after three days, he was buried in a grave at his wife's side. Some now say that he dug his own grave and lay down in it to die, demonstrating his power to know the future. Others do not believe this. Whatever the truth may be, the exposures of the bodies represent gifts of the flesh to the animals that ate them and to the god on whose mountain they were offered.

A Shiva lingam (an icon of Shiva) has been placed above Karuppan-aswami's grave; above his wife's grave there is an image of Parvati, Shiva's consort. To the uninitiated, the appearance of the graves is like that of a small temple. A *gurupuja* (a worship in honor of a religious teacher) is performed annually at the site of Karuppanaswami's grave on the anniversary of his death.

In 1962, a shrine to Karuppanaswami was built, a stone statue (*silai*) in his likeness was installed, and the statue was purified by a Brahman priest with a ritual purification ceremony (*kumbaabisheekam*). This ritual cleansing is done for all holy images at the time they are installed in a temple and periodically thereafter. This ceremony removes any impurities transmitted to the stone by the stone carvers or others. The image is then believed to be entered by the spirit; as I was told, "it gets power." The Brahman priest of the Kumaragiri Murugan temple daily performs a puja to Karuppanaswami before he climbs the mountain to the temple. He washes the statue and places leaves (*patirapushpam elai*) over the image. He dresses the image, burns camphor, and dis-tributes ash (*vibuuti*) to any worshipers who may be present. Some persons worship at the shrine and believe Karuppanaswami to be a minor god who can aid them, but not everyone agrees on this point. The Brahman priest says that Karuppanaswami was a powerful devo-tee of God, but he was not *sittan* – a perceiver of the future – nor is he a god. Others are quick to agree, pointing out that gods do not die; but Karuppanaswami died, as all men do.

Both the OTTakkuutar and Karuppanaswami stories depict the sac-rifice of the human body in devotion to gods. They relate the exchange of human sacrifices offered to Shiva and Murugan in return for special honors and notability. OTTakkuutar offered heads and poetry; Karup-panaswami offered his body and those of his mother and wife, as well as the temple he built. In exchange, Karuppanaswami was given the honor of sitting at the feet of God, and he receives veneration and devotion from the temple Brahman priest and from worshipers. Like OTTakkuutar, Karuppanaswami symbolizes the Kaikkoolars' excep-tional if unorthodox devotion to Shiva, their closeness to this deity, and their special place in the universe.

All of this violent devotionalism appears to conflict with the nonvio-lent vegetarian values described by south Indians as central to the Saivite sect. Shiva and Murugan are depicted in south India as benevo-lent gods. Their priests must be vegetarian, and worshipers abstain from meat before their weekly worship of Murugan. Worshipers also abstain from meat during the month of Kaarttikai, Murugan's month. Karuppanaswami was himself vegetarian. Yet most Kaikkoolars in the Salem-Erode region are nonvegetarian, and their myths and heroes portray them as born warriors who kill in the service of their kings and kingly gods. Nonetheless, they consider themselves devout, despite many customs that contradict Brahmanical niceties. This explains the appeal of the myth of Karappan Aiyanaar to Kaikkoolars.

Painted prominently on the wall of the Kaikkoolars' Subramaniyam temple in Ammapettai is a picture depicting Karappan Aiyanaar's worship. The painting displays a lingam showing the face of Shiva with a bleeding eye. Karappan Aiyanaar is attempting to stem the flow of blood by placing his foot against the eye, while he gouges out his own eye in an effort of transference. Here again is the element of physical self-sacrifice as a form of devotionalism. But the myth involves another element. A person's foot is ritually unclean, but the uncouth Karappan Aiyanaar is only aware of the suffering Shiva, whom he wishes to aid. He loves Shiva with his heart. Unaware of Brahmanical niceties, he commits a major ritual faux pas. He offers meat as a sacrifice to Shiva, who is a strict vegetarian, because as a hunter he considers it his finest offering. He does everything contrary to Brahmanical rule, but he is closer to God than the Brahman shown in the picture, who is standing in the surrounding forest. The Brahman is an addition to the picture, and is not always represented. The Kaikkoolars have added him in part because, like Karappan Aiyanaar, they are nonvegetarian, yet they can be closer to God than the Brahman. Karappan Aiyanaar is loved by God because his heart is pure in its love of Him. The message is clear: You do not have to be vegetarian to be close to God, nor do you have to be Brahmanical. What is important is the sincerity of your devotion and what is in your heart. Nonetheless, the Kaikkoolars are aware of the contradiction between their nonvegetarianism and the vegetarian ideal of these high gods. It causes them some discomfort.

Until the 1920s, another important feature of Kaikkoolar devotionalism was the deeva-daasi tradition that was described previously. It, too, causes the Kaikkoolars discomfort, and may also be described as a type of sacrifice involving redistributive exchange between Kaikkoolars and their kingly gods. This now-defunct practice involves the dedication of daughters, often by prominent families, to Saivite temples. The complexity of the relationship of donor families and castes to the daasis and the persons they served is apparent. As wife givers and givers of services (through the daasi women), the Kaikkoolars ranked transactionally as subordinates to the kingly god and the temple court. However, the symbolic marriage alliance underscored their devotion and special status next to God (as affinal kin). But Kaikkoolars did not want these same principles of alliance and exchange extended to incorporate the communities the daasis served as concubines and prostitutes, because this extension was degrading. Accordingly, only the sacrifice to God was valued by Kaikkoolars as a devotional act. The daasis themselves were outcaste and their offspring disowned.

The interior realm: family gods and personal well-being

In the exterior realm of kingly gods, the Kaikkoolars sacrifice themselves and receive in return their status marked by special temple honors. Through their links to high god temples, they receive the symbolic integration of their caste territory, organized by the temple puja networks and the systems of redistributive exchange.

These networks link the caste localities supralocally in conjunction with the pyramidal naaDu hierarchy that once culminated in Conjeepuram. However, the interior realm of the Kaikkoolars' sacred cosmos has a different focus. It is concerned with families and kinsmen, and it has a definite sublocality basis. The gods of this interior domain are locality-based family gods (kuladeevam). These gods command the somewhat reluctant devotion of the Kaikkoolars by the fear they produce in human hearts. Kaikkoolars do not sacrifice themselves to these small, malevolent gods; they sacrifice the blood of cocks, goats, and pigs, and make offerings of food, limes, salt, red dyes, liquor, cigars, and their own hair. These gods are to be placated. They are neither kingly nor noble. They do not define caste territories or establish supralocal networks, nor do they give status. They are terrible, often depicted as fanged, red-faced, monstrous women and their lesser consorts, or as fearsome men. In exchange for their sacrifices, individuals hope to receive reprieve from illness or misfortune, or to preserve their families' well-being and prosperity.

It is believed that a family will not prosper unless it worships its kuladeevam appropriately with sacrifices. These sacrifices must be made at particular times, such as childbirth or other life transition points. The first hair-cutting ceremony of an infant, as well as ear and nose piercing, are done at the kuladeevam shrine. These are rituals of transition for a child during the dangerous early years when children seem to die so easily. The cut hair is given to the kuladeevam.

Many Kaikkoolars believe that family gods demand blood sacrifices, whereas others say that milk offerings are sufficient. Here is one source of the Kaikkoolars' practical ambivalence about their nonvegetarian practices caused by their belief in kuladeevams and their acceptance of the vegetarian ideals associated with their high gods, Shiva and Murugan. I know one Kaikkoolar who was caught squarely between this demand for sacrifices and his ideals. When his first son was born, he gave a milk sacrifice to his kuladeevam. But his son soon became ill; the man, fearing that his offering had been insufficient, hastily made the prescribed blood sacrifices.

The goat and chicken are cooked at the place of sacrifice and are eaten by the worshipers. Usually the pig is given to untouchables, but many Kaikkoolars eat a portion because of the belief in this meat's great potency. For example, the child just described is thought by his family to have an unusually cool body, a characteristic that makes him susceptible to colds. South Indians classify people as having "hot" or "cold" physiologies, and believe that health and well-being require a balance of these two aspects. Once, after making a sacrifice to their kuladeevam, the child's family fed the boy a piece of pork wrapped in other food in order to induce heat in his body.

The purpose of relating these specific aspects of kuladeevam worship is to demonstrate the immediate and practical value of this worship to Kaikkoolars. The kuladeevams' sphere of influence includes individuals and families, but kuladeevam temples lack extended territories. Their realm is that of kin, a focus reflected in the locality basis of their identity.

The kuladeevam of each family is associated with the particular locality from which the family's agnatic kin are said to originate. A woman worships with her husband, and although many unrelated families and castes may worship at the same shrine, Kaikkoolars believe that they must worship only at the shrine located at their own ancestral place of origin. Different families, therefore, worship at different localities even if they reside next door to one another. The deity(s) they propitiate, however, are regionally known; they are not locality specific. Thus, different families may worship the same deity but at different locations. Table 1 lists the common family gods.

Kaikkoolar kin ties reflect this limited territoriality. As we have seen, marriage is narrowly confined by sublocality identity. Endogamy based on locality prevents kinship from organizing supralocal relations. The weak role that kinship plays in caste organization, however, is not necessarily a result of the Kaikkoolars' extensive itinerant commercial interests, which contrast so clearly to the locality interests of landowning castes.

The Tamil-speaking Muslims, for example, are a mercantile community that uses kinship as the basis of its interregional ties (Mines 1972:85; 1977). I believe that the existence of the naaDu system and its associated kingly god temple hierarchy, and in the twentieth century the establishment of other supralocal corporations, allow this split be-

Table 1. *A list of common family gods (kuladeevam)*[a]

Devam	Consort
Ambayamman (F)	Ambayaram (M)
Periyandachi (M)	Periyandamman (F)
Periyannan/Cinnannan (M)	Angayyi (F)
AngaaLammaa (F)	Cinnaiya (M)

[a]Names given by Kaikkoolars in Salem.

tween domain and kinship. These corporations are forms of organization not found among Tamil-speaking Muslims. Furthermore, the Kaikkoolars' supralocal organization is a response to the need for interaction between the locality and the state; but the kinship-based organization of the Tamil-speaking Muslims, who do not expect to benefit from interaction with the state, is simply a business network.

What has happened to the Ammapettai sannyaasi, Karuppanaswami, since his death dramatizes the dichotomy between the political domain of the exterior cosmos associated with high god temples and naaDu territories, and the narrowly confined, kin-based realm of the interior cosmos associated with small gods. Although Karuppanaswami was a devout worshiper of Murugan and a vegetarian, his descendants believe that he came to one of his sons in a dream and told him that his lineage (*pangaaLi*) should worship him in the manner of a kuladeevam, with blood sacrifices. Annually, on the anniversary of Karuppanaswami's death, they take his begging bowl and annakaavaDi out and carry them around the streets in his old manner. The sacrifices cannot be held near Karuppanaswami's shrine, because it is within the god Murugan's Kumaragiri temple area, so they are performed in the family home.

It is possible that Karuppanaswami is in the early stages of becoming a minor god. Other men, such as Madurai Viiran, have become gods, and there are many people who already believe that Karuppanaswami is a deity. Everyone agrees that he is at least a holy man with power (sakti) who sits at the feet of God. Evidence supporting this hypothesis of potential deification is found in another, but socially disapproved attempt to deify a dead human. The wife of a local businessman died a short time ago. Kaikkoolars say that she came to one of her sons as a ghost. In response, and to honor her, her husband and sons built a temple with her image as a manifestation of God. They hired a priest to perform kumbaabisheekam and named the temple the "Shivagaviyamman temple" after the dead woman. The local townspeople were scandalized by the family's behavior and insisted that the woman was not a manifestation of God. By contrast, no one questioned the appropriateness of the shrine dedicated to Karuppanaswami or the daily puja performed there. One Kaikkoolar informant speculated that time would obscure the controversy, and that both persons may eventually be regarded as gods. This informant felt that kuladeevam may in fact have their origins in circumstances similar to these. Kuladeevam may once have been real persons of unusual character.

Karuppanaswami clearly reflects the division between the realms of the high gods and those of the family gods. He was a devotee of Murugan and a vegetarian, but he virtually gave up his life as a sacrifice to God. His body and those of his wife and mother were exposed on the mountain so that the birds could feast on them. He had sufficient power to perform difficult tasks. In return for his service and sacrifice, he is said to sit at the feet of God. Karuppanaswami's grave site has been enshrined with a lingam, and the shrine containing his statue is attended each morning by a Brahman whose ritual tasks honor him and mark his special status as a devotee. His identity has received a degree of sanctity that is accepted throughout the Salem Kaikkoolar community and by people of other castes throughout Tamilnadu. Kaikkoolars are proud of this unusual devotee and claim that they share the intensity of his devotion. Karuppanaswami, therefore, belongs to the realm of the high gods, to sacrifice and devotional service, and to the realm of honors.

But Karuppanaswami was a man and a householder, and to his sons, who live in Salem today, he is an ancestor who has had a profound effect on their lives. Tamilians believe that the ghosts of unusual persons or those who died unfulfilled may afflict the living. It is not surprising, therefore, that this exceptional man is thought by his descendants to affect their lives directly. They believe that he must be propitiated, not as they worship Shiva or Murugan, but as they worship family gods. After all, that is how supernaturals who directly affect life must be placated.

Family gods and the high gods are not the only deities worshiped by Kaikkoolars. There are other supernaturals who fall within the small god category. Muniyappa, the warlike hero god who protects the village locale; Maariyammaa, the goddess of smallpox; the street gods Madurai Veeran, Karappana, and Aiyanaar; and the *moohini,* evil female ghosts that are believed to possess the living, are among the multiplicity of supernaturals associated with localities, geographic features, and unusual lives and deaths. All of these deities affect limited domains but are not specific to kin groups. Kaikkoolars worship them according to their personal preferences in order to avoid illness or to improve their lot in life. Many Kaikkoolars make blood sacrifices; others do not.

Some of the supernaturals are believed to possess worshipers who are attuned to them; they enable these worshipers to perform great feats or foretell the future. At the annual Maariyammaa celebration, for example, two men from Ammapettai dress as the goddess (*saambaveesam*) and her consort (*puundaarikaarar*). The saambaveesam sews limes to his skin, but he is said to feel no pain because he is possessed by the goddess's power. Together the two men dance in procession through the temple streets. All of these small gods directly affect people's lives, but their domains are limited to the locality of their shrines, although they are regionally known.

Moohini, their male counterparts, and a variety of drishtis (evil forces) are among the supernatural dangers that do not take the form of deities, but that Kaikkoolars attempt to control or influence. Specialists called *mantiravaadis,* who are believed to know spells that control good and evil forces, are sometimes used to rid people of such evil possessions, to cause harm to others, and to aid in the search for lost objects.

Kaikkoolar control of temples

Kaikkoolars wish to control temples and the priests who serve them because of the roles these high gods' temples and priests play in forming the caste's regional organization, status, and identity. The VeLLaaLas and other castes have shown a similar interest. The result has been disputes among castes such as those described in the previous chapter as characterizing left-hand/right-hand confrontations. The political and social importance of what might appear to be disputes about largely symbolic rights is also apparent. Disputes between Kaikkoolars and VeLLaaLas were not merely about rights to use symbols and signs; they were disputes about the definition of caste domains: whether one or the other community was to be given precedence, whether Kaikkoolars were to have administrative autonomy matching their economic autonomy, or whether they would be administratively dependent upon and commanded by the economically dominant agriculturists. Temple honors were also used to define the boundaries of the caste community at any particular hierarchical level, clearly marking those who were in and those who were out. When sections of the community were outcaste or, as in the case of the Moolakkaarans, when a group was attempting to gain status as part of the caste, the issue of who was to participate as representatives of the caste defined the composition of the group.

The following case illustrates the manner in which groups could be defined through temple rights. In 1930, in an article entitled "Bavani Real Sengunthars [Kaikkoolars] Deserved Success: Again Defeat for the Moolakkaarar" (*Senguntha Mittiran* 1930:132), the Kaikkoolars' caste journal reported that Moolakkaarars, who had apparently become temple trustees, wished the privilege of raising the temple flag for the Sellaandiyamman festival, an act that had been performed by Kaikkoolars. The Moolakkaarars were demanding this right as part of their claim to be Sengunthars, which the Kaikkoolars opposed. The Moolakkaarars wanted the dispute to be settled by the temple trustees, but the Kaikkoolars turned to the police and were able to prove that the privilege was theirs by custom because they had been granted the right for the preceding twelve years. This dispute and others like it were critical to Kaikkoolars because at this time they were adamantly opposed to Moolakkaarar claims to Sengunthar status. The dispute, therefore, was not just about raising the flag, but also about who was a Kaikkoolar and so had the right to perform this act.

Kaikkoolars attempt to control temples in a variety of ways. As we have seen, a commons (paavaDi warp-stretching grounds) and a Murugan temple form the symbolic center of each local Kaikkoolar community. In each locality I visited in the Seven-City Territory, the Murugan temple is directly administered by local Kaikkoolar community leaders. This management gives them symbolic control over their own locality. They have also replaced the Brahmans who once served the Murugan temples with Kaikkoolar priests (teesikar), a process that began fifty years ago.

Another method Kaikkoolars have used to control the ritual sphere is withdrawal from temples controlled by castes that do not ritually acknowledge the Kaikkoolars' status. If necessary, they build their own temples to avoid being controlled in the existing ones. As noted previously, the VeLLaaLas have also used this method to avoid Kaikkoolar control (for example, in Kolanalli). It should be noted that this withdrawal and temple replication have not been forced on Kaikkoolars because they have been ritually unclean. Untouchables engage in replication because their ritual impurity makes it impossible for them to enter high caste temples. Thus, untouchable status remains in the control of high castes because the untouchables are excluded. Kaikkoolars have historically been ritually clean, and frequently have used multicaste temples until disputes led to their withdrawal. They have withdrawn in order to avoid being controlled ritually by VeLLaaLas.

The convention of settling disputes between right-hand and left-hand castes by the spatial and ritual separation of the contestants is another reason for the replication of temples. Kaikkoolars occasionally withdrew from wide-ranging conflicts because they were no match for the VeLLaaLas. Kaikkoolars followed this pattern in the Erode region during the 1920s, when they fled from the countryside to Erode City. Finally, Kaikkoolars attempted to acquire ritual markers of status, domain, and identity by controlling temple boards and offices. These markers of status, which are still sought and maintained by Kaikkoolars today, included the right to raise the temple flag at the beginning of festivals (Bavani); to give particular offerings such as coconuts, cloth, and, before 1927, deeva-daasis to the temple god (Trichengode); to enact particular ritual roles in temple processions (Ammapettai); to sing ritual songs during festivals (Akkamapettai); and to sponsor major pujas in the bigger temples (Trichengode). They also included the right to administer temples and to control temple funds, which even today, as we shall see, give temple officers access to riches that may be used for personal business or political purposes (Ammapettai). In Salem today, local leaders base their strength not only on their involvement in political and economic institutions but also on their control of temple boards. It is alleged that this control has enabled them to divert funds for political purposes, which is one reason why political parties at the state level also attempt to control temple boards.

Kaikkoolar beliefs and anthropological models of caste in south India

It is generally accepted by Indianists that south Indians model their caste identity and behavior on two primary reference categories: the Brahmanical system of beliefs, which is based on priestly behavior and ritual purity, and the kingly category, which is based on the command of economic and political temporal power. Merchants have traditionally followed a Brahmanical model for behavior insofar as it emphasizes vegetarianism, emotional restraint, and ascetic control; these are elements of ritual purity rather than temporal power. Service castes that rank lower follow a model of deference to and dependence on those whom they serve (Mandelbaum 1970, vol. II:447-467). Castes aspiring to high status choose, therefore, to style their customs and behavior as either priestly or kingly.

These two models depict contradictory qualities of behavior. They embody an inner conflict, as Heesterman (1973) has phrased it, between the Brahmanical qualities of purity and independence from subordinating service transactions, and the kingly emphasis on the ability to command the services of subordinate castes and to control the sources of power based on political-economic resources. In contrast to the nonviolence, asceticism, and emotional control that mark the

Brahmanical model, kingly castes usually claim a ruling or warrior tradition involving violent action and emotional expression.

Heesterman (1973) and Beck (1970, 1972) have argued that the left-hand castes follow the Brahmanical model, but this conclusion is misleading because left-hand castes appear to have mimicked the full range of right-hand caste behavior. The two divisions of castes were integrated differently.

Today, castes of the right-hand section studied in the context of villages are found to be locality oriented, because for centuries states have attempted to prevent the development of strong regional sodalities among agriculturists as part of their policy of control. They are members of caste hierarchies that have been worked out locally through the service and ritual transactions that accompany socioeconomic interdependence (Marriott 1959, 1968). Castes that command the services of others rank above those they command, and the summation of these relationships, when coupled with food transactions, replicates closely the local ranking of castes (for a summary of these ideas applied to Jaffna castes, which are similar to those of Salem, see David 1974:46-50).

Brahmans in south India also fitted the model of transactional integration, although traditionally they stood above and apart from the right-hand/left-hand distinction. The Brahmans' involvement in transactional ranking was an element of their importance as a secular force in south India. They were a major landowning caste category and held a majority of the important government posts open to Indians. In these roles, they commanded services from subordinate castes while refusing food from all but their own caste section. They also wielded power in the temples, for in the performance of their priestly services they received and shared in the services and sacrifices offered by others. Further, they carried out and partook of the public display of temple honors offered to worshipers. Therefore, the Brahmans' secular and ritual powers were both acted out transactionally in a manner that reflected favorably on their status. Accordingly, Heesterman's characterization of Brahmans as independent of service transactions must be considered misleading.

Castes of the left-hand section were not usually integrated transactionally through service or food exchanges in local hierarchies, but clearly they were ranked by the nature of their transactions with priests in ritual contexts and temple pujas. Brahmans conducting life-crisis ceremonies or acting as priests in temples symbolically marked the statuses of the castes they served. Therefore, each time Kaikkoolars sponsored a puja at their paavaDi temple or conducted a family life crisis ceremony in which they employed a priest, they engaged in transactions that publicly ranked them. But this ranking was not a result of political-economic interdependence. Even today, Kaikkoolars and other high-ranking left-hand castes such as the Aachaaris and Beri Chettiars are given relatively high local status, although they are non-dominant and are unable to command the services of others. They lack the traditional secular transactional relations that define superordination and subordination in intercaste relations (Mines 1982). As one informant told me, Kaikkoolars can be defied even by untouchables, over whom they lack economic control.

In contrast to the agriculturists, the Kaikkoolars have been integrated supralocally by their corporate organizations, which both link the caste segments interlocally and tie them to state systems at the regional level. The Kaikkoolars' integration into local caste hierarchies is vague and ambiguous compared to the clarity of their supralocal organization. The interlocal temple hierarchies associated with the pyramidal organization of the naaDu territories, the caste association or Sangam, and the hand-loom weavers' production cooperative system – all of which are discussed in later chapters – are organizations used by the Kaikkoolars to achieve this regional integration. Their purpose has been to administer caste relationships among localities and with state organizations. As this state organization has changed, the caste leadership has responded by utilizing new voluntary organizational forms better suited to their own changing political and economic needs.

The caste ideology of the EeRuurunaaDu Kaikkoolars, expressed in their myths and stories about their caste heroes, reflects a warrior model for behavior. Kaikkoolars are men of strong emotion and belli-cose disposition. They are meat eaters and are defiantly proud. They make blood sacrifices, are reputed to drink liquor, and allow widow remarriage. But they do not command the services of others. In their myths they are the close associates of kings and gods, for whom they perform services. Thus, they reflect the kingly model of dominant right-hand castes but lack an important ingredient of that model: the ability to command.

In other localities in Tamilnadu, Kaikkoolars combine elements of the priestly and kingly models for behavior, as they do contextually when they act as Saivite priests in the EeRuurunaaDu. Thus, in Conjeepu-ram, Kaikkoolars are Brahmanical in some of their traits. They are vegetarian, apparently do not make blood sacrifices, emphasize greater emotional control, and do not drink liquor. However, they also ac-knowledge and emphasize the Kaikkoolars' warrior past, so their caste ideology in this locality reflects a mixture of priestly and kingly features.

Clearly, Kaikkoolar ideology contains many symbolic components of both the priestly and kingly models, but the meaning of the myths and tales is different. These stories do not detail Kaikkoolar integration as a commanding caste at the local level, and certainly not as a priestly caste except in the limited contexts in which they serve as their own priests. Instead, these stories portray the nature of Kaikkoolar integration into the state, which is symbolically depicted as organized around redistributive exchange relations between Kaikkoolars and the regnal courts of gods and ancient kings.

The Kaikkoolars follow a third model for caste identity that may be called "castes organized as sodalities." These castes integrate their locality-based endogamous segments by means of their interlocal networks of exchange. These networks of exchange are of three closely intertwined types: (1) ritual exchanges that take place in temple contexts and define the caste's membership and territorial domain; (2) economic exchanges associated with trade and the caste's self-administration of interlocal relations among their naaDu territories; and (3) political/economic exchanges that occur in the context of the caste's interactions with the governing state. This third type of exchange is expressed in the Kaikkoolars' narratives of their warrior service in the armies of the Cholas, as well as in the state's taxation and administration of the textile trade. It is also expressed in the contemporary state's exchange of welfare benefits for political support.

Heesterman's proposal and Dumont's analysis of low-caste beliefs

My analysis of Kaikkoolar beliefs in this chapter suggests a different perspective from which to view what Heesterman (1973) has called the "inner conflict of Hinduism," and challenges Dumont's analysis of low-caste beliefs. The conflict is between the vegetarian, nonviolent beliefs associated with the priestly castes and the Brahmanical high gods such as Shiva and Murugan, and the nonvegetarian, violent beliefs associated with small gods and castes following the kingly model. The two traditions are distinguished by their conflicting values.

Heesterman attempts to explain the existence of this conflict in terms of two differently organized caste orders: the kingly order, which is formed around agriculturists and their interdependent service castes, and the priestly order formed by castes that enjoy economic separation from agriculture and stress their independence. This order includes primarily Brahmans, merchants, and independent artisans. Heesterman argues that this distinction in south India is institutionalized as a division between the left-hand (priestly) castes and the right-hand (kingly) castes.

As we have seen, this explanation is flawed. Left-hand castes can be both priestly and kingly, and not all left-hand castes are merchants or artisans. Furthermore, the Kaikkoolars, who are artisan-merchants, stress their warrior character, not a priestly heritage. What is the explanation? First, the left-hand castes exhibit independence from traditional service and food exchange relationships at the locality level. This is partly a product of their economic independence from agriculture. But there are some nondominant agriculturist castes that are identified as left-hand castes. Their status must be explained as a result of their attempt to avoid being dominated by more powerful agricultural castes. There is some evidence for this explanation in northern KonkunaaDu, where the Padaiyaachi agriculturists and the VeeTTuva Gounders are said to have once sought the protection of Kaikkoolars and, as allied castes, to have paid tribute to the Kaikkoolars for the sponsorship of pujas.

Second, the Kaikkoolars are distinguished from the right-hand castes by their structural emphasis on maintaining relationships between locality and state. They are supralocally organized. To attempt to classify the whole left-hand section as priestly obscures this point and oversimplifies the complexity of their beliefs.

Dumont (1970a:27-28) recognizes the dichotomy between vegetarian and nonvegetarian traditions and its parallel among high gods and small gods, but he offers a different solution to the problem. He sees the opposition as a "particular form of the opposition of purity and impurity, which is the principle of the caste system" (Dumont 1970a:28). In the caste system, pure castes need impure castes to perform necessary but impure services for them. This protects them from ritual pollution. The impure castes "absorb" impurities to preserve the purity of higher castes. The small gods who receive blood sacrifices stand in a similar relationship to the purer high gods.

Dumont notes that low castes such as the Kallar (a dominant but low-ranking non-Brahman caste) nonetheless worship both categories of gods. The reason, he argues, is that although they do not identify with high gods, they mimic the worship of high castes that worship high gods. They identify "only with the impure gods who occupy a position in the pantheon homologous to their position in society" (Dumont 1970a:28). Consequently, there are not really two traditions at all, but one hierarchical system integrated by an ideology of purity and impurity.

A similar analysis cannot be used to explain Kaikkoolar beliefs. Kaikkoolars identify closely with their impure family gods (kuladeevam), but also trace their origins and identity to Shiva and Murugan. They identify with both traditions. Their identity with the high gods is just as important as their belief in small gods.

Kaikkoolars view their world as being composed of two spheres. One emphasizes the interior realm of the cosmos, the domain of kin and small gods; the other emphasizes the exterior realm, the domain of the state, kings, and regnal gods. Both realms are needed to describe and classify the order of the social world in which they see themselves, for in fact the Kaikkoolars conceptualize their caste as organizing interaction in a dichotomized society. The Kaikkoolars are a sodality of locally endogamous segments organized to interact with each other and with the states within which they have lived since they were first named in epigraphs over eight hundred years ago. They sacrifice to small gods in order to effect the well-being of their kin and their locality, and they serve the high gods to establish their naaDu territorial identities and their social position within these territorial realms.

5 The naaDu system

. . . those who have the lion flag, tiger flag, cow flag, cock flag and *anna* [a mythical bird] flag; those who received [as honors] *pilittaNDai* and *lavaNDai* [ankle ornaments worn by women], those who received [as honors] *viiraseekaNDi, viirataaLam,* and *viiratundipi* [warriors' victory gong, cymbal, and kettle drum], those who have an umbrella the color of the cloud . . . those who are courageous army men; Hear yea brave Sengunthar Mudaliyars, people vested with great strength, the great *Seela NaaDu MeeLuur, Seela NaaDu KiiRuur* [councils of the Salem Kaikkoolars], *Periyathaanakaarar, Kaariyakkaarar* [officers of the council]; and other community members; and to others, what *Seela NaaDu* makes known.

(Translated from the Kaikkoolars'
Seela NaaDu letterhead, dating
from the 1940s)

A striking contrast between historical northern and southern India is the absence of Kshatriya institutions in the south. "The normal political condition in Northern India during ancient and medieval times was its division into a great number of small territories under kin-linked warrior families of high status. Such was the nature of Kshatriya raj" (Stein 1980:48). Morris E. Opler and others have found that the organization of this old order is still apparent in the social geography of north Indian villages. For example, the village of Senapur in Uttar Pradesh is part of a larger territory that was divided into village areas by the descendants of the original Kshatriya chief who conquered and settled the region. Most of the village's panchayat (village council) and *jajmani* (traditional intercaste redistributive system) ties are confined to this territory, known as the "Dhobi Area." Villages adjacent to Senapur but outside the territory have fewer institutionalized ties with the Dhobi Area than do more distant villages located within the territory. The subdivision of the Dhobi Area's social geography and Senapur is locally explained in terms of the genealogical history of the conqueror's family (Opler and Singh 1948).

Brahmans, naaDus, and the left-hand/right-hand division

By contrast, the social order in south India, in the absence of Kshatriya raj, has consisted of a tripartite division since ancient times (Stein 1965:53; Stein 1980:49-51). One division was composed of Brahmans who sought to control society through both their religious dominance and their secular dominance as landowners. A thousand years ago, they lived in Brahmadeyas (Brahman villages) and ruled by *sabhaa raj* (rule by assembly). In more recent times, after the disappearance of Brahmadeyas, the dominance of Brahmans was based on their ritual position as priests in the kingly temples of south India, where they occupied a pivotal role in the recognition and bestowal of temple honors and the association of large temples with urban market and production centers. As will be explained subsequently, within the market systems of artisan-merchants these temples formed a central element defining membership in trade networks. The Brahmans' dominance was also based on their continued control of land and on alliances with high non-Brahman landed castes, particularly VeLLaaLas.

The second important administrative division after sabhaa raj was the hierarchically organized naaDu system. These chiefly territorial segments of south Indian states were dominated by the important agriculturist castes, especially the VeLLaaLas, which administered their subordinate dependent castes. The third institutionalized division of society was the separation of non-Brahmans into right-hand and left-hand sections.

Burton Stein (1980:52) has succinctly stated the three elements that gave south Indian society its special nature:

The uniqueness of this [south Indian] variant of Indian social structure is based upon three persistent and related characteristics: the great secular authority and significant secular functions of South Indian Brahmans; the dual division [the right-hand and left-hand divisions] of lower social groups; and the territorial segmentation of all social hierarchies in the south Indian macro region [the naaDus].

Within this structure, Brahmans held a special position at the top of society, for they were not only secularly powerful landowners with their own network of interdependent castes, but also the mediators of the right-hand/left-hand division. As temple priests, they held a pivotal position between the temples they served and the left-hand and right-hand castes that used temple worship as a means of establishing caste identity and status.

There was a natural alliance between Brahmans and the dominant *Sudra* landowners based on similar political-economic interests supported by Brahman ideology. Land provided the wealth of both groups, and the Brahmans sanctified a society of ranked, interdependent castes dominated by landowners. In this social context, the artisan-merchants, including Kaikkoolars, strove for symbolic status equal to that of the landowning castes. However, the ties of artisan-merchants to Brahmans did not constitute a natural alliance based on shared landowning interests, but were instead based on the wealth that artisan-merchants could offer temple Brahmans in return for ritual honors. Ties were also based on the association of large temples with urban market and production centers, where temples were the integrating institutions defining membership in trade networks.

All three characteristics of medieval Tamil society – the secular and ritual dominance of Brahmans, the dual division of society into right-hand and left-hand sections, and the naaDu system – continued in various forms to be important components of south Indian social organization well into the twentieth century. Recent social change has greatly altered these characteristics, but all three are important for understanding Tamil society today.

Until modern times, political control was highly segmented and localized despite the presence of kingly states. In KonkunaaDu, the landowning VeLLaaLas and the artisan Kaikkoolars were the two main warrior communities in medieval times (Arokiaswami 1959:273), and constituted the two main chiefly castes prior to colonial times (Murton 1979:30).

The nature of naaDu organization in history

From medieval times until well into the twentieth century, Brahmans, VeLLaaLas, and artisan-merchants locally attempted to regulate their own internal affairs and those of their lesser dependent castes. This governing was done by VeLLaaLas and Kaikkoolars in northern KonkunaaDu within the context of naaDus, which were named territories. NaaDu territories such as KonkunaaDu formed the "basic unit of government" in rural south India (Stein 1980:109) from Chola times through the nineteenth century. The naaDu was a territory without clear boundaries because it was defined by the interrelationships of the towns and villages comprising its membership, rather than by precise borders (Stein 1980:90, 93):

The *nadu* was the basic peasant unit of the age, it was also an ethnic region to which the later, prestigious Brahman villages and the great overlords adapted themselves. The essential governmental significance of the *nadu* was its ethnic coherence. All persons and groups directly involved in the peasant agrarian system of a locality and jointly dependent upon the successful exploitation of the land tended to constitute a discrete social universe. Where land capable of being turned to the plough ceased, where slope, aridity, hazards to human or animal welfare, or the presence of a hostile people – peasant or non-peasant – who could not be displaced occurred, the locality ended. Within that spatial universe, in most parts of the macro region, those with sufficient authority to compel it forced the acceptance of social rules based upon hereditary hierarchy and segmentation. Those whose military power and agricultural skills had originally converted a tract of land to peasant cultivation maintained authority through control over cultivable land and through connections with supra-local chieftains. (Stein 1980:109)

Stein emphasizes the power of the main landowning castes in defining the territorial units. The Brahmans and VeLLaaLa Gounders were the most powerful landowning castes in KonkunaaDu, and at least the Gounders' naaDus were ordered into kin-based subunits (Beck 1972:19-109). In general, naaDus have been treated as if they were associated solely with land ownership (Beck 1972:108; Stein 1980:109); but there is evidence that high castes of the left-hand section also regulated their own internal affairs and were independent of the agrarian system. Hall (1980:202, 205), however, argues that in Chola times, artisan-merchant associations were fully integrated into the agrarian naaDus, and at the end of the Chola period (thirteenth century) forged alliances with these naaDus "for protection against brigands" and for the purpose of opposing Chola efforts at taxation.

Nonetheless, the artisan-merchant castes, including the Kaikkoolars and Kammalars (Aachaaris), also formed their own caste networks, and at least by Vijayanagar times (fourteenth to seventeenth centuries) were organized into naaDus (Buchanan 1807, vol. II:265; Arokiaswami 1959:273; Murton 1979:30). Judging by my fieldwork among the Kaikkoolars, these left-hand caste organizations were very different from the naaDus of landowners. They were integrated into supra-local pyramidal hierarchies and were organized to administer trade. The left-hand naaDu territories were defined, as we have seen, by the joint sponsorship of pujas at naaDu temples. In this manner, the locality-segmented subunits of the castes were formed into territorial confederacies.

Stein mentions that in medieval times, artisan-merchants such as the Kaikkoolars played the important role of linking isolated nuclear peasant localities through trade. These artisan-merchants were able to pass through hostile, unsettled areas where feared tribals lurked because they maintained their own armies. They represented not only a military force but also a number of mobile, supralocally organized caste segments. The famous merchant organizations of the medieval period, such as the Ayyavole 500 (Stein 1965), were such supralocal mercantile organizations. It is reasonable to conclude that artisan-merchants developed pyramidal naaDu hierarchies in order to administer trade interactions among a number of localities.

Even today, the extant naaDu systems of artisan-merchants reflect this need to regulate interlocal transactions. Weaving and the weavers' trade networks formed an important feature of the segmented states' political economy both before and after the coming of the British. In the seventeenth and eighteenth centuries, weaver trade networks in northern KonkunaaDu linked the administrative towns of the indige-nous states (Murton 1979:23-24). The trading towns (*kasba*) closely correspond to the membership of the Kaikkoolars' naaDu system in the locality today (Map 2). Northern KonkunaaDu was linked through the textile trade to Madras City and formed an important source of textiles in the region. Major temple centers were located at these administrative towns and, as meeting places, served as the head-quarters of the Kaikkoolars' naaDus.

The naaDu organization of VeLLaaLa Gounders in contemporary Coimbatore District

Descent is the basis of the organization of the locality-oriented naaDus of agriculturists. It is, however, of relatively little importance in the organization of the supralocally oriented naaDus of artisan-merchants. Beck (1972:108) notes this distinction, although in the area in which she worked, left-hand castes lacked territorial organization:

The right division – those groups which have rights in land – has an elaborate internal descent structure which is intimately linked to local territorial boundaries. The left division – those who live by various traditional and specialized skills – place little emphasis on descent and have no important ties to territory.

Beck found that in KonkunaaDu the VeLLaaLa Gounders' descent organization was associated with a hierarchy of kin-owned and highly localized temples that marked the subunits of the naaDu. The Gounder family (*kuDampam*) and lineage (*gotram*) were associated with a local village (*uur*) council and a goddess temple; the clan was associated with a localized *kiraamam* (the village revenue area) coun-cil and a goddess temple; and the subcaste was associated with the naaDu. Thus, the kin-based subcaste was identified with the territory of the naaDu. Further, adjacent naaDus were sometimes joined by crosscutting kin ties created through marriage alliances. Kinship struc-ture and naaDu structure, therefore, closely corresponded and were tied to a system of kin-dominated temples. Above the naaDu level, however, kinship structure no longer played a part, and all the Gounders of the KonkunaaDu region came under the authority of powerful regional leaders known as *pattakkaarar* (Beck 1972:66ff).

Beck observed in KonkunaaDu an adaptation of segmentary line-age organization to the regulation and organization of small localities. NaaDus of small size are characteristic of agriculturists. Stein (1980:95) notes that in medieval times in CholamaNDalam – a region in what is today Tamilnadu – most naaDu boundaries encompassed an area ranging from fifteen to thirty square miles. Arid regions had larger naaDu territories of up to 200 square miles in area (Stein 1980:97). This size range is commensurate with what is still found today in arid KonkunaaDu.

The Gounders' naaDu territory is segmented along descent lines that correspond to the division of kin-owned temples. At each point of linked kin and territorial segmentation, there is a temple owned by the kin segment. These temples are dedicated to goddesses who are specific to the locality, and they are presided over by Gounder priests. At the subcaste level of the naaDu, the goddess is replaced by a temple dedicated to Shiva; although it is presided over by a Brahman priest, the temple is controlled by the Gounders. This marks the juncture at which kin organization is superseded. Below this point, the goddesses are specific to particular kin groups and localities, but Shiva is a god worshiped by all Gounders. Shiva temples are not inherently associated with a particular territory. As I argued in Chapter 3, this association must be established by the caste segments that jointly sponsor pujas in a particular Shiva temple. A single temple, therefore, can serve the same function for several castes.

The naaDu level also marks the point of articulation with Brahmanical Hinduism. It is the level of the general rather than the specific; the union of localities rather than locality segmentation; and segmented state organization rather than kin-based, local caste organization. In medieval times (eleventh to thirteenth centuries) the naaDus were the local semi-independent administrative units of the kingly state. They were also units of taxation. During the period of the Vijayanagar kings (A.D. 1350-1650), naaDus encompassing larger territories were formed by powerful warrior chiefs who maintained alliances with the kingly state. Their chieftain territories (*paalaiyams*) were often composed of several naaDus. The chiefly paalaiyams lost their importance in the late seventeenth century, but the naaDus continued as a form of local political organization (Murton 1979:15-17). It is worthwhile to emphasize the clear correspondence between Gounder naaDu and temple organization and what is described in the previous chapter as the Tamilians' sense of the cosmos as divided into the domains of small, kin-oriented gods (kuladeevam) and high kingly gods such as Shiva. The Gounders' kin-organized naaDus have small-god temples, whereas the locality naaDu has as its focus a Saivite temple. The distinction between kin and kingly domains is maintained.

Councils headed by persons holding named hereditary offices occur at each level of segmentation. At the level of the settlement is the uur Gounder. At the kiraamam level the headman is called *muppaaTTukkaarar*, whereas at the naaDu level the caste officer is called *naaTTan-*

maikkaarar, or *naattu* Gounder, or simply *naaTTar* (Beck 1972:66ff).
According to Beck, the uur Gounder–the village-level officer–has
important dispute settlement responsibilities, not only for his own
caste but for dependent castes as well. The naaTTar and muppaaT-
Tukkaarar, however, seem to have lost their function in the last thirty
years, and their purpose is no longer clear. They appear to have once
had largely ceremonial roles relating to the goddess temples. They act
as representatives of their own naaDus at the important ceremonies of
neighboring naaDus, and they collect funds for worship at the goddess
temples.

Within KonkunaaDu, but above the level of the naaDu, the
Gounders' pattakkaarars still have some dispute settlement functions,
and their duties as caste officers are closely associated with Shiva
temples. Beck (1972:108) also notes that adjacent naaDus were once
linked by ritualized marriage ties. These caste endogamous marriages
occurred among a number of castes of the right-hand section. Consequently, right-hand castes were linked vertically by political-economic
interdependence and horizontally by marriage alliances.

It is apparent that the Gounder naaDu polity is founded on land
ownership and kinship, and is symbolically integrated by joint worship
at Shiva temples at the naaDu level and kin temples at lower levels.
Land is owned by Gounders and is distributed along kin lines; the
territory they dominate through their control of land is subdivided
along naaDu lines. Temples below the naaDu level are kin specific and
linked to the segmented kin units of household, lineage, clan, and
subcaste. The offices of the caste are hereditary and are also linked to
the different levels of kin segmentation. Kinship, ownership of land,
settlement pattern, temple geography, the juncture of small-god (the
kin-linked goddesses) and high-god (Shiva) ritualization, and political
organization all appear to be isomorphic and parallel components of
the Gounders' locality-based naaDu structure.

Beck notes (1972:70) that leadership at the extremes of the system,
at the level of the uur Gounder and pattakkaarar, still has some importance in settling disputes. However, the officers in between, at the
level of kiraamam and naaDu, have lost their importance. Beck
(1972:97) also notes that the Gounders' descent-group organization
and its associated temples are neglected compared to those of other
right-hand castes. She argues that the "lack of interest in descent-
group activities among KavuNTars [Gounders] today is associated with
a gradual shift of emphasis away from collective ritual toward the
affirmation of individual family status" (1972:97). The loss of naaDu
leaders, she suggests, has occurred "perhaps because of endemic disputes between those qualified to hold these intermediate titles"

(1972:70). In effect, since the 1950s, the naaDus have lost their political importance.

In postcolonial India, kin organizations and temple hierarchies no longer structure politics and economic power; they have been superseded by elected councils and representatives, and by the institutions of modern bureaucracy and statecraft such as cooperative banks, government officers, and marketing societies. The uur Gounders continue to function amid these changes because caste and kinship remain important for settling disputes at the village level, and because the power of the landowners over dependent castes is still real, if no longer absolute. At the other extreme, pattakkaarars symbolize the greatness of the caste beyond the local level and are important to the Gounders' caste image.

Beck notes that other relatively high-ranking, landowning castes are organized like the Gounders, whereas dependent castes are administered by the Gounders' naaDu organization. The necessities of land ownership and agriculture gave the organizations of the right-hand castes a strong kin-based, locality focus. Their organizations were allied to the Gounders' naaDu structure; the different degree of each caste's subordination was determined by the extent of its dependence.

According to Beck, the high left-hand castes contrast sharply to the Gounders. Left-hand castes lack local political organization, but in the past were loosely organized under regional religious leaders. Without the locality orientation that agriculture produces, the left-hand castes lack all of the characteristics of right-hand naaDu organizations. Except for the Kaikkoolars, whom Beck considers aberrant, none of the left-hand castes has any clan organization. Kaikkoolars do have clans (*kuuTTam*), but these are important only for defining exogamy. This lack of kin-based local organizations is characteristic of the other left-hand castes as well. Descent organization is not associated with caste organization, territorial identity, or local temple organization.

Whereas right-hand castes worship locality goddesses specific to particular kin groups, Beck argues that the left-hand castes worship regionally known small gods specific to neither kin groups nor castes. These small gods and goddesses, such as AngaaLammaa, lack locality identity. Further, the left-hand castes do not provide their own priests at goddess temples, as do the right-hand castes.

Beck concludes that high left-hand subcastes "have no political organization of their own" (1972:77). They lack titled caste offices. And in contrast to the integration and interdependence of the right-hand castes, the high left-hand castes are independent of each other. Each caste negotiates its own disputes and never appeals to other communities for assistance in reaching settlements. The contrast, as drawn by

Beck, is between locality-based right-hand castes and guru-affiliated left-hand castes. The former are dependent upon the land and interdependent among themselves, and are organized by their kin-based system; the latter lack locality-oriented characteristics and have no political organization.

Kaikkoolar (left-hand) naaDu organization in contemporary Salem District

Perhaps because of the decisive dominance of Gounders in the area of her research, Beck overlooked the Kaikkoolars' naaDu organization and the regionwide caste organizations of other left-hand castes such as the Kammalars (Aachaaris) (Thurston 1909, vol. III:109-110). I shall describe the organization of the Kaikkoolars of northern KonkunaaDu first, since this description is based on my fieldwork in this region. I will then refer briefly to the extensive political organization of the Kammalars.

Kaikkoolar polity combines locality organization with a supralocal naaDu tradition that incorporates what is today Tamilnadu, Sri Lanka, and much of Kerala. In theory, the Kaikkoolars' system of naaDus incorporates all localities where a Kaikkoolar population may live (*Senguntha Samuuha Kaittari, Maatar, Maanila MaanaaDu* 1976).

At the local level in the Seven-City Territory, Kaikkoolar social geography always follows the same form. In villages and towns, it centers on an area of common land known as the paavaDi, used for stretching paavu, or warps. The paavaDi is located near the caste's Murugan temple, typically in front of the temple's entrance. In urban settings, the temple and its maaDa viiti (temple streets) demarcate the community's geographic center and incorporate the paavaDi ground and often a caste meeting hall, which in the villages is the Murugan temple. In urban areas, a school founded by caste members may also be located here. In towns and cities, another source of pride is the festively lit marriage hall (*kalyaaNam maNDapam*). The marriage hall is a relatively recent form of ostentation for the middle- and upper-class Kaikkoolars, whose marriages during the last twenty years have become large, expensive affairs. The hall also offers a display of pictures of prominent caste leaders who donated large sums of money for the hall's construction; pictures of these donors' families may also be shown. In addition, engraved lists of names categorize the important donors by the size of their donations. To outsiders, the marriage hall is a display of the community's affluence, whereas for the community it is a public record of the caste's most prominent families, as well as a demonstration of the caste's wealth and a symbol of community unity.

The meeting hall or the Murugan temple is the assembly place of the Kaikkoolar community's paavaDi council (paavaDi naaDu), the lowest level in the Kaikkoolars' hierarchy of naaDu administration. At this level the council is composed of three named hereditary offices and incorporates the territory of the local community. The naaTTaaNmaikkaarar, also sometimes known as the *naaTTavar* or *periyathaanakaarar*, is the presiding officer of the paavaDi assembly. He is assisted by one or two lieutenants, *kaariyakkaarar*, and a peon, or *taNDalkaaran*. This latter office is filled by a dependent untouchable, who acts as the council's "crier" and supplicant when the council appears before a higher council. The peons of paavaDi councils outcaste by higher-level councils will lie prostrate with their arms outstretched on the ground before the officers of the higher council, symbolizing the recalcitrant council's submission to the higher council. The outcaste community's officers stand off to one side. They tie their shoulder cloths around their waists as a symbol of their respect for the council. Kaikkoolars fill all council offices except that of the taNDalkaaran. Until recently, offices at all levels of the naaDu system were hereditary, but officers are now elected in some areas, such as Trichengode.

The paavaDi councils settle disputes, collect taxes for ceremonial functions, and represent the community at important locality pujas and higher-level naaDu councils. Today, paavaDi councils settle minor disputes involving family partitioning, disagreements between husbands and wives that have become public, and cases of misconduct. They settle disputes only for Kaikkoolars, although forty years ago, Kaikkoolars say, the councils also handled cases involving washermen, potters, barbers, and in some areas Padaiyaachis and VeeTTuva Gounders (nondominant, agriculturist castes). Serious criminal cases are not handled by the council. They are taken to the police and the courts, as are most cases involving wealth in which a mutually satisfactory settlement cannot be achieved.

PaavaDi councils no longer function in urban communities such as Ammapettai, Salem, and Erode, where there has been considerable Kaikkoolar emigration. Kaikkoolars in these cities have lost the sense of community consensus on which their councils' authority was based. Nonetheless the geographic organization of their communities remains essentially the same. Interested residents from these localities still attend the annual Vaikasi Teer festival in Trichengode as representatives of their sublocalities. The joint sponsorship of a puja at this festival by the Seven-City Territory's Kaikkoolars symbolically defines their territorial identity and the caste membership of the participating sublocalities. Functioning councils are commonplace throughout most of the rest of the Seven-City Territory. Kaikkoolars nonetheless believe the system to be less important than it was seventy years ago.

PaavaDi councils collect taxes from Kaikkoolars to fund local ceremonials, particularly for Murugan and Maariyamman festivals. At the paavaDi council level, the most important festivals involving the participation of the entire caste community are the Suurabatman festival and the annual Maariyamman festival. Kaikkoolars in Ammapettai and Salem City stage elaborate processions for both of these festivals. Since the paavaDi council is now defunct in Ammapettai, the celebration is financed by the local Murugan and Maariyamman temples. In addition, I found that in the Seven-City Territory, taxes from each paavaDi community are collected to sponsor the Vaikasi Teer festival puja previously mentioned. Trichengode is the location of the locality's highest caste council. It ranks next in jurisdiction to the castewide council once located in Conjeepuram. Thus, local paavaDi councils are linked by ceremonial involvement with increasingly higher levels of caste aggregation. The paavaDi officers attend these affairs as community representatives, publicly donate their paavaDi councils' collected taxes, and participate in the meeting of supralocal naaDu councils.

These supralocal councils handle a significantly wider range of affairs than do the paavaDi councils. They adjudicate political disputes between naaDu officers and the public, disagreements among officers of the paavaDi councils, and questions of precedence among member councils. They also settle disputes similar to those heard by paavaDi councils. The supralocal naaDu councils also bring cases before the third tier in the naaDu system involving disputes between naaDus.

According to my informants, thirty-two or thirty-three contiguous paavaDi councils form a naaDu. For example, Ammapettai's paavaDi council belongs to Seela naaDu, with headquarters in Salem city. Similarly, Trichengode is headquarters for the EeRukarai naaDu with its own group of thirty-two villages (see Table 2). Within the naaDu, one paavaDi council is designated as *meeL uur* or *meeL graamam* (West Village), and one as *kiiR uur* or *kiiR graamam* (East Village).[1] These councils are notified in writing when the naaDu council meets, and in turn notify surrounding paavaDi councils. Matters of importance to the naaDu must always be considered in the presence of officers of these councils. Thus, in 1979, the officers of one naaDu were admonished by their superior council in Trichengode for opening a letter without first notifying the meeL graamam or kiiR graamam. Seela naaDu's kiiR graamam (East Village) is Ammapettai; its meeL graamam (West Village) is Venanduur. At ceremonials, honors are given first to the

---

[1]These are also called *meeL naaDu* and *kiiR naaDu.*

Table 2. *The Kaikkoolar's NaaDu hierarchy*

				Chief Officer: AaNDavar
Highest	IV	MahaanaaDu		
		Headquarters:	Conjeepuram	
		Membership:	Four thisainaaDu	
	III	ThisainaaDus (e.g., Salem district, northern KonkumaNDalam)		
		Headquarters:	Talamai naaDu	(Trichengode)
		Membership:	EeRuuru naaDu	(Seven City Territories)
			EeRukarai naaDu	(Trichengode)
			Inai naaDu	(Taramangalam)
			Seela naaDu	(Salem)
			Mallesamutram	(Mallesamutram)
			Pachchal naaDu	(Rasipuram)
			Eluur naaDu	(Komarapalaiyam-Edapadi)
			Araiya naaDu	(Paramuthu and Eluur)
	II	NaaDus (e.g., Seela naaDu)		
		Membership:	meeL graamam (West Village): in Seela naaDu, Venanduur	
			kiiR graamam (East Village): in Seela naaDu, Ammapettai	
			Each naaDu has as members 30 to 33 paavaDi naaDus.	
Lowest	I	PaavaDi naaDu (e.g., Ammapettai council)		
		Membership:	Local community	

84

officers of the naaDu headquarters, followed by the West Village and East Village officers, respectively.

Contrary to Beck's findings, therefore, the Kaikkoolars have a caste-wide naaDu organization, and their system clearly has a territorial basis. The titles of the naaDu offices are the same as those of the paavaDi councils. The naaDu councils hear similar kinds of disputes involving localized caste affairs, but in addition they hear cases involving disputes between paavaDi councils and among their officers. These are cases brought before the naaDu council as appeals, and are paid for by the plaintiffs. NaaDu councils act both as local councils for their own community and as courts of appeal for disputes handled first at the paavaDi council level.

Above the level of the naaDu councils are the thisainaaDus (places of jurisdiction). There are four thisainaaDus, but Trichengode's is the only one I have observed in session. In addition to being headquarters of a naaDu, the EeRukarai naaDu, Trichengode is headquarters (*talamai naaDu*) of the Seven-City Territory's place of jurisdiction (the EeRuurunaaDu thisainaaDu), which includes seven naaDu territories: EeRukarai naaDu (Trichengode), which is the head naaDu (Talamai naaDu); Inai naaDu (Taramangalam); Seela naaDu (Salem); Mallesamutram (Mallesamutram); Pachchal naaDu (Rasipuram); Eluur naaDu (Komarapalaiyam), and Araiya naaDu (Paramuthu and Eluur) (Map 2). This is a ranked order of naaDu territories. The last three listed correspond to three of the twenty-four naaDus that have constituted KonkumaNDalam (KonkunaaDu) since Chola times (Arokiaswami 1959: 221-222). The correspondence, however, may be in name only, since the VeLLaaLa Gounder-dominated naaDus to which the twenty-four naaDus correspond are clearly separate from the Kaikkoolar-controlled administrative bodies. This is evident in the separate jurisdictions of the two sets of naaDus. Neither VeLLaaLas nor Kaikkoolars maintain institutionalized relationships with the other's naaDus. Further, four of the naaDus do not correspond to any of the traditional twenty-four naaDus of the Konku area. This indicates that the two systems overlap territorially but are not identical in extent, and that they are administratively distinct. The image this evokes is one of a tier of administratively distinct local and supralocal networks that partially overlap territorially.

This system of naaDu organization is more complex than has been commonly supposed. Thus, Stein (1980) and Hall (1980) describe naaDus as centered on the dominant agricultural caste of an area, and Beck (1972:77) says that the left-hand castes lack any kind of political structure similar to the VeLLaaLa Gounders' naaDus. The evidence of the Salem-Erode locality indicates that the Kaikkoolars in fact have a parallel naaDu organization that mirrors the Gounders' system in some features, but that is different in its organization, in its supralocal extent, and in its dissociation from kinship and land ownership.

The officers of the (thisainaaDu) bear the same titles as the officers of the lower councils, and divide their attention between local affairs and cases appealed from lower councils. The main difference is that there are two presiding officers, periyathaanakaarar, instead of one heading the Trichengode thisainaaDu because of this council's heavier case load. The two decide cases jointly. Before hearing a case, they require the disputants to agree to accept their decision. If they do not, they are expelled from the caste until they agree to comply, apologize publicly, and pay a symbolic fine. This procedure is followed for disputing naaDu councils as well as for private cases.

For example, in 1968 Trichengode's thisainaaDu decided a case in a manner with which none of the other six naaDus agreed. All six naaDus were expelled until they accepted the decision, at which point they were readmitted. Trichengode again expelled all the member naaDus of the Seven-City Territory in 1978. This expulsion involved a case that had been appealed to Taramangalam, which ranks as the second highest naaDu of the Seven-City Territory. Taramangalam settled the case, but when it was subsequently appealed to Trichengode's council, Taramangalam insisted that Trichengode rubber-stamp its decision. This was contrary to customary rule, which requires that the case be reheard. Taramangalam and the lower naaDus that supported it refused to comply and were accordingly expelled. The lower naaDus, except Mallesamutram, then supported Trichengode and were readmitted. Finally, in June 1979, representatives from Taramangalam appeared in Trichengode to apologize before naaDu representatives from all parts of the Seven-City Territory. They paid a fine and were readmitted as members of the Territory. Mallesamutram had yet to seek readmission in 1979.

Like the lower councils, the Seven-City Territory Council (EeRuurunaaDu thisainaaDu) is associated with a Saivite temple, the Ardhanaari-isvara temple in Trichengode, a major pilgrimage temple. Each year at the Vaikasi Teer festival – the temple car festival – the Trichengode thisainaaDu council meets in conjunction with representatives of all its member councils in good standing for the dual purpose of jointly sponsoring a special puja and of reaffirming the office holders of the member councils. This latter function is performed by a Brahman priest, who presents yellow turbans of office to the naaTTaaNmaikkaarar and kaariyakkaarars of each attending council in the order of the councils' rank. Expelled councils, of course, are not allowed to attend.

As observed in June 1979, the meeting consists of four main parts.

First, there is the gathering of the representatives of the Seven-City Territories under the presiding Trichengode naaDu council. During the meeting, great formality is observed. Speakers before the dais wrap their shoulder towels around their waists to show deference. Issues important to the Kaikkoolars' Seven-City Territory such as out-casting and readmission are considered. All decisions are repeated by the council's crier (taNDalkaaran), so that everyone hears clearly. Over one hundred men are present on the dais. Persons leaving the meeting ask formal permission of the presiding officers. The criers of penitent councils prostrate themselves before the body while suitable but largely symbolic fines are discussed. A formal roll call of naaDus is taken and representatives reply, indicating how much their village is donating for the Kaikkoolar-sponsored puja of the god Ardhanaariis-varar that occurs early the following morning.

Next, the Seven-City Territory Council travels in a procession led by drums and *nagaswarams* (a double-reed instrument used on auspicious occasions) to the meeting place of Taramangalam's council, the Inai naaDu (equal *naaDu*). Taramangalam's council, which had previously been invited to come to Trichengode, has been meeting elsewhere in the town. The Seven-City Territory Council now invites the Inai naaDu to come to its meeting place. They return together in proces-sion to the dais. Taramangalam's council is invited each year to the Trichengode car festival, and in return the officers of the Seven-City Territory Council are invited to the Taramangalam car festival. Al-though officers of the member naaDus are normally invited to attend important functions of the Territory, Taramangalam is the only mem-ber council of the Territory given this special recognition of rank.

The third activity of the meeting involves the reinvestment of au-thority in the officers of the different village paavaDi councils and naaDu councils. The two top officers of each council – the naaTTaaN-maikkaarar and kaariyakkaarar – are given turbans as signs of office in the order of their council's rank among the attending councils. The turbans are tied by a Brahman *Iyer* priest, a rare instance today of a Brahman being used to legitimate ritually the authority of caste officers.

The final activities of the gathering occur when the Kaikkoolars as a community jointly sponsor a puja for Ardhanaariisvarar, using the funds collected from the paavaDi councils. The Kaikkoolars say that the bestowal of turbans and the worship of God are the main pur-poses of the meeting. The meeting occurs in the course of a single night, and the attendant pomp and circumstance create a feeling of great dignity and importance. The meetings, the money, and the puja similarly underscore Kaikkoolar unity, the extent of their domain and constituent membership, their religiosity, and their importance among other worshipers.

These two features, domain and worship, are outstanding and basic to Kaikkoolar identity in the Seven-City Territory. First, there is the reaffirmation of the caste's structural order, its constituent membership, its territorial configuration, and the sources of the council's power and authority. Second and equally important, there is an emphasis on the gathering of Kaikkoolars as worshipers of Shiva, their mythical father, and Murugan, their mythical military commander. In this way, two aspects of Kaikkoolar identity – the territorial and the sacred – are reaffirmed through ritually enacted reciprocity among the worshipers and their gods. The worshipers' actions define the order of their social world, and their relationship to the sacred defines their territorial domain and warrior status among men. The structural and the symbolic are interwoven and are mutually reinforcing.

The Kaikkoolars' naaDu system still operates to the level of the Seven-City Territory Council, the EeRuurunaaDu thisainaaDu, although the Seven-City Territory itself is spotted with places, especially in cities, where local councils are defunct. Throughout the twentieth century, naaDu officers have complained that they no longer have the authority or political importance of former years.

Fifty years ago, all levels of the system's pyramid were complete. At that time, the top tier of the naaDu pyramid still functioned in Conjeepuram. Conjeepuram was the religious-political apex of the Kaikkoolar caste. Conjeepuram's council, the MahaanaaDu, was the ultimate court of appeal within the naaDu system and had final jurisdiction over all lower Kaikkoolar councils. It heard cases appealed from lower councils, and its presiding officer, the hereditarily selected aaNDavar, acted as the symbolic head of the Kaikkoolar caste. Conjeepuram was also the location of the Kaikkoolars' head temple, the Eekaambanaatar Kooyil, and of their caste goddess, KaamaakshiyammaaL. Therefore, at this highest level of the system, there is a correspondence between a naaDu council's jurisdiction and its territorial domain established by temple worship. At least until the late 1920s, the supralocal character of the naaDu system was also ceremonially reinforced by caste gurus from Conjeepuram. Brahmans who regularly toured the naaDus gave sermons on ideal behavior and dispensed ritual blessings. The use of Brahman gurus and priests was largely given up with the rise of the non-Brahman movement, and today even in Conjeepuram, Kaikkoolars use Kaikkoolar teesikars (priests) for household ritual.

The last major caste dispute handled by an aaNDavar occurred in Gudiyaattam, North Arcot District, in 1905, and its proceedings were published under the title *Nadavadikkai*. Unlike the officers of the lower-level councils, those of the MahaanaaDu apparently traveled to the location of the dispute. The aaNDavar was always accompanied by ceremonial pomp. In 1905 his procession from the train station to the meeting place included deeva-daasis who fanned him while he was carried in a palanquin, nagaswarams and drums, and scepters of office. The procession was led by torch bearers, their torches lit even in daytime, and eighteen flags. Each of these processional features was an emblem of the honor and status that were aspects of the aaNDavar. Their use was a right Kaikkoolars maintained as a high left-hand caste (for comparison, see Mackenzie 1875:344-346). The last aaNDavar was appointed to office in 1914, but by the late 1920s he had lost power and the MahaanaaDu was defunct. The MahaanaaDu functioned primarily by customary rule. Disputes were brought before the council by appeal and were settled on the basis of prevailing local customs which varied significantly from locality to locality. The MahaanaaDu could not directly legislate or dictate new codes. Consequently, the council's orientation was conservative.

Although the form of the Kaikkoolars' naaDu structure is still clear today, the weakening of the system's functions, which Kaikkoolars say has been occurring since the nineteenth century, obscures much of its former importance. As noted earlier, artisan-merchant organizations (nagaram) in the eleventh and twelfth centuries appear to have been incorporated into agrarian naaDu structures. According to Hall (1980:202), each naaDu had a marketing center (nagaram) administered by its artisan-merchants. Armed itinerant merchants linked naaDu localities, but there was no hierarchy of artisan-merchant organizations. Artisan-merchants and agrarian naaDus were both political forces that formed important segments within the south Indian states. They regulated many of their own affairs and attempted to balance the advantages they gained from the state, including status, honors, security, and financing, against the disadvantages of state control, taxation, and plundering (Hall 1980:185ff).

In Vijayanagara times, the artisan-merchant naaDus took on their pyramidal form and itinerant trade lost its military aspect. Vijayanagar chiefs attempted to destroy the military capabilities of both local agrarian warriors and merchants. It was during this time period (1350-1650) that the great merchant associations disappeared. I suspect that under the Vijayanagar kings, the Kaikkoolars' naaDu system took shape as a marketing network for textiles that gave rulers a means of taxing production and trade while providing the Kaikkoolars with security and a means of marketing textiles. In this system, paavaDi naaDus were local production centers, whereas higher levels in the naaDu system formed points in the textile market networks that brought textiles up from their producers to centers that redistributed some cloth downward into the local markets and traded some cloth products outward into regional and international markets. Each naaDu center provided a location for marketing and a place where agreements among weavers and merchants could be made and disagreements settled. Today the marketing functions of naaDus have been replaced by legal contracts and wholesale marketing. Perhaps one reason why naaDus nevertheless have persisted is that they still provide a context in which contacts between localities are maintained. These contacts are an important ingredient in caste identity, help to establish a political following for local leaders, and establish a sense of good will among weavers and traders from different places.

The weakening of the Kaikkoolars' naaDu system

The location of Conjeepuram near Madras City played an important part in the MahaanaaDu's demise in the late 1920s and 1930s. At that time in Madras, a small number of young Sengunthar men from several districts were among the first of their caste to pursue university and legal educations. When, in the late 1920s, the caste founded a statewide caste association, these young men formed a youthful, progressive, and energetic cadre within the corporation. In contrast to naaDu leaders, whose authority rested on conservatism, these men advocated change. They formed a new, Western-educated caste elite employed in nontraditional jobs, and they sought to lead the caste through a series of social and economic transformations in order to bring about its general uplift. They were to play pivotal roles in the formation of the handloom weavers' cooperative movement, the creation and administration of the caste association, and the transcendance of conservative localism. In 1978-1979 the surviving members of this group were in their seventies, and either still held important roles in Kaikkoolar affairs or were only recently retired.

The last hereditary aaNDavar was a conservative, uneducated man who favored traditional caste localism at a time when the emerging leadership saw several advantages in creating a socially and politically unified Kaikkoolar caste. University-educated Kaikkoolar men were rare, numbering fewer than fifty in 1930. Since their numbers were small, they found it difficult to form suitable marriage alliances with similarly advantaged families within their own localities. Consequently, they sought marriages with families living beyond their traditionally endogamous localities. One such educated man who played a pivotal role in the confrontation between the new elite and the caste conservatives was the son of a Conjeepuram Kaikkoolar merchant. While this

young man was in law school, his family arranged his marriage with a
Madras girl from an educated family. The aaNDavar adamantly opposed this marriage because it violated locality endogamy, but in so
doing he split Conjeepuram's Kaikkoolar community into opposing
factions. This proved to be the aaNDavar's undoing. The new elite felt
that the naaDu system, which weakly organized a highly localized and
segmented confederation of subcastes, no longer provided a framework for caste unity. Times had changed in Madras Presidency.

In 1918, the British had promised Indians dyarchy, a system of government that was to allow democratically elected officials to administer
local affairs. Many castes saw this change in government as offering
opportunities to any caste that could act effectively as a united political
force. In 1927, with new elite members playing a prominent role, the
first all-Kaikkoolar caste meeting was held in Erode, pointedly not in
Conjeepuram, the seat of naaDu organization. As part of their effort
to unify the caste, leaders at this meeting advocated extralocality marriage. Opposed by the aaNDavar, this meeting was a success for progressive leadership, and new-elite families began to arrange extralocal
marriages in the face of the aaNDavar's threat to outcaste transgres-
sors of caste law. The aaNDavar in Conjeepuram was unable to carry
out this threat, however, because the progressives received too much
support. The outcome was the resignation of the aaNDavar and his
replacement by an elected new-elite leader, M. Shanmugam Mudaliyar, a flag raiser at the first all-caste association conference held in
Erode and a Madras municipal board member. Families were split on
this issue of extralocal marriage, and in the hinterland regions of Tamilnadu some still are. But the MahaanaaDu had lost its authority and
was never to regain it.

We see in this confrontation the broader conflict between the traditional hereditary leadership and the emergent educated progressives.
The former leadership was suited to the locality-based naaDu system
and the highly segmented structure of the caste. The new leadership
wished to transcend the confines of the locality because it was too
small a social arena for the changed political system, and could not
offer the marriages and other opportunities that Western education
and nontraditional occupations opened to the new elite. They wished
to create a unified, educated caste with greater political clout. This
conflict also shows that the naaDu system had more than ceremonial
importance. In the early twentieth century, when most Kaikkoolars
were poor and geographically immobile, it provided a powerful link
among localities on which to base regional leadership. In a more limited way, the Seven-City Territory still provides a political base for
Kaikkoolar leaders in Trichengode, where the Kaikkoolar population

has remained homogeneous and where elected presiding officers have created enough flexibility to allow expression for new leadership.

The importance of the naaDu system as a powerful framework for political leadership is also illustrated by the demise of the Ammapettai paavaDi council located in Salem. The dispute that led to the capitulation of Ammapettai's paavaDi council officers illustrates a similar conflict between a progressive leadership that organized its power around the growing handloom weavers' cooperative system in the late 1940s and early 1950s, and the conservative, hereditary naaDu leaders.

A Brahman, C. Rajagopalachariya or "Rajaji," as he was better known, was elected as the first chief minister of Madras in 1937 and became head of the Provincial Congress Committee. His home constituency was Trichengode. In the 1940s, a non-Brahman congressman, Kamaraj Nadar, challenged him for leadership of the party. This was the first serious split within the Provincial Congress Committee. It was settled by Mahatma Gandhi in favor of Rajaji, but was subsequently reflected in the political structure of Ammapettai during the 1946-1947 municipal elections.

During these elections, two political factions emerged among the Kaikkoolars of Ammapettai. One faction, led by P. Mariyappan, a kaariyakkaarar of the Ammapettai paavaDi council, supported Rajaji and is described today in Ammapettai as a group of older, conservative men. The other faction was led by A. Mariyappan, a young local leader and later the president of the Ammapettai Handloom Weavers' Cooperative Society. This faction supported Kamaraj. Each faction put up two candidates for the municipal council seats. When this occurred, the paavaDi council fined A. Mariyappan and ordered him to withdraw his candidates. He appealed to the Trichengode territorial council, but Trichengode was Rajaji's stronghold. The territorial council upheld the fine and A. Mariyappan was outcaste (*tallivaittal*), subject to his complying with the Ammapettai paavaDi council. Shortly thereafter, the Rajaji faction won the election, but found that A. Mariyappan had a sufficient number of supporters in Ammapettai to make his outcasting unenforceable. Outcasting required total social ostracism. If a Kaikkoolar interacted with the outcaste person, then he and his family were outcaste as well. A. Mariyappan was visited by so many supporters that soon he and his followers formed a significant minority within the community and his outcasting became meaningless. Lacking the effective support of the community, the paavaDi leaders dissolved the council. They had won the election and their position was upheld by the territorial council, but they lacked the true consensus on which the enforcement of such decisions must rest.

In 1952, A. Mariyappan's faction gained dominance in the area, and he was elected president of the Ammapettai Handloom Weavers' Co-operative Society, a position he was to hold for twenty years. At this time, the cooperative system of handloom weavers partially displaced the naaDu system as the main locality-based organizational framework for Kaikkoolar leadership. Some leaders continued to maintain naaDu offices, but in Salem, Trichengode, Ammapettai, and elsewhere, the handloom weavers' cooperative system increasingly became the organizational base for local political power during and after the 1940s.

The cases just described suggest that the naaDu councils formed the main political structure for the Kaikkoolar caste in the Salem area and provided it with leaders at least until the late 1940s and early 1950s. The first half of the twentieth century, however, was a period of tremendous social change, and the naaDu system had been profoundly affected. In many localities, the system appears to have been too rigid to accommodate the transformations wrought by political change. The system was disrupted by the desire of the emerging new leadership to integrate the caste within a caste association and to push for the economic and social transformation of the caste. In their view, Western-style education would bring about the caste's social and economic uplift. The Kaikkoolars' caste association was to organize the caste as a corporation in order to pressure the government to respond to the caste's particular needs. As part of this effort, the new leadership vigorously sought to improve the condition of the common weaver by instituting handloom weaver cooperative societies. As self-styled leaders of the common man and the poor weaver, they drew political backing from their local communities and from the political parties that sought their leadership in organizing grass-roots support. Many joined Mahatma Gandhi and the Congress Party and fought for independence. Others were influenced by Periyar, the anti-Brahman leader, and the non-Brahman movement that emerged with dyarchy, and couched their mobility aspirations in a language that emphasized escape from the religious oppression of Brahmanical Hinduism.

By contrast, the traditional leaders were usually older and well established in their communities, and consequently were not inclined to change. They based their power on their prestige and on their reputation for upholding local customs. They lacked power beyond the support they could muster within their naaDu areas. The new leaders were interested in transcending naaDu localism which they considered too provincial in the more centralized atmosphere of dyarchy and the growing expectation of self-rule. To them, the politically relevant arena was the province and state. The locality could be an important grass-roots focus of support, but it had to act as part of the greater caste to gain the benefits sought by the new leadership. As a result, the caste association first displaced the naaDu system as a more effective statewide political organization, and then in the 1960s was itself displaced by the statewide system of handloom cooperative societies. These societies, in turn, provided many leaders with a popular local seat of power based upon the welfare benefits they brought to weavers in the societies they headed.

The new leaders never directly attacked the naaDu system. They were proud of the system as part of their caste's ancient legacy. However, when they found themselves in conflict with naaDu localism and traditionalism, their leadership roles in cooperative societies, their political affiliations, and their caste association ties provided them with enough public support to undercut the traditional leaders' authority. Where this occurred, it spelled the demise of the naaDus. These conflicts destroyed the Conjeepuram MahaanaaDu and many other councils as well, including Seela naaDu and the Ammapettai and Erode paavaDi councils. In general, at the village level and in towns and cities such as Trichengode and Taramangalam, where the caste population has remained relatively undisturbed by emigration, naaDus in modified form have continued to function. In some areas, the naaDus survived because their leaders were supplanted by elected officers or because they were fortunate to have enlightened leaders. However, surviving naaDus were not as powerful as before. They considered a smaller variety of subjects, and the authority of their officers was more tentative.

The weakening of the naaDu system, therefore, was not solely a result of the Kaikkoolars' adoption of the British-founded legal system to settle disputes and regulate trade. There were several causes, including the rigid conservatism built into the naaDu structure as a locality-based, segmented system of caste organization in a time of increasing governmental centralization and the acceptance of interests couched as generalized caste concerns. The system was also weakened by the conflicts between new and traditional leaders. These confrontations were created by the distinctive power bases of these two types of leaders. One base was hereditary and flowed from the consensus of the caste's segments; the other was popular and arose from a leader's ability to benefit his caste fellows. The system was further weakened by the increase in social and geographic mobility among Kaikkoolars and the increase in Western education and extra-local marriages among the elite. This mobility created socially heterogeneous Kaikkoolar communities whose leaders thought that a caste association led by Western-educated men could transform the caste and bring about its social, political, and economic elevation. They wanted to create a uniform caste code for behavior, make the caste a single political unit, and transform the caste's economic behavior.

Kaikkoolar and Gounder naaDus

Comparing the naaDu system of the Kaikkoolars with that of the Konku VeLLaaLa Gounders described by Beck, we see both similarities and differences. Clearly, Beck errs when she says that high left-hand castes do not have naaDu systems. As we have seen, the Kaikkoolar system is extensive, is still active at many levels, and has an ancient history. In addition, Thurston reports that the Kammalars, or Aachaaris, have also had an extensive system of caste organization, with appointed officers bearing titles similar to those of the Gounders and Kaikkoolars (Thurston 1909, vol. III:108-110). The Kammalar system seems to have been hierarchical and supralocal, much like the Kaikkoolar system. The supreme office holder is called *Anjuviittu NaaTTaaNmaikkaarar*. Thurston does not call this organization a naaDu system, but from its titles of office and its association with temples and locality, it appears to be one version of such a system. In addition, Buchanan (1807, vol. II:268; 1:77) and MacKenzie (1875:345-346) both refer to the Kammalars as being the head of the left-hand castes as a group. There is no evidence for this in the Seven-City Territory today. Nonetheless, it is clear that high left-hand castes do have extensive caste organizational and political systems.

A second similarity is that the Kaikkoolars' system has a clear territorial and locality base. This is reflected not only in the existence of a hierarchy of territorial councils, including the paavaDi councils, the naaDu councils with their meeL graamam and kiiR graamam, and the thisainaaDus and mahaanaaDu, but also in the association of each council at all levels with specific Saivite temples – especially Murugan temples – that form the temple geography of the system. As for many other castes, the ritual center of the system is Conjeepuram, the location of the MahaanaaDu. During the early twentieth century in Conjeepuram, right-hand and left-hand castes had, as in other shared pilgrimage locations, separate rest houses (maNDapam) and separate groups of deeva-daasis. I believe that the separate maNDapam Kaikkoolars maintain in Trichengode today are a vestige of this distinction. The separation of left-hand and right-hand maNDapam at the major naaDu temples reflects the juxtaposition of the naaDu systems of the two moieties. Their naaDus exist as parallel networks of administration.

A third similarity is the fairly close correspondence between the office titles of the Kaikkoolars' and the Gounders' respective naaDu systems. The titles differ, however, at the extremes of the systems: the highest officers (pattakkaarar, Gounder; aaNDavar, Kaikkoolar) and the lowest (uur Gounder, Gounder; naaTTaaNmaikkaarar, Kaikkoolar). Kaikkoolars also apparently lack a naaDu division at the revenue village level.

Another important difference between the two naaDu systems is that the Kaikkoolar system lacks the Gounder system's close correspondence with descent organization. This is also reflected in the temple structure of Kaikkoolar naaDus. Kaikkoolar naaDu temples are dedicated at all levels to Saivite deities, whereas Gounder naaDu temples at the lower levels of organization are dedicated to locality goddesses associated closely with descent groups. Kaikkoolar temples belong to the community, not to specific descent groups, and are open to worship by other castes.

These differences are indicative of the differences in the universes of these two castes. As agriculturists, Gounders are tied to particular naaDus by descent and inheritance, as well as by their worship of small gods. Kinship corresponds to the lower levels of their naaDu system. But Kaikkoolars are not tied to territory by land ownership, so they do not worship small gods at any level of their naaDu system. Their connection with naaDu territoriality is defined by their joint sponsorship of pujas at Saivite temples. Their territoriality is not kin based; it is contractual. Both the Gounder and Kaikkoolar systems, therefore, correspond to the Dravidian division of the cosmos into interior and exterior realms. The interior is kin based and is associated with the worship of small gods. The exterior is associated with the worship of high gods and is concerned with domain and state.

An intriguing question is whether the Kaikkoolar and Gounder naaDus are geographically coterminous. As shown earlier, some of the Kaikkoolars' naaDus from northern KonkunaaDu have the same names as naaDus in the Gounder-dominated system. However, the evidence suggests that the two castes in this area of Tamilnadu maintain administratively separate systems. Beck notes that the former left-hand castes still maintain independence from the jurisdiction of the Gounder naaDus. Further, the temples of the two systems are different at the lower levels of organization; where they are shared, they have different maNDapam to house members of the two moieties separately. The division of deeva-daasis and the strict rules about which moiety they might serve also suggests that socially and administratively the Gounder and Kaikkoolar systems were separated even when they shared the same temple. This evidence indicates that the Kaikkoolars' naaDus are not territorial units with clear borders, but rather social-administrative networks that join locality-segmented subcastes into a loose hierarchical confederacy or sodality.

In the eighteenth century, the councils that formed the nodes of the Kaikkoolar networks were trade centers located at major temple and

administrative centers throughout the northern KonkunaaDu area
(Map 2). The structure of the Seven-City Territory still reflects this
organization (Murton 1979: especially 23-24). The Kaikkoolar system
is designed to link towns in a hierarchical trade network organized to
move textiles throughout the region, and wealth back to weavers and
presumably to the towns. As we have seen, the social networks of
Kaikkoolars and Gounders are differently constituted; the Gounders'
system is kin based and agriculturally centered, whereas the Kaikkoolars' system is urban based and trade centered. Thus, the appearance
of correspondence in the southern part of KonkunaaDu may be attributed to temple geography and the dominance of Gounders. Elsewhere in northern KonkunaaDu and in Conjeepuram, the separate
networks appear to overlap territorially, but they differ functionally.
Kaikkoolars and Gounders may share common temples, towns, and
villages as loci in their respective systems, but the systems are organized differently. The Gounders' system defines locales; the Kaikkoolars' defines hierarchical trade networks. The two systems are differently oriented administrative organizations that territorially overlap
but do not correspond.

The differences that distinguish the naaDu systems of Kaikkoolars
and Gounders reflect the legacy of the left-hand/right-hand distinction
expressed in duplication and separation and in Gounder attempts to
dominate the Kaikkoolars in KonkunaaDu. These attempts are seen in
the disputes between Gounders and Kaikkoolars. The superior
strength of the Gounders, which Kaikkoolars acknowledge and which
led to their flight to Erode in the 1920s, is undoubtedly in part a
consequence of the impoverishment of weavers that followed the loss
of much of their market during colonial rule. The world market for
textiles was and continues to be volatile. This impoverishment and
Gounder dominance may well explain why Beck (1972) found no left-
hand naaDus in her area of KonkunaaDu. It is telling, however, that
the Gounders in Beck's study area claimed no authority over Kaikkoolar affairs. These they recognized as the Kaikkoolars' own concern.
This indicates that Gounders did not see Kaikkoolars as their dependents. On the contrary, the disputes described in Chapter 3 suggest
that Kaikkoolars were a caste with which they competed for status and
for control of local institutions.

The differences in the two naaDu systems also reflect their different
functions. The Gounders' system had a strong local focus that reflected
the caste's agricultural interests, but the Kaikkoolars' system fulfilled a
dual purpose. One was to administer a pyramidal network of trade
centers associated with weaving and the textile trade, and to settle
disputes arising from this trade; the other was to define the caste's

membership, which shares a domain and so forms a confederacy. At this level, the naaDus administered the problems spawned by supralocal interaction, and as a unit formed one component in the social segmentation of south Indian states prior to Indian Independence. In this manner, the Kaikkoolar naaDu organization bridged the caste fragmentation that was a product of locality segmentation, and provided an organization for trade and interlocal administration within the segmented state.

Administrative centralization begun in the nineteenth century spelled the end of segmented state organization. With it ended the tripartite organization of south Indian society, which had existed for nearly one thousand years. The Kaikkoolars' naaDu system had organized the caste so that they could trade and move throughout the Tamil-speaking region. Its system of hierarchical jurisdiction and pyramiding domains provided a basis for shared identity and a means of defining membership, taxing localities, and settling interlocal disputes. These functions organized the Kaikkoolars' naaDu areas into a sodality that formed part of the organization of segmented south Indian states. As the warriors described in myths and as the sponsors of pujas in kingly temples, Kaikkoolars depict themselves even today as an integral segment of these past states.

Centralized administration, dyarchy, and the democratization of India destroyed segmentation by creating a unified political field and a social environment that demanded a new kind of organization for castes such as the Kaikkoolars. They responded by forming caste associations that had a popular base and could represent the interests of the caste as a whole. NaaDu organization continued to have some local importance as a source of prestige for locality leaders and as an aspect of caste identity, but in the 1920s and 1930s the representation of caste interests in statewide politics shifted to the caste associations.

6 The caste association: the Senguntha Mahaajana Sangam

Between 1914, when the last aaNDavar of the Conjeepuram Mahaa-naaDu was selected, and 1929, when the first castewide meeting of the Kaikkoolar caste association, the Senguntha Mahaajana Sangam (hereafter Sangam), was held in Erode, south Indian society underwent a number of profound social changes. Like other castes, the Kaikkoolars were swept up in these changes, and the structure of their caste was transformed. The Kaikkoolars' naaDu system was weakening, and the caste's MahaanaaDu in Conjeepuram ceased to function. Textile trade had become increasingly internationalized, and Kaikkoolars saw their own fortunes as directly affected by competing foreign textiles (Irschick 1982). Dyarchy was implemented, and the Congress Party became the national party of Indian independence. But the implementation of the Congress's *khaadi* policy, which advocated handspun, handwoven cloth, was opposed by the Kaikkoolars, who wove with mill-produced yarn. This issue made Kaikkoolars aware of the effects of government policy and desirous of finding an effective means of influencing policy to their advantage. The formation of the caste Sangam was in part a way to achieve influence in national politics.

Parallel with these political and economic changes, a new elite leadership with Western education was emerging among the Kaikkoolars. The role these men played in the formation of the new caste order was critical. As we have seen, they opposed the locality orientation of the old leadership and the segmented organization of the naaDu system, and strove to unite the caste by means of a new corporate order, the Sangam. The caste Sangam was to act as a special interest pressure group to lobby the government on behalf of all Kaikkoolars. As men of the future, some of these caste leaders and their supporters became active participants in the nationalist movement of the 1930s. Their

99

orientation was toward the regional society that they hoped would offer greater opportunities to their caste and to themselves. They were reformers and transformers of society, rather than supporters of the status quo.

Another great societal change of this period was the development of the non-Brahman movement. The supreme secular and religious status of the Brahmans in Madras Presidency was being challenged. Kaikkoolars participated in these efforts to displace Brahmans, not because they opposed Brahman custom but because they associated Brahmans with government and government with adverse policies and, in time, with the Depression (Baker 1976:192). After 1929 the Kaikkoolar Sangam opposed the use of Brahman priests both in temples and in household ritual, and encouraged the training of their caste fellows to act as priests.

A further area of great change was the demise of the right-hand/left-hand caste division in south India. In 1909, when Thurston published *Castes and Tribes of Southern India*, he wrote vividly of the moiety's importance for dividing deeva-daasis into two sections (1909, vol. II:128, 366), for determining Conjeepuram's temple use, for explaining the maintenance of separate temple maNDapam, and for ordering Tamil castes (e.g., 1909, vol. III:117; vol. II:40). Although the importance of the division in urban conflict appears to have peaked in the mid-nineteenth century (Appadurai 1974), Kaikkoolars in Erode say that intense moiety conflicts still occurred in the region during the 1920s. Nonetheless, by the 1930s, these conflicts had stopped entirely.

Three factors were important for ending the moiety distinction. First, the right-hand/left-hand distinction had involved status competition between castes at the local level. After 1918, the locality politics of which this competition was a part became secondary to the expanding political involvement of Indians in provincewide and national politics. The new political arena being created gave no recognition to the division of castes into right-hand and left-hand sections. Castes of different sections could not compete, therefore, for separate rewards and honors. They had to compete with each other for the same potential rewards in a unified political field. Second, the role of temples as the symbolic integrators of society was undercut by the weakening of naaDus as the primary political institutions creating supralocal caste ties among the non-Brahmans. Temples had also been an important arena for the expression of moiety distinctions mediated by Brahmans, but non-Brahmans now sought to avoid such distinctions and to replace the segmented caste domains defined by the temples with Sangam organizations. The 1930s was a period during which caste Sangams vied for political attention (Baker 1976:196-198). By paying heed to caste demands, the British encouraged their proliferation (Baker 1976:196). Third, non-Brahmans saw that it was to their political advantage to forget old distinctions and to unite against Brahmans in their competition for social and political dominance of the Presidency.

Brahmans in 1918 represented only a small percentage of the Presidency's population, but they were major landholders and held a disproportionate share of the government jobs available to Indians (Irschick 1969:5-26). Telugu and Tamil Brahmans represented only 3.2 percent of the total population of Madras Presidency (Irschick 1969:5), but they dominated

> . . . in many upper levels of government service. The distribution of appointments among deputy collectors, sub-judges, and district *munsifs* [native judges] (all high positions so far as Indian employment was concerned) showed that Brahmans in 1912 held 55, 82.3, and 72.6 percent of the posts then available to Indians. (Irschick 1969:13)

At lower levels of government service and in education, Brahmans were also disproportionately represented. Further, Brahmans were prominent in the growing independence movement. In the 1920s, the chief independence party in India, the Congress Party, was considered by south Indians to be essentially Brahman controlled (Irschick 1969:186, 337-339). Given these conditions, non-Brahman leaders in Madras Presidency feared that unless they took decisive action to displace Brahman dominance, they could play only a small role in an Indian-constituted government.

The Montagu-Chelmsford Report of July 2, 1918, played an important part in bringing non-Brahman sentiments to a head and in creating a regionwide arena for the political involvement of Indians. Although Indian involvement in government had been increasing for decades (Washbrook 1976), this report "committed the British government to the principle of increased participation by Indians in the administration of India, by means of a constitutional system called dyarchy" (Irschick 1969:89). Dyarchy involved the administration of local affairs by elected Indian officials within the context of continued British colonial rule. Even if tightly circumscribed, the chance for real political power, with all of its concomitant benefits, was being further opened to Indians. The political field was expanding, but non-Brahman leaders generated the belief that the privileged position of Brahmans gave the latter a clear advantage over all other castes. Accordingly, many non-Brahmans opposed the Congress Party and the Home Rule movement, which they saw as a fulfillment of Brahman aspirations for power. Instead, non-Brahmans sought to secure special communal concessions from the British in the new Madras Legislative Council formed in 1920.

During this early period, non-Brahmanism was an ideology created to produce a fabricated sense of the non-Brahman need for political concessions rather than to represent a widely felt dislike of Brahman control in politics. It was only in the 1930s, especially "in the cotton tracts of interior Tamilnad," that non-Brahmanism became a popular movement (Baker 1976:192). Non-Brahman challenges to Brahman supremacy have been an important characteristic of Tamil politics ever since. Leaders encouraged castes to stop using Brahmans as priests, to oppose their secular and ritual influence, and to refuse to accept Brahmans as the arbiters of social and ritual status. They also sought education – formerly a Brahmanical perquisite – and the professions, government positions, and political influence available to the educated.

Kaikkoolars, a large but poor and mostly uneducated caste in 1918, at first appear to have had no direct involvement in the non-Brahman movement. The first to respond to the new politics had been the better-educated and wealthier non-Brahmans, but the Kaikkoolars' educated elite was influenced by the ideas current among non-Brahmans and espoused by leaders such as E. V. Ramaswami Naicker ("Periyar").

It is not surprising, given British propensities to acknowledge caste interests, that the Kaikkoolars later formed their own caste Sangam. Like other castes, the Kaikkoolars did so partly in the hope of being better able to represent their special interests to the government. Positions of influence and special concessions had been sought and obtained by other castes such as the Nadars, *Naattukottai Chettys* (Hardgrave 1969:131), VeLLaaLas, and *Nairs* (Irschick 1969:17). Kaikkoolars also felt that their interests could be more effectively presented through an association that would act on behalf of all of the caste's localized segments. An examination of the caste association's journal, the *Senguntha Mittiran,* indicates that seeking concessions and representing caste interests to the government were the central purposes of the Sangam from its inception to the present.

At this time in south India's political development, caste was seen by the British as the only widespread basis for political organization other than political parties. As we have seen, all three of the prior characterizing features of the south Indian state – the naaDus, the division of society into right-hand and left-hand sections, and the secular and religious supremacy of Brahmans – had a caste basis. The British saw caste as a natural framework for representing the shared special interests of its members, and Kaikkoolar Sangam leaders responded to this perception.

Interests that could be represented as jointly held were the association's strongest asset and gave it political power. Despite its radical views on intracaste marriage, the success of the Kaikkoolars' Sangam in subsequent years in gaining the support of caste members indicates that Kaikkoolars felt there were real advantages to their union as a single corporation. The success of the Sangam also demonstrates that most Kaikkoolar leaders shared a common sense of their caste's needs. This indicates a degree of uniformity in the condition of Kaikkoolars. Despite the wealth of some, they saw themselves primarily as poor, uneducated weavers with little influence on the government. They joined the Sangam in order to change these conditions and weaknesses.

Compared to the castes previously mentioned, the Kaikkoolars, or Sengunthars as they preferred to be known, were late in organizing their association. For example, the Nadars' association, founded in 1910, after some floundering was operating effectively by 1920 (Hardgrave 1969:131-133). The Naattukottai Chettys had already obtained special representation to the Legislative Council before 1910. The explanation for the Kaikkoolars' slowness seems to be twofold. First, the caste was still generally engaged in handloom weaving, and was extremely poor as a result of the nineteenth-century industrial transformation of textile production. Caste associations require a degree of affluence to finance caste congresses, and the leaders must be able to afford time to promote their association's interests. Non-Brahman castes that had earlier formed associations had significant wealthy and well-educated segments, but the poverty of most Kaikkoolars was abject (Raghavaiyanger 1893; Naidu 1948). Second, the caste lacked Western-educated leaders who could form an association and provide its driving spirit. By the late 1920s, both of these conditions were beginning to change in a few urban centers such as Madras, Conjeepuram, and Erode. Finally, as noted by Baker (1976:192), during the late 1920s and 1930s, the British inadvertently encouraged Sangam growth and politics. The Kaikkoolars formed their Sangam at a time when this type of organization was particularly effective in dealing with the government. Caste had become the language of special interests.

The formation of the Kaikkoolars' caste Sangam

In 1927 some Western-educated men and a few successful Kaikkoolar merchants founded the caste Sangam and organized the first castewide meeting, held in Erode in 1929. Their purposes were multiple. It is widely stated as fact by Kaikkoolars that the ostensible reason for forming the Sangam was to distinguish "true" Sengunthars from Moo-

lakkaarars, the descendants of deeva-daasis. The association of Kaikkoolars with the daasi tradition was a legacy of the right-hand/left-hand
distinction. The custom was part of the old Brahman-dominated system of status reckoning defined by the reciprocal exchange relationships between worshipers and the temples through which caste territories, temple rights, and caste honors were established and given.

By the 1920s, in the political atmosphere of dyarchy, the daasi
tradition no longer suited the times from a number of viewpoints.
The greater society thought the practice immoral because of its association with concubinage and prostitution. It was a temple-centered,
moiety-based aspect of Kaikkoolar status, and daasis themselves were
used as signs of rank and office by naaDu officers when they traveled
in procession. Neither the moiety division nor the prestige of locality
officers fitted well with the unified political field created by dyarchy
or suited the modernizing goals of Kaikkoolar leaders. Being grouped
with daasis and their descendants had become a status liability. The
Sangam was formed in part, therefore, to define who was a Sengunthar and who was not, and to deny that status to the Moolakkaarars.

In Kaikkoolar terms, this distinction made sense. Kaikkoolars dedicated girls as daasis, but the daasis' descendants, the Moolakkaarars,
were of mixed ancestry, the offspring of unwedded unions. Kaikkoolars, therefore, opposed Moolakkaarar claims to Sengunthar identity
for two reasons. First, Moolakkaarars did not share the same ancestry,
so that they were by reason of pedigree a different caste. Second, they
were of inferior status because of their licentious origins, and were
consequently unsuitable for intermarriage even if they were of the
same caste.

It was, however, difficult to identify Moolakkaarars who claimed to
be Kaikkoolars. Even today, Kaikkoolars say that the only clue to
Moolakkaarar heritage is a person's place of origin. Sengunthars from
locations with large temples where many daasis were known to live are
viewed with suspicion. The old custom of locality marriage limited the
worry about forming inappropriate marriages, but the era of the Sangam, with its emphasis on interlocality marriage, made it important to
distinguish Moolakkaarars. But there is another reason why Kaikkoolars want to be distinguished from Moolakkaarars. They do not want
Moolakkaarars to share their status rights, which would imply that the
two castes were of the same rank. Early issues of the *Senguntha Mittiran* (see, for example, 1930, vol. 4 [*Chittirai* issue]:132) record conflicts
between the Kaikkoolars and Moolakkaarars over the latter's claim to
the temple rights held by Kaikkoolars.

In 1978-1979, because of the notoriety of the daasi tradition, the
separation of the two communities was still discussed, although much

less openly. The two castes are so closely associated that intermarriage is inevitable; when sexual misconduct occurs in the community, there are often whispered allegations of Moolakkaarar connections.

Leaders involved in the early years of the Sangam describe a second and, I believe, more important reason for the corporation's formation: the desire to establish caste unity (*Senguntha Mittiran* 1930, vol. 4) in order to influence government policies that affected Kaikkoolar economic and social interests. Misunderstanding the segmented nature of the naaDu system's organization, Kaikkoolars believed that the caste had been united at one time under the executive authority of its naaDu officers. As we have seen, this was a type of authority the naaDus actually never had. With the changing social order of the 1920s and 1930s, even the authority once exercised by the naaDus had been weakened.

Leaders saw the Sangam as a mechanism for achieving changes in caste behavior. The association meetings and the caste journal were used as vehicles to overcome what the founders saw as the parochialism that kept Kaikkoolars socially backward and poor. The Sangam was to introduce Kaikkoolars to modern ways, suggest improvements in diet, teach healthful habits, and discourage "barbarian" religious practices. Leaders encouraged the spread of Sangam branches, advocated in meetings and in the caste journal the advantages of Western-style education as a means of opening up new economic opportunities, encouraged economic diversification, sought to redefine the caste as a single endogamous unit, acted as a pressure group to obtain civic improvements in Kaikkoolar areas, and sought to protect and improve the handloom industry. Segments of the Sangam also supported the non-Brahman movement and advocated anti-Brahman ideology. The Sangam was seen by Kaikkoolars, therefore, not only as a vehicle for representing the caste's shared interests to the government, but also as a means of reorganizing Kaikkoolars to serve personal self-interest and facilitate the social elevation of the caste in terms of the values of the times.

What Kaikkoolars were doing can be seen as the reaction of one caste to the dramatic transmutation of south Indian society which was coming to a head in the 1920s. At this time, the last of the left-hand/ right-hand disputes between Kaikkoolars and VeLLaaLas in the Erode region occurred; simultaneously, Kaikkoolars displaced Brahmans with priests of their own caste in their temples and household rituals. In 1929 the first all-Sengunthar Sangam met in Erode, signaling the end of the naaDu system as the primary organizational framework for caste leadership and rule, and declaring a new caste identity and organization for interacting with the state.

The decline of the caste Sangam: 1960-1979

Although the Sengunthar Sangam is still extant and still publishes the caste journal, the vital years of the association were between 1929 and 1960. During this period, twelve castewide Sengunthar conferences were held, about once every two and one-half years. The thirteenth and last meeting was held sixteen years later, in 1976, in Erode. It is unclear whether another will ever be organized. The current editor of the *Senguntha Mittiran* says that the journal at its peak sold approximately 4,000 copies monthly (Baker 1976:199; Irschick 1982:45), but in 1979 as a bimonthly publication it sold less than half that number. Another informant says that the number of subscribers is even lower, between 500 and 1,000 (C. Balasubramaniyam, personal communication, March 1979).

There are several reasons for the diminished importance of the caste Sangam among Kaikkoolars. First and foremost, the Sangam has accomplished most of its objectives. Second, when the Sangam was founded, the caste's poverty and handloom-weaving occupational focus provided a basis for appeal to the majority of caste members. Since that time, the number of educated and relatively prosperous members of the caste has dramatically increased, and their economic and political interests have diversified, as have the economic and political interests of the caste's rank and file. Diversity has given rise to conflicts of interest. For example, leaders of the Sangam during its most active years were supporters of the old Congress Party and more recently have supported Indira Gandhi's Congress, the Congress (I). This is because the handloom industry, especially the cooperative sector, has fared well with Congress support. But by 1960 the non-Brahman separatist party, the Dravida Munnetra Kazhagam (DMK), was gaining strength in the state, and was in a few years to become its ruling party. Whereas the aging leaders of the Sangam were Congress supporters, many younger Kaikkoolars turned to the DMK for various reasons, not the least of which was the presence of Kaikkoolars in the party and the chances for new local leadership opportunities. The handloom cooperative system was well established, and DMK policies continued to support cooperative production.

The Sangam, therefore, was no longer able to unify the aspirations of the Kaikoolars or direct their political interests. The advantages of cooperation under Sangam leadership no longer seemed great. It had no new programs to offer, let alone programs with broad appeal. Instead, the Sangam was perceived by many as the seat of conservative and politicized leadership when, if it were truly to represent shared caste interests, it would have to be politically neutral. In 1976 many

Kaikkoolars complained bitterly that the Sangam's all-caste meeting was heavily politicized and pro-Congress (I). Reflecting this political bias, the meeting's memorial publication opened with a series of full-page photographs, which in order are: the caste goddess, Conjee Kaamaakshi; Mahatma Gandhi; Indira Gandhi; C. Subramaniyam; Sivaaji Ganeesan; and the guru, Goondaa Lakshman Baabuji. Goddess and guru aside, all of these persons are important Congress leaders. Critics felt that the political views of Sangam members were diverse and, despite the existence at that time of Indira Gandhi's "emergency rule," that the pro-Congress (I) orientation of the meeting alienated many Kaikkoolars.

But the primary reason for the association's decline is an economic one. As the Kaikkoolars have prospered, their economic interests have diversified, dividing them into sections with their own special and sometimes opposed economic aspirations. The textile industry has grown in complexity. Handloom producers and their advocates oppose the spread of powerloom producers and have attempted to control their growth. The interests of textile exporters promote the growth of the small-producer powerloom sector, whereas government policies discourage powerloom production and encourage handloom weaving for export. The economic interests of the educated and employed are different from the interests of those who are in traditional occupations or self-employed. Textile merchants and yarn dealers commonly oppose the cooperative system or at least do not support it, and handloom producers often feel that they are at the mercy of these businessmen. Kaikkoolars tied to the textile export market have interests different from those of Kaikkoolars engaged in the domestic market. The interests of the wealthy have become dramatically diverse, whereas those of the poor weavers have remained remarkably the same.

The wealthy have formed their own associations. Powerloom owners and wholesale exporters, for example, have formed associations to protect their economic and political interests. By the 1960s, the handloom weavers' cooperatives had reached a point at which they were able to provide benefits to poor weavers independently of the Sangam. This independence has separated the interests of cooperative handloom weavers from those of their caste fellows who are not members of cooperatives. Consequently, the Sangam can no longer represent the caste as a community with shared economic concerns.

A final reason for the diminishing importance of the Sangam is the growing feeling that such associations promote casteism. Although this is not the main reason for the difficulties the Sangam faces, it is sufficiently important to cause Sangam leaders today to deny casteism in public speeches. The charge is significant in another way. It occurs at a time when there is no caste unity based on social, economic, and political interests. There is little basis for an appeal for unity except appeals to caste sentiment. When the Sangam was formed, caste was seen as a natural vehicle for the expression of political interests, but the postindependence efforts to discourage casteism has changed this situation. Government is unresponsive to special caste interests. Even within the caste, this kind of appeal is no longer acceptable to many, and so the period when caste identity could form a basis for political organization has passed. Since 1960, the influence of the Sangam has been weakening. It lingers on as an ineffective representative for large segments of the caste, more as a cultural club than a political pressure group.

Thus, contrary to the beliefs of some who have studied caste associations (Rudolph and Rudolph 1967), the Kaikkoolars' caste association has not been a new beginning for caste, but its very end. Caste can no longer be used as a basis for political-economic associations. Hardgrave has argued that a growth in political and economic differences weakened the Nadar's caste Sangam (Hardgrave 1969:266), and it is easy to assume that this has been the case with the Kaikkoolars' Sangam as well. But this is not the only reason for the Sangams' end, since the caste has always been highly differentiated by special and local interests. These interests, Sangam leaders learned, had to be tolerated while a sense of caste unity was preserved. Although political-economic differentiation is important, the Kaikkoolar Sangam's loss of influence must be seen in part as a consequence of government caution in responding to interests expressed in terms of caste. It is precisely at this point, when caste loses its political justification, that Kaikkoolar leaders shift their focus to the handloom weavers' production cooperative system as the primary organization for furthering their own interests and those of a large segment of their caste. Without a widespread sharing of political and economic interests, the Sangam has lost its intensity; without government support of caste Sangams, it has lost its legitimacy.

The accomplishments of the Kaikkoolars' caste Sangam: 1929-1960

What did the Sengunthar Mahaajana Sangam accomplish during its active period? The founding of the Sangam was an effort on the part of the new elite to restructure the caste and to form a vehicle for their leadership and aspirations, both for the caste's general welfare and for themselves. They fostered an image of caste unity symbolized by the heritage of the naaDu system and based on a common identity as

Kaikkoolars. The Sangam leaders ignored locality segmentation and locality endogamy, emphasizing instead the common interests and needs of caste members and their common heritage and pedigree. The appeal for unity was widely accepted because the economic and social benefits to be achieved were significant. Acceptance of this unified image of caste was among the Sangam's first accomplishments.

Although extralocality marriages are today still considered risky, they are almost everywhere accepted as morally appropriate. Only a few places such as Chennimalai, a small town near Erode, have reportedly remained exclusively endogamous. In these times, when there is no economic or political basis for caste unity, marriage rules continue to be central to establishing and maintaining caste identity. But this caste identity is a broadened one that, because of the cultural variation among Kaikkoolars, has required a relaxation of locality codes of behavior. Within limits, conformity in caste behavior is no longer important for determining marriage suitability. Thus, in Salem, a Kaikkoolar raised by a Padaiyaachi family was married to a Kaikkoolar girl, although he is described as behaving just like a Padaiyaachi. Before the advocacy of the Sangam, behavioral differences such as this were thought to make such marriages unthinkable. This is a significant change in the rules of caste identity. Caste pedigree has become the primary criterion determining caste identity; intracaste segmentation based on variations in local codes of behavior has largely disappeared.

Aside from the redefinition of caste in this broadened form, most of the goals of the association were aimed at advancing the well-being of the caste and its membership. These goals took several forms. First, the association sought special government concessions. In the early years of the organization, Sangam leaders urged the British to appoint a Kaikkoolar representative to the Legislative Council (*Senguntha Mittiran* 1930:439). This goal was never accomplished, in part because of the Kaikkoolars' internal conflicts over whom to select as a representative, and in part because many British by 1919 (Irschick 1969) wished to avoid such appointments, which they saw as divisive.

The Kaikkoolars did manage to be listed as an educationally backward caste, enabling students to receive financial assistance from the government when they pursued Western-style education. The Sangam also sought to have the caste classified as "most backward," so that members might receive additional support. Although this attempt failed, they were able to keep the caste on the "backward" list despite the government's periodic threat to remove them.

A continuing theme of Sangam propaganda has been the need for education, especially at the college and university levels. Education was seen throughout the Sangam period as creating economic opportunities, and some early articles in the caste journal emphasized that Kaikkoolars should give up handloom weaving and seek new sources of modern employment in order to escape poverty. For this reason, the Sangam opposed the manufacture of khaadi, handspun handloom cloth, which was Mahatma Gandhi's special symbol of an economically self-sufficient India. They did so because the income to be earned from its manufacture was too small. To the present day, Kaikkoolars oppose khaadi production for this reason.

Throughout the Sangam's history, efforts were also made to establish scholarships for Kaikkoolar students and to raise funds to build hostels for them. The Sangam failed in both endeavors. As far as I know, only one hostel was ever begun; located in Madras, it had not yet been completed in 1979. Nonetheless, Sengunthar interest in education grew dramatically during the Sangam years. The number of Kaikkoolar university graduates expanded from approximately 15 in 1927 to over 2,000 in 1979 (interview, Nachumuttu Mudaliyar, March 27, 1979). C. Balasubramaniyam, professor of Tamil at the University of Madras, says that fully 25 percent of all Tamil-language teachers at all levels of education today are Kaikkoolars. Similarly, although Kaikkoolars have not funded scholarships, they have individually founded a number of private high schools. One of these, located in Erode, has achieved national fame as an exemplary secondary school.

Education has been instrumental in improving the Kaikkoolars' social conditions. Most Sangam leaders and some of the leaders of the handloom weavers' cooperative movement have received university educations; several have received law degrees. According to these leaders, however, the general growth in prosperity experienced by the caste over the last thirty years has occurred not because of education-related economic diversification but because of developments in the textile industry.

These developments have occurred primarily in three areas: the sponsorship and spread of weavers' cooperatives, a significant increase in textile exports, and the spread of small powerlooms operated by small-scale producers. The handloom weavers' cooperative movement grew rapidly following Indian independence under the leadership of caste reformers and the advocacy of the Sangam and the Congress Party. The reason for cooperative development was the widespread poverty of weavers. Since the end of the nineteenth century, a series of inquiries into the economic conditions of weavers revealed them to be impoverished. It was found that wages as such were not the cause of this poverty. Rather, the seasonality of weaving resulted in prolonged periods of unemployment, forcing weavers to borrow from their masterweavers in order to live. In this manner, a cycle of debt and economic dependency on masterweavers was created, which was difficult for weavers to escape.

Cooperatives were designed partly to mitigate this problem by offering weavers continuous employment and by forbidding cooperative members from working for masterweavers. It was also felt that the weavers' poverty was an outgrowth of their helplessness in the face of the vicissitudes of the yarn market, and of their inability to market their products independently outside of their localities. As a consequence, cooperative leaders eventually came to realize that they had to act as procurers and manufacturers of elements such as yarn, dye, gold thread, and textile design, and as marketing agents for their weaving members. Since the early 1960s, the cooperative system has expanded to fulfill these needs.

The cooperatives have not brought prosperity to the weavers. As politically supported social welfare programs, however, they have raised thousands of weavers out of the abject poverty described by earlier governmental reports. By 1979 the handloom cooperative system in Tamilnadu had become big business, with important ties to local, state, and national governments. It produced annually 200 million meters of cloth worth 430 million rupees, nearly a third of the state's total handloom production, and incorporated almost 37 percent of the state's handloom weavers.

The most dramatic growth in Kaikkoolar prosperity has occurred because of two recent developments affecting small-producer textile manufacture: the growth of the export textile market and the spread of small, inexpensive powerlooms among small producers. During the 1970s, the export market in handloom textiles and clothing grew at a rapid rate, from approximately 1 million rupees in net worth in 1970 to over 30 million rupees in 1979. This occurred because of the establishment of favored-nation treaties with Western countries and Australia, which have partially opened their doors to handcrafted textiles. Indian government policies have also encouraged independent exporter participation. Thus, in Tamilnadu, three cities with large handloom industries – Erode, Karur, and Madurai – have been designated as export centers, and merchants applying for permission to export have found it easy to obtain export licenses from the central government. From 1975 to 1979 these government policies, including special government-funded "discount" loans and "key" loans, transformed Erode.

Erode holds a weekly market in handloom goods in which daily sales amount to hundreds of thousands of rupees. The officer of one of the many banks involved says that his bank handles weekly about 100,000 rupees generated by textile sales. Actual sales values of exports are undoubtedly much higher than official figures indicate. The town boasts twenty-seven banks, modern hotels to accommodate buyers and agents, a cosmopolitanism characterized by multilingual signboards, north Indian restaurants, many modern taxis, and in the heartland of Dravidian India, the frequent sounds of spoken Hindi. These are all indications of an expanded market and a prosperity unusual for a town the size of Erode. Many Kaikkoolar merchants have become wealthy in the process, as have some textile merchants from other communities.

This dynamic export market has stimulated weaving in surrounding towns and villages. Skilled weavers are in high demand, and their wages have risen steadily. In Chennimalai, a few miles from Erode, the wage of a skilled weaver in 1979 was twenty rupees a day, double the average wage of powerloom operators in Salem. Ancillary industries, including dye manufacturing, yarn marketing, sizing, and transportation, have also been stimulated. The net effect has been to spread the prosperity widely among Kaikkoolars and others within the surrounding ten- to twenty-mile area.

A paradoxical by-product of the growing export market for handloom textiles is the spread of small powerlooms among small-scale producers. According to exporters of handloom goods in Erode, handloom weaving is too slow to produce the yardage ordered within the time period that export demands. Consequently, masterweavers farm out their orders to small powerloom owners, who mimic handloom material but weave faster and at lower cost. Erode producers insist that as much as 90 percent of exported "handloom" textiles are imitations.

Again, this has led to growing prosperity among Kaikkoolars who have been able to finance the purchase of powerlooms for themselves (about 7,500 rupees in 1979). Earning twice what handloom weavers make, hired powerloom operators have also prospered. In Akkamapettai Village, located ten miles from Erode, over 100 powerlooms were installed between 1968, when the village produced only handloom textiles, and 1978. This created a small industrial revolution in the village and brought about several social changes. A few families have become wealthy manufacturers and operate ten or more looms. The increase in powerlooms has raised the demand for labor to run them and has changed hiring practices. Families can no longer meet all their own labor needs, and Kaikkoolars have hired outsiders as operators as they have acquired powerlooms. This has put pressure on the available labor pool of the village. The village's largest landowner, a VeLLaaLa Gounder, says it is now difficult for him to hire fit, young adult permanent agricultural laborers. The men from whom he used to draw his workers today prefer nonagricultural labor, and an increasing number of opportunities are now open to them. The economic dominance of agriculturists has been lessened by these new labor opportunities.

Employed powerloom weavers earn an average of 50 to 100 percent more per day than do handloom weavers, and about three times the wage of permanent agricultural laborers. Another result of this labor demand has been the weakening of the caste-exclusive nature of weaving. It is now common to see representatives of several castes, including untouchables, employed on the basis of their skills as loom attendants. But the spread of powerlooms is a mixed blessing, according to handloom advocates. They argue that each powerloom puts at least two handloom weavers out of business. Consequently, the spread of powerlooms has led to growing prosperity in one sector of the caste, while contributing to the displacement of ordinary handloom weavers.

Akkamapettai's prosperity has enabled the villagers to raise their educational expectations. The village in 1965, with a population of about 500 persons, had one college graduate. In 1979, with a population of 700 to 800, the Kaikkoolars of the village boasted fifteen university graduates, including three M.A. degree holders. Persons who have completed high school or vocational school are commonplace.

The role that the Sangam has played in achieving the relative prosperity of the caste today has been, therefore, both direct and indirect. Its role in enlightening the caste to the benefits of castewide organization and to education has had indirect benefits. The Sangam's advocacy of the handloom, the formation of cooperatives, and the formulation of protectionist and special interest policies have had direct benefits. The Sangam still acts in this capacity to affect government policies in order to secure and improve the livelihood of the average weaver. For example, at a castewide meeting in 1960, the Sangam sought to limit mill production of textiles, proposed that sari and dhoti production be produced solely by the handloom sector of the industry, advocated preventing the licensing of additional powerlooms in south India, and asked the central government to subsidize export transportation costs. This lobbying has generally been effective, and by 1979 many of the concessions sought by the Sangam had been achieved.

Education, special government concessions and recognition, caste unity, and the development of the handloom industry were the most important issues of the Sangam's most vital years between 1929 and 1960. In addition, there were a few other issues and aims in which the Sangam was involved. These included local interests such as community improvements and services, the paradoxical advocacy of Brahmanical customs and rituals, which some Kaikkoolars hoped would replace "undesirable" and "backward" elements of Kaikkoolar behavior, and the simultaneous support of non-Brahmanism. None of these issues ever enjoyed the uniform support of all Kaikkoolars. For example, in the early years of the caste journal, a number of articles advocated eliminating from the caste's religious repertoire all animal sacrifice and the worship of small gods. Other journal articles advocated vegetarianism. These "sanskritizing" efforts represent attempts on the part of vegetarian sections of the caste to purify the caste's rituals in order to make them conform better to high-caste Brahmanical, or "sanskritic," standards.

Many of these advocates were Kaikkoolars from Conjeepuram, Pondicherry, and Tanjore, where Brahmanical influences were strong and Brahmans, as important landowners, were still dominant. The Kaikkoolars' gurus from these areas preached the value of Brahmanical high-caste Hinduism. One such influential guru in the 1930s was GnaaniyaswaamihaL of Tirupadaripuliyuur from near Cuddalore, Tanjore District. Although these advocates were influential among Kaikkoolars, their success was only partial in the Seven-City Territory and in KonkunaaDu, where the non-Brahman Gounders were the dominant landowning caste. Gounders themselves were meat eaters and animal sacrificers. In Akkamapettai the Gounders in those days still sacrificed water buffalo to the goddess Badara Kali. And Kaikkoolars, mirroring this caste with which they were in status competition, made similar sacrifices. One Kaikkoolar, for example, told me in 1969 of his intent to perform a buffalo sacrifice in appreciation of his having obtained a government job (the sacrifice was never carried out). Like Gounders, Kaikkoolars felt that sacrifices were essential for ensuring the well-being of household members.

Today animal sacrifice is illegal in Tamilnadu, but many Kaikkoolars still consider it necessary to their health and prosperity. Caste members generally agree that the majority of the caste has remained non-vegetarian despite efforts to advocate vegetarianism as a more desirable practice. As a consequence, the promotion of vegetarianism has been dropped as a Sangam goal. Similarly, early Sangam leaders encouraged abstinence from liquor with mixed success since, among other uses, liquor is an offering to small gods. In the 1930s, liquor was an important source of taxation. Consequently, abstinence was for some an aspect of independence agitation. Of course, this is no longer an issue.

Efforts at sanskritization by segments of the Sangam were unevenly successful, in part because of the growing influence of the non-Brahman movement. The movement argued that Brahmanism was an Aryan import from the north and that the true culture of the south was Dravidian. Brahmanical customs and rituals were to be shunned in favor of what was purely Tamil. Paradoxically, it appears that Dravidianization, which included efforts to give up using Brahmans as priests, was most successful in Salem and Coimbatore, where Brahmans were not the main landlord caste, and least successful in Conjeepuram, Tanjore, and Pondicherry, where Brahmans were dominant.

In Salem, Ammapettai, and Akkamapettai, Kaikkoolars have not used Brahmans to conduct household rituals and marriages or to act as priests in Sengunthar-controlled temples for approximately fifty years. The reason Kaikkoolars give for this rejection is that Brahmans, in their ritual behavior, do not acknowledge the status Kaikkoolars demand for themselves. On the other hand, in Conjeepuram, Kaikkoolars still use Brahman priests. The explanation for this dichotomy in behavior seems to be that Kaikkoolars, in their competition for status, imitate the dominant agricultural community of their area. Thus, Gounders frequently act as their own priests, especially in household ritual and in their worship of small gods. In the Seven-City Territory, Kaikkoolars do the same. On the other hand, Brahmans are vegetarian, do not make animal sacrifices, and do not worship small gods; Kaikkoolars from Brahman-dominated areas use Brahman priests, are vegetarian, and also do not sacrifice animals. Kaikkoolars, I believe, are in linked competition with the dominant landowners of their region. Consequently, a castewide policy regarding Brahmans has not been achieved, and the desire for caste uniformity has been dropped by the Sangam as an issue in the quest for social improvement.

The Sangam has been more successful in sanskritizing some aspects of marriage customs. In the 1930s, dowries were unknown among the caste, but a token brideprice (*parisam*) was paid. In addition, there was the custom of giving gifts to sons-in-law, called *maapiLLai siir*. The brideprice was considered a low-status custom, and because the amount given varied among Kaikkoolars, it was considered a symbolic point of division among subgroups. MaapiLLai siir was thought to cause hardship because it was payment that extended over several years. The Sangam sought, therefore, to abolish brideprice and limit siir gifts to the first year of marriage (*Senguntha Mittiran* 1931-1932:131). Both customs have now been dropped, but the practice of dowry has replaced them and has become a burden on the middle class and the wealthy. In fact Kaikkoolars have become notorious for the size of their dowries even outside their community. The Sangam now advocates eliminating dowries. It is perhaps only coincidence that the present editor of the caste journal is the father of five daughters.

Another activity of the Sangam, which involved only limited sections of the caste, was lobbying of regional governments for community services and civic improvements in various Kaikkoolar-dominated urban residential areas. The effectiveness of this lobbying was a product of the Sangam's structure, which at the local level consisted of primary societies. These included societies of various kinds: youth societies, Sengunthar religious societies, women's societies, and branches of the Sengunthar Mahaajana Sangam. All came under the aegis of the Sangam and utilized the *Senguntha Mittiran* as their journal to promote social programs and to report social events, marriage proposals, festivals, and the progress of disputes among Kaikkoolars and between Kaikkoolars and other communities. Thus, for example, in 1930 (*Senguntha Mittiran* 1930:138-139) the Ammapettai Senguntha Mahaajana Sangam of Salem recorded a series of requests made to the provincial government designed to benefit its own community. These covered a wide range of topics: the abolishment of brideprice and the limiting of siir gifts, the elimination of toddy (liquor) shops in the area, a formal request for a local post office and a records office, a request to establish a speed limit of five miles per hour because of crowding, a request for a vegetable market to improve the area's sanitation, and a request for a *jatka* (horse-drawn taxi) stand so that horse carts would not have to park in front of shops and thus block the way of customers. All of these requests were achieved through the Sangam's ability to lobby on behalf of local Kaikkoolar communities.

Local societies were enfranchised by the castewide organization in at least three ways. At the second castewide meeting held in Conjeepuram in December 1929, it was decided to form for conferences an advisory board composed of representatives from the primary societies. In this manner, local leaders were given an opportunity to express their views and the Sangam achieved a wide base of local support. Second, the Sangam's journal was designed to act as a forum for the regular expression of ideas concerning the caste. Even views unpopular with the Sangam leadership were sometimes published. For example, in the early days of the journal, an article opposing extralocality intermarriage was published. Third, the Sangam meetings were shifted sequentially from one district of the Tamil area to another in order to incorporate Kaikkoolars from all areas. The origins of Sangam leaders reflected this geographic diversity. They came from many places, including Salem, Erode, Chennimalai, Conjeepuram, Madras, and locations in Tanjore and Pondicherry, and thus represented different customary views. In these ways, the Sangam was able to make a general appeal to all Kaikkoolars. The Sangam leaders also made a bid for unity by downplaying topics over which Kaikkoolars were divided. In time this practice contributed to the blandness of the caste journal, and, as the issues faced by the Sangam diminished, the journal was left with very little to say.

By 1960, the Sangam as a force within the caste was spent. It could no longer generate new goals around which to rally diversified interest groups within the caste. The time when caste could be used as the basis of political associations had passed in Tamilnadu.

The protection of the handloom industry remains the Sangam's most important line of advocacy directed toward the state and central governments, whereas education and scholarships for needy Kaikkoolars constitute the main thrust of intracaste aspirations. The Sangam continues to support handloom weaving, the weavers' cooperatives, and the institution of protectionist policies, but the effective leadership of these interests has passed to the administrators of the state's handloom cooperative system. These men are often also Sangam leaders. However, their power and influence stem not from the Sangam but from their role in the cooperative structure. Since the 1960s, the Sangam has lost much of its political influence at the state level. Its leaders have lost their special ties with the state.

Since the late 1930s, the leaders of the Sangam have been closely involved with the Congress Party. Economically, the connection was a natural one; Congress supported the handloom industry because for Mahatma Gandhi it symbolized a return to small-scale indigenous production and a turning away from foreign imports. Kaikkoolars saw this support as beneficial. As the cooperative system grew with government help, they benefited from the building of cooperative housing projects, cooperative spinning mills, and dyeing factories; government-underwritten marketing; control of the licensing of powerlooms; and the reservation of certain fabrics for the handloom sector. The benefits gained by the caste leadership were considerable, and by the 1960s made the handloom cooperative system an independent basis of power for caste leaders. It is only natural that Sangam leaders and the leaders of cooperatives who had benefited from Congress policies remained loyal supporters of the party. But in the late 1960s and early 1970s, although retaining control of the Sangam, the Kaikkoolar leadership began to lose control of the cooperative handloom industry and its special place in the political structure of Tamilnadu. The first blow came when the DMK (Dravida Munnetra Kazhagam) Party wrested control of the state from the Congress Party. Sangam leaders no longer had direct ties with the party in power, and the effectiveness of the Sangam was reduced. However, the cooperatives retained close ties with the state government for a time.

Political interests among the Kaikkoolars were already diverse, and many Kaikkoolars were supporters of the DMK. One by one, Congress Party supporters in cooperative management were replaced by DMK supporters. A new younger leadership among the Kaikkoolars, with their own political ties, seemed to be emerging without strong Sangam ties; the Sangam and the *Senguntha Mittiran* remained in the hands of the old leadership, as did political ties with the Congress-controlled central government. Then, amid accusations of corruption, the DMK splintered and in a general election lost to its offshoot, the Anna Dravida Munnetra Kazhagam (ADMK). Accused of corruption in many localities, Kaikkoolar cooperative leaders were displaced from their controlling positions on handloom boards, and the Kaik-koolars lost the special influence in local politics they had enjoyed since Independence.

Today the Sangam is divided by its caste members' diverse political views. Its leaders find themselves without the power or the influential ties they once had because they are still closely tied to the Congress (I) Party. Many of the most important leaders of the past are dead, re-tired, or in poor health.

In addition, the economic growth of the caste has created diversified economic aspirations. Persons who have grown wealthy through ex-ports and the spread of powerlooms favor more lenient licensing and a loosening of production controls. Supporters of handlooms and the cooperative movement favor the retention of tight regulations. Expo-nents of both economic views have formed voluntary associations at the grass-roots level to promote their viewpoints and protect their interests. The caste has become crisscrossed by ties that link and op-pose people because of their economic interests and divide them be-cause of their political interests.

It makes little sense to say that Kaikkoolars are divided by class interests defined by the sharing of roughly the same amounts of power, wealth, income, or prestige. The 600 plus workers of the Salem spin-ning mills, for example, belong to eight unions, which reflect a variety of political affiliations and the political aspirations of union leaders. It also makes little sense to describe the Kaikkoolars as divided by Marx-ian class. There are no political and economic interests that unite owners and managers against nonowners and workers. Indeed, the cooperative system has helped to prevent such class distinctions. The development of Marxian classes has also been discouraged by the di-verse political affiliations of workers and by the self-interest of the persons and groups involved in different kinds of enterprises. The Kaikkoolars have not only undergone considerable occupational diver-sification, but have also developed overlapping roles in the production process. It is common for weavers to own their looms and to produce privately for the market. Other members of the household may be members of a handloom cooperative. In fact, the same weaver may do both. Other members of households may work for masterweavers, run small shops, or even act as moneylenders, financing the production of other weavers. Marxian class structure is unsuited to the analysis of inequality in this situation.

Yet clearly, state governments and the Kaikkoolars themselves are concerned with inequality and poverty. On the one hand, state policies seem designed to respond to what are seen as the interests of the poor. Many government policies have been implemented to protect the handloom sector from competition with other modes of textile production. On the other hand, most weavers are governed by self-interest, and at times see the government's rules of cooperation and production as things to be outmaneuvered. Thus, a cooperative weaver may work for a private masterweaver or for himself when the market is good, and produce for the cooperative sector only when the market is poor. This is contrary to cooperative rules. Similarly, almost without exception, handloom weavers prefer powerloom production because it is more profitable than handloom weaving, and they will work on powerlooms if given the chance. Yet government policy limits the use of powerlooms to protect handloom production. The protector becomes the perpetrator of an archaic mode of production in the eyes of some of the workers. It is a benevolent force in the eyes of others. More typically, it is viewed as a bureaucracy around which to maneuver.

It is too simple to say that some unified class interests have replaced caste interests, because members of the same economic class support different political parties and have diverse economic interests. It is more accurate to say that shared occupational, political, and institutional interests have promoted a variety of self-interests over either economic class or caste interests. Kaikkoolars still see the value of cooperation, but they make alliances when it suits them. A unified Sangam welded by castewide interests is no longer obtainable. Former Kaikkoolar leaders have lost control of their caste and can no longer deliver caste support to any political party.

The ADMK's response to this situation is understandable. In the 1970s, the party replaced many Kaikkoolars in cooperative management with government-appointed "special officers," and appointed a dynamic non-Kaikkoolar, Subbalakshmi Jagadeesan, as Minister of Handlooms for the State. Through her leadership, the ADMK hopes to revitalize the flagging cooperative system and appeal directly to weavers of all caste backgrounds, not just Kaikkoolars. The ADMK seeks to bypass the quagmire of caste leadership and diverse political and economic loyalties. At this time, one result of the effort to solicit occupationwide political support among weavers appears to be a continuing need for the government to support the industry financially. The Kaikkoolars, therefore, have lost control of the major economic institution that their Sangam helped to create. It is unlikely that the caste, without its former singleness of purpose, will be able to regain control. A new stage in the social evolution of the Kaikkoolars is developing.

Because of the importance of the handloom cooperative movement to the economic and political development of the Kaikkoolars since Independence, a more thorough examination of it is warranted. In the next chapter, I review and analyze the development of the system, its rationale, and its economic and political realities. It will become apparent that the system has been used by Kaikkoolar leaders as a mechanism for attracting government-funded benefits for the caste and, in turn, has been used by the government in power as a means of garnering the votes of the caste. Kaikkoolar leaders have similarly used the system to ensure their positions of influence within their own localities and within the networks of state political leaders on which political parties build their organizations.

7 Caste, politics, and the handloom weavers' cooperative movement: 1935–1971

Handloom cooperative societies and Kaikkoolar political influence

Political change provided the incentive for the formation of the Sengunthar Mahaajana Sangam, and the political unity it created increased the caste's political influence among both state and national parties. The importance of the handloom industry in Madras Presidency made the provincial government sensitive to the weavers' welfare, and the Kaikkoolars were nearly the largest textile-producing population. Next to agriculture, weaving was the largest sector of the regional economy. According to the Directorate of Handlooms and Textiles for Tamilnadu, the handloom sector in 1978 produced about 22 percent of the industrial sector's contribution to state income, and 6 percent of Tamilnadu's working population was supported directly or indirectly by handlooms (1978:2; Census of India 1961 vol. 9, part XI-A:65). These percentages were probably much larger before World War II, since the industrial sector of the economy has grown and diversified since Indian independence, and handloom weaving has declined (Census of India vol. 9, part XI-A:13, 31, compared with 66). It is not surprising, therefore, to find that early Sangam leaders were concerned with improving the handloom industry as one way of elevating the caste's social and economic conditions, and in turn that the provincial government and later the state government supported their efforts.

Although earlier attempts to establish handloom weavers' cooperatives had been made, it was not until 1935, when the statewide association was formed, that the modern structure of the cooperative system was established. The first viable production cooperatives were founded shortly thereafter. The first statewide cooperative was the

Madras Provincial Handloom Weavers' Cooperative Society, later called the Tamilnadu Handloom Weavers' Cooperative Society, Ltd., or "Cooptex," its brand name. Kaikkoolars formed handloom weavers' cooperatives in Salem and Trichengode by 1938, and in Chennimalai in 1941. In these towns, young Kaikkoolar leaders organized primary handloom production societies with Congress Party backing in order to improve the economic conditions of local weavers. After World War II, primary societies proliferated with local political support, so that by 1960 the cooperative structure, which was controlled largely by Kaikkoolars, had replaced the Sangam as the institutional base for caste leadership.

After Independence, the Congress Party pursued a policy favorable to handloom production and the cooperative effort, so that in time cooperatives became the primary means of channeling economic and social benefits originating at the state and national levels to the common weaver. In this manner, local leaders used the societies they headed to establish a dependent clientele among their weaver membership and among those employed in other capacities by their societies. These same leaders acted as local grass-roots leaders for the Congress Party. In other words, their influence traveled in two directions: downward to the weavers in the cooperative societies, and to their communities in general, and upward to the Congress Party, which controlled the state and central governments. For example, throughout the 1950s and 1960s, Cooptex was governed at the state level by a board controlled by a Kaikkoolar president and vice-president, both of whom were also Congress Party members. These same men also served on important state and national boards affecting handloom policies. In the Salem-Erode region, they headed their own primary handloom weavers' societies and acted as political and economic brokers, pivotally serving their local weaver clientele, on the one hand, and the supporting Congress Party on the other. At home, they often held central positions in the Congress Party structure.

In contrast to the cooperative structure, the Kaikkoolars' Sangam organization was less directly a part of any corporate political or economic institution. It mainly played a pressure group advocacy role, supporting weaver interests. The Sangam had no direct institutional ties with weaving. After its initial years, the Sangam, despite its political interests, was too factionalized to channel political favors effectively to the community. As the cooperative movement developed, real power passed from the Sangam to those leaders within its fold who were also leaders in the handloom cooperative sector. Weaving, however, was not a domain occupied exclusively by Kaikkoolars. *Sowraashtraas,* *Saliars,* and Thevangar Chettiars were also important weaving castes in the state, and their communities formed handloom weavers' cooperative societies as well. Indeed, Kaikkoolars represent only 18 percent of Salem District's weaver population, whereas Thevangars, for example, comprise some 50.4 percent. Kaikkoolars are only marginally the largest community of weavers in the state, representing 32.5 percent of the total weaver population in 1960. Thevangars are next, with 30.4 percent, followed by Saliars with 11.4 percent and Sowraashtraas with 8.2 percent (Census of India 1961, vol. 9 XI-A:63-64). Although Kaikkoolars were only one of many weaver castes and a minority in Salem District, they dominated the cooperative structure by being among the first to form successful cooperatives in northern KonkunaaDu and by controlling the top positions in Cooptex, the state's apical society.

The establishment of weavers' cooperatives created a shift away from caste identity as a source of political organization. Although Kaikkoolars were often the chief beneficiaries of the cooperative movement, the structure of cooperation was designed potentially to benefit weavers of all castes. Therefore, by the 1950s and 1960s, Kaikkoolars no longer used caste identity and unity as the basis for political influence or as the chief means of gaining benefits for the caste. This shift of leadership affiliation from caste Sangam to the cooperative system had the effect of broadening the latter institution's political value in the eyes of the ADMK, the party that succeeded the DMK in the mid-1970s.

Because the cooperatives lacked clear caste ties, the ADMK could focus on an important sector of the economy without having to appeal to a particular caste community. This was a time when such caste-exclusive appeals made little sense, for two reasons. First, the growth in the export market created economic growth in the handloom industry, which drew weavers from a wide variety of castes. Second, the lack of caste unity made caste-exclusive appeals ineffective, while simultaneously state and central governments sought to downplay caste, further reducing the effectiveness of Sangams. By the mid-1970s this trend ended the dominant influence of Kaikkoolars in handloom cooperatives, for the ruling government removed Kaikkoolars belonging to opposition parties one by one from the governing boards of primary societies and from Cooptex. The governing party no longer needed Kaikkoolars to reach weavers. For the first time in recent history, Kaikkoolar leaders were left without control of an institutional structure on which to build their influence and power at the state level.

The discussion of the evolution of Kaikkoolar relations with the state would be incomplete without an analysis of handloom production cooperatives. The development of the cooperative sector incorporates the shift in Kaikkoolar leadership strategy that marks a movement from using caste as a basis of appeal, defining social, economic, and political interests, to using occupations as the vehicle that allowed leaders to address these issues. The cooperative sector displays the current interplay between state government and the Kaikkoolars' attempts to pursue their interests in the context of changing political circumstances. Caste leaders are balancing several types of interests. They support political parties whose policies benefit them. They seek to influence policy. They seek benefits for a major sector of their constituencies, basing their leadership on doing so. And they promote their own careers as community leaders and as entrepreneurs.

The examination of handloom cooperatives offers another installment in the description of the Kaikkoolars' economic and occupational behavior. The historic organization of handloom textile production and trade and the development of the small-scale textile industry since the 1960s have been detailed in previous chapters. This chapter focuses on the political economy of handloom textile production cooperatives, where more than a third of handloom production takes place today.

Leadership, cooperatives, and politics: three life histories

An examination of three prominent leaders from within or near the Seven-City Territory locality demonstrates the evolution of Kaikkoolar leadership in the handloom weavers' cooperative effort. The life histories of these men[1] illustrate the importance of their political ties for gaining benefits for their caste within the cooperative system and, reciprocally, for supplying political parties with grass-roots leadership and providing a way to garner votes. The first and oldest to be considered is Kasiviswanathan Mudaliyar of Trichengode.

Kasiviswanathan of Trichengode

Kasiviswanathan was born in 1912. His father was a wholesale cloth merchant of imported English textiles, and the owner of three acres of urban land and two acres of agricultural land. His grandfather operated a toddy (native liquor) shop. As a young man, Kasiviswanathan met C. Rajagopalachariya, "Rajaji," an important Congress Party man from Salem District, and through his influence became a follower of Mahatma Gandhi. Kasiviswanathan joined the Congress Party in

[1]These life histories are based on interviews and materials I collected during 1978–1979. A. Mariyappan's story is reconstructed from interviews with associates and materials collected during this period.

1930 at the age of eighteen. His father was also caught up by Gandhian ideas and discontinued importing English cloth in order to trade exclusively in handloom and Indian mill cloth.

Inspired by Rajaji, Kasiviswanathan's earliest goals were political. He served as secretary of the Trichengode Congress Committee from 1928 to 1935, and was president of the Taluk (subdistrict) Congress Committee from 1935 to 1957, the period of greatest Congress strength in this region of south India. Kasiviswanathan supported Rajaji, a Brahman, in a factional dispute with Kamaraj, a non-Brahman, over control of the state's Congress in 1946. Kamaraj eventually won control of the state Congress and then of the national Congress, and Kasiviswanathan's political influence in the party declined. He attributes his own loss of support within the Congress structure to his support of Rajaji. He believes this is the reason why he never achieved his dream of becoming a member of the Legislative Assembly. Nonetheless, he remained active in Congress politics until 1967, when, somewhat embittered, he withdrew completely from politics. He turned exclusively to his own businesses and to his involvement in the handloom weavers' cooperative effort.

Kasiviswanathan's involvement in cooperatives began in 1937, when he organized a primary handloom weavers' cooperative society in Trichengode. Initially, he did this as part of his Congress activities. Congress sought to encourage handloom weaving as a part of its drive to promote indigenous production and redevelop household industry. But Kasiviswanathan also became involved because of his desire to benefit the weavers of his community. From approximately 1955 to 1975, he served as vice-president of the governing board of Cooptex under the presidency of another Kaikkoolar, Nachumuttu Mudaliyar. He was simultaneously a member of the Madras Handloom Board for a period of ten years and director of the Cooperative Union in Tamilnadu, an advisory board to the government on cooperatives. He served as director of three cooperative spinning mills located in Ammapettai (Salem), Tirunelveli, and Srivellapatur. His first daughter's husband was the purchasing officer for the Ammapettai mill. Kasiviswanathan's influence in handloom cooperatives ramified throughout the state.

When Kasiviswanathan joined the cooperative movement, there were nine primary societies in Salem District; by 1971, the number had expanded under his leadership to approximately 170. Salem District today, with 30 percent of Tamilnadu's weavers, has sixty-five more cooperative societies than Coimbatore District, which, with 16 percent of the state's weavers, has the next largest weaving population in Tamilnadu. Together these two districts have nearly a third of all the societies in the state. Coimbatore District is the home of Nachumuttu

Mudaliyar, who was president and chairman of the Cooptex board from about 1955 to 1972. These two men, Nachumuttu and Kasiviswanathan, aggressively built the cooperative structures of their home districts while in office.

At about the time Kasiviswanathan left the Congress Party, he was elected president, naaTTaaNmaikkaarar, of Trichengode's Kaikkoolar naaDu and co-naaTTaaNmaikkaarar of the Seven-Town Territory's territorial council of jurisdiction, a post he has held intermittently ever since. He occupies the highest naaDu office still extant within the Kaikkoolar caste, a post that carries great symbolic meaning even if little real economic or political power. This post easily makes him one of the most respected caste members in Salem District. Yet Kasiviswanathan is no longer a supporter of the caste Sangam, which he feels is too politicized to be representative, and he did not attend the last conference of the Senguntha Mahaajana Sangam held in Erode in 1976.

The basis of Kasiviswanathan's local influence among weavers stems from the benefits weavers' cooperative societies provide their members. They employ weavers on a year-round basis in order to alleviate the hardship produced by seasonality in the private sector. Weavers may also borrow from their societies; they are given special textile loans for festivals, and earn year-end dividends. Giving gifts of textiles is an important aspect of certain festivals in Tamilnadu, so textile loans are designed to meet the special financial needs of members. The hope is that weavers will request loans from their societies, and will avoid turning to masterweavers for help. The aim of the cooperatives is to avoid the exploitation of weavers by masterweavers to whom they may become indebted. Reformers believe that this kind of indebtedness is an important source of the widespread poverty of handloom weavers. The primary societies also provide marketing and design development with the aid of Cooptex. In this manner, wider markets are opened to weavers who otherwise would be restricted to the uncertainties and limitations of their local markets.

Societies also provide housing, medical assistance, and sometimes school facilities and meeting halls. Among the benefits Kasiviswanathan brought to Trichengode's Kaikkoolars was a housing colony with associated amenities, financed inexpensively by government and society funds. Housing colonies have been built to provide society members with a chance to own their own homes and to give them an alternative to the poor-quality housing otherwise forced upon them by poverty.

One of the continuing difficulties handloom weavers have had to face in the twentieth century is the unpredictable yarn market. The development of cooperative spinning mills in Tamilnadu during the 1960s was designed to alleviate the problems of yarn procurement and the harm caused by fluctuating prices, which periodically exacerbated weaver unemployment. Thirteen mills were developed during this period and now account for 80 percent of the yarn needs of the state's 940 primary cooperatives. Further, Kaikkoolars have benefited from the additional employment generated by these mills and ancillary enterprises. The Salem Cooperative Spinning Mills, Ltd., for example, employs about 650 workers and has a cooperative membership of 747 shareholders. The managers of these cooperative enterprises are placed in positions in which they can both benefit weavers and obtain opportunities for personal gain. Through the successful operation of cooperatives, the influence of managers increases among weavers and with the government, and the managers' exposure to the networks of suppliers and buyers provides these men with an array of economic and political opportunities.

In this manner, the Trichengode weavers' society formed the local base of Kasiviswanathan's power. He was its president from 1937 until about 1973. His directorship of spinning mills gave him district and statewide influence, and his role in Cooptex and in the other cooperative organizations gave him state and national influence.

The political importance of these cooperatives is underscored in several ways. First, the state and national governments are directly involved in promoting handlooms. They subsidize the marketing of handloom textiles. Tamilnadu has a minister of handlooms and textiles as well as a directorate of handlooms. Since 1956, a succession of state and national governments has provided a variety of loans for cooperative expansion and to encourage exports. They have underwritten spinning mills, marketing, and research.

Second, the state and central governments have instituted several regulatory and promotional policies designed to benefit weavers. They have limited the licensing of powerlooms in Tamilnadu, restricted certain kinds of textile production to the handloom sector, invested in the technical development of handloom production, and have pursued different marketing ideas in their efforts to promote handlooms.

Third, handloom production is still a hot political issue. Like mother and apple pie in the United States, it is a topic in Tamilnadu that no politician can slight. At the national level, khaadi textiles and handlooms in general still have an almost religious importance because of their connection with Mahatma Gandhi. Articles appear regularly in the local newspapers on the development of handlooms and report governmental policies and efforts at promotion. In addition, state and national politicians make a point of achieving exposure and popularity by promoting handlooms. For example, important politicians are regularly invited to attend the dedication of cooperative projects. The Salem mill was founded by Kamaraj Nadar, once the president of the Congress Party, and its foundation stone was laid by Lal Bahadur Sastri, India's second prime minister, while he was home minister in 1961.

In 1971 Kasiviswanathan ended his twenty-year career as vice-president of Cooptex's Committee of Management when this board was displaced by a special officer designated by the director of handlooms and textiles. Since 1971, a large number of elected officers within the cooperative structure have been similarly displaced by the state's governing party. Reasons for removal have ranged from charges of misusing cooperative offices to achieve political ends to charges of corruption and general mismanagement to the need to achieve policy compliance with the minister of handlooms and the directorate of handlooms and textiles. In the 1970s, the ADMK sometimes took control of cooperative management to revitalize inactive societies. Since 1961, the number of active cooperatives has declined to roughly 750 from 1,064 (Census of India 1961, vol. 9, 11-A: 29). In other instances, the ADMK has appointed special officers to displace local leaders who oppose the ADMK and seek to thwart its policies. In 1973, at the age of sixty-one, Kasiviswanathan retired as manager from the Trichengode Handloom Weavers' Cooperative Society.

Since 1973 he has spent his time furthering his family's businesses, which include powerloom and handloom enterprises and a sizing factory. In addition to his naaDu posts, he has been elected to the presidency of the local sizing factory association, which is today a thriving business in Trichengode. He is president of seven religious institutions and of the building fund-raising committee of Trichengode's Government High School. As a promoter of community projects, he has also built a Kaikkoolar marriage hall (kalyaaNam maNDapam) in Trichengode dedicated in his family's name. Kasiviswanathan, therefore, has managed to maintain a leadership role among Kaikkoolars in Trichengode and the Seven-City Territory, although his political influence and that of the Congress Party have declined.

Kasiviswanathan has personally experienced what has happened in more general terms to Kaikkoolars as a whole. In 1930 he became a Congress Party member and supporter. Kaikkoolars benefited greatly in the 1950s and 1960s from Congress policies that encouraged and supported the development of handloom weavers' cooperative societies. But as Congress lost power in the 1960s, so did Kasiviswanathan. By the mid-1970s, changes in government had forced him to give up his offices in the cooperative structure, and with them his brokerage of state and national policies affecting weavers. In a similar manner, numerous Kaikkoolars elsewhere also lost their managerial positions, first to Kaikkoolar supporters of the DMK in the late 1960s and early 1970s, then to special officers appointed during Indira Gandhi's "emergency," and later to ADMK appointees during the mid-1970s. The governing of cooperatives by special officers is limited by law to a maximum of three years, at which time an election must be held to enable the cooperative membership to select a new board. The ADMK government, however, has allowed special officer control to continue beyond this time period for certain cooperatives, including the apical society, Cooptex, and the Ammapettai Handloom Weavers' Cooperative Production and Sale Society, the largest weavers' cooperative in Tamilnadu.

Kasiviswanathan's biography of leadership and involvement in weaver cooperation is distinctive in certain ways. For example, his support of Rajaji shows him to be politically more conservative than the less affluent supporters of Kamaraj. Kamaraj is seen today by many Kaikkoolars as having been more of a leader of the common man than was Rajaji. Indeed, during the 1940s, the division of support within the Kaikkoolar community between these two Congress leaders reflects the growth of economic disparity between the average Kaikkoolar weavers, who were poor, and those who were becoming increasingly prosperous, primarily through the growth of ancillary textile enterprises, including yarn production, textile design, sizing, printing, and marketing. Nonetheless, Kasiviswanathan's involvement in the cooperative system is characteristic of leaders who used the system not only to benefit their community but also to form the basis of their leadership among a largely poor constituency.

Kasiviswanathan's career also illustrates how the cooperative system formed the basis of its leaders' political power. Through this system, Kasiviswanathan delivered Kaikkoolar support to politicians and, in turn, distributed the cooperative benefits offered by favorably disposed state and national governments. Kasiviswanathan's loss of power came when his faction within Congress lost its dominant position, and his status worsened when Congress lost control of the state government. Even so, it was not until the early 1970s that he lost his position of leadership in the cooperative system. In these respects – in terms of the basis of caste leadership within the cooperative systems, in terms of the benefits the Kaikkoolars gained, and in terms of the subsequent loss of special influence concomitant with the loss of leadership positions within the cooperative system – Kasiviswanathan is like other Kaikkoolar leaders in the postcaste Sangam period. This pattern is well illustrated by the biographies of two other leaders from the region: Nachumuttu Mudaliyar of Chennimalai and A. Mariyappan of Ammapettai.

Nachumuttu Mudaliyar of Chennimalai

"Chentex," the Chennimalai Weavers' Co-operative Production and Sales Society, Ltd., was founded by Nachumuttu Mudaliyar in Chennimalai, a small but productively important handloom center near Erode in Coimbatore District. In 1941 the president of the Madras apical society came to the town to encourage the establishment of a primary cooperative. But the town's masterweavers feared the spread of cooperative societies because they thought that they would have to pay a higher competitive wage to attract weavers and that they might lose financial control over their indebted weavers. It is not surprising that the cooperative effort made masterweavers anxious; an explicit aim of cooperation was to displace masterweavers, who were characterized as exploiters of their employees.

Unable to find a local organizer, the president approached Nachumuttu, a Sangam advocate who was practicing law in Erode. Nachumuttu agreed to found a society, and Chentex was organized in 1941 with forty-five members. Nachumuttu has been president ever since; by 1978 he had increased the society's membership to nearly 600. The boundaries of the society include the town of Chennimalai, four surrounding villages, and their hamlets.

Nachumuttu, a long-time Congress Party supporter, is one of the few who has maintained control of the society he founded, and, through his astute leadership, has used the cooperative to channel a wide range of benefits to his society's members. Since 1970 the society has operated its own dye factory. With the help of government loans and a grant, it has constructed a housing colony of 100 units that is occupied by society members. It has constructed and rents out a marriage hall. It operates a cooperative store in the colony, has built a Vinayakar temple for its residents, and in 1978 opened an elementary school in the colony with the support and attendance of the state's minister of education and minister of handlooms. The society operates its own warehouse, has constructed a Mahatma Gandhi Community Hall and Library, runs a dispensary, employs a part-time doctor for members, and maintains two guest houses for visitors.

For the society of 600 members, most of whom are Kaikkoolars, the scope and range of benefits are as substantial as the government's investment in the society. In addition to direct government grants-in-aid and loans supported by the cooperative bank, the society receives financial support from both state and central governments. With these it underwrites sales of handloom textiles at 30 percent reductions at special fairs and at festivals. This is a general sales-promotion policy that benefits all weavers' societies. The state and central governments and the societies each underwrite a third of the subsidy. The bulk of handloom textiles are sold during these seasonal sales. At other times, the handloom market is sluggish and textile stocks pile up, an indication of the size of the price reduction that cooperative-produced handlooms require to be competitive with mill-produced goods.

Society marketing is another benefit members receive from Chentex. Besides a local showroom in Chennimalai, it operates two other outlets, one in Madras City and one in Hyderabad. Chentex participates in textile exhibitions in Madras, Bangalore, Mysore, Coimbatore, Salem, and Hyderabad, where it sells directly to consumers. Most of its products, however, are supplied to Cooptex and to the All-India Handloom Fabrics Marketing Cooperative Society, Ltd., which exports textiles to foreign countries. In 1978 the retail sales of the society amounted to 9,080,677 rupees. Chentex is recognized statewide as one of the best-run production cooperatives, but its development and functions are essentially similar to those of societies in Trichengode, Salem, and elsewhere in the state.

Through his successful operation of Chentex and his leadership role within the handloom industry at state and national levels, Nachumuttu has built a reputation as a strong supporter of the handloom industry and as an important Kaikkoolar leader. He has campaigned vigorously against the licensing of powerlooms in Tamilnadu, because he feels that they benefit the wealthy rather than the average weaver. He served as president of Cooptex, with Kasiviswanathan as vice-president, from the mid-1950s to the mid-1960s, and then as chairman of its governing board for seven years. Nachumuttu is currently a member of the All-India Handloom Board, an advisory board to the government of India, and has served on the Handloom Export Promotion Council.

The key to Nachumuttu's power is his former position as president and chairman of Cooptex, his affiliation with the Congress Party, the success of the primary society he headed, and his close friendship with powerful Congress politicians. During the period of Congress rule in Tamilnadu, and primarily during his tenure as head of Cooptex the cooperative system took its basic form, including the character of its capital development. Among its more spectacular achievements were the construction of the cooperative spinning mills and several cooperative housing ventures, all of which were underwritten by the central and state governments. These projects represent the two most visible capital investments designed to assist the handloom cooperative system and its members. For example, the capital outlay for the Salem Cooperative Spinning Mill[2] was 18,355,000 rupees in 1961, the bulk of which was government financed. In 1979 this mill had a paid-up share capital of 7,337,500 rupees, 5,874,000 of which were held by the government of Tamilnadu. The Chennimalai housing scheme was financed similarly, largely in the form of a state government loan (340,000 rupees) and an outright grant (120,000 rupees). The cooperative society's investment amounted to 37 percent of the total (168,530 rupees).

The other major investment, which was also developed during the period of Nachumuttu's association with Cooptex, is in the cooperative marketing structure. This is largely handled through Cooptex. In April 1978, Cooptex's share capital amounted to 28,297,800 rupees, of which 23,450,000 were subscribed by the government of Tamilnadu. These figures indicate the state government's considerable investment in the cooperative system. Without governmental financial support there would be no cooperative system, no housing projects, no spinning mills, no government-subsidized procurement, no marketing and financing, no textile trade fairs, and no government-subsidized sales with price reductions of 30 percent. Without question, the Kaikkoolars have benefited greatly from all this governmental support. It follows, therefore, that where the spread of cooperatives has been greatest, so have the benefits received by weavers. Under Nachumuttu and Kasiviswanathan, the greatest number of primary societies were developed in their home districts of Coimbatore and Salem, primarily within or at the edge of the traditional Seven-City Territory (see Census of India 1961 vol. 9, XI-A: map facing p. iv).

After the DMK came to power, Nachumuttu decided not to run again for the chairmanship of Cooptex and advised Kasiviswanathan not to run for his office on the Cooptex board. Nachumuttu felt that as a Congressman he could not win the election, since the DMK was too powerful and had strong support among Kaikkoolars. As Nachumuttu predicted, the next chairman of Cooptex was a DMK supporter and a Kaikkoolar, S. K. Sambandam. Kaikkoolars today say that several of the DMK's leading members were Kaikkoolars, including the late C.

---

[2]Statistics were collected at the mill in 1978-1979, "Short Notes of the Working of the Mills" (typescript). Chentex statistics are derived in part from "Short Note on the Working of the Chennimalai Weavers' Cooperative Production and Sale Society Ltd., No. K.885, Chennimalai" (mimeo). Information on Ammapettai's cooperative is derived in part from a booklet published by the society: "Amkoo Texs: Ammapettai Kaittari Nesavaalar KuuTTuravu Urpatti and Virpanai Sangam, Ltd., No. S.532," and from "A Short Note on the Working of the Society" (mimeo). Information on Cooptex was collected from the assistant director of handlooms, Madras. Additional information was collected from the Census of India, 1961, vol. 9, Part XI-A, "Handlooms in Madras State."

Annadurai, chief minister of the state and head of the DMK party until his death in 1969, and Polivar Govindar, speaker of the State Assembly. Consequently, as control of the state shifted from Congress to the DMK, Kaikkoolars were able to maintain their influential ties within the DMK and their special leadership role within the cooperative system.

However, when Indira Gandhi in 1975 declared an emergency in India, the DMK government and the Cooptex board were dissolved, the latter purportedly because of its close connections with the DMK and because of corrupt practices. After the emergency the ADMK, a splinter party, succeeded the DMK. However, the ADMK was a party without a strong base among Kaikkoolars. Kaikkoolars with DMK connections still controlled segments of the cooperative system, but they have not regained control of the system at its apical level. It is not surprising, therefore, to find that in 1979 an ADMK-appointed special officer was heading the system. This appointee belongs to the Gounders, the Kaikkoolars' old competitors in the left-hand/right-hand moiety division.[3]

Nachumuttu's status as a leader and advocate of the causes of handloom weavers was weakened by his loss of control of Cooptex. His local leadership role continues, but he no longer has strong state-level ties with the party in power. Nachumuttu, however, has managed to retain control of Chentex. Three factors seem important. First, he has run a showcase society that has been notably successful. Second, he has maintained ties with the central government's advisory boards, which makes him a power to be reckoned with by any state party seeking to support handloom production. Third, he has long been an outspoken advocate of handloom weaving and a key public figure in the industry's support. To remove him from the board of his home society, therefore, would cause more trouble than it would be worth. As a prominent advocate, Nachumuttu works primarily to support handloom production. Thus, he does not openly oppose the ADMK, the party in power in 1979.

Since the mid-1970s, the ADMK has been especially vigorous in its efforts to extend the system to more weavers and to promote marketing. In the sixth five-year plan for India, the state's Department of Handlooms and Textiles proposed drawing 60 percent of the state's

[3]It is perhaps no accident that a Gounder VeLLaaLa was appointed to this position, for the aim appears to have been to separate the weavers' interests from those of cooperative society administrators. This was a sharing of interests that made the societies a separate power base. When the British had wished to break the tie between textile merchants and weavers, with their overlapping interests, in the eighteenth century, they also appointed VeLLaaLas as their agents (Arasaratnam 1980:272-273).

weavers into the cooperative sector by 1983-1984 (personal communication, joint director of handlooms and textiles, Madras City, March 8, 1979). This drive to promote cooperation is partly a response to the development of a vigorous export market in the 1970s. This new market has been dominated by private producers. The cooperatives under Cooptex administration hope to obtain a slice of this market and are developing a number of new projects designed to generate more competitively marketable products.

In addition, the growing Indian involvement in the world textile market has drawn new communities into weaving. Thus, the ADMK views the development of weaving as a means of not only benefiting the large traditional weaving population but also improving the welfare of the very poor, including tribals and untouchables. The present government, therefore, is supporting the development of the cooperative system as a method for distributing economic benefits among the poor, but not as a means of maintaining a leadership clientele among Kaikkoolars, who in the past delivered the political support of their societies' memberships to the political parties that nurtured them.

A. Mariyappan of Ammapettai

The third biographical example illustrating the use of the cooperative structure as a basis for Kaikkoolar caste leadership and political party brokerage is that of A. Mariyappan, president of the Ammapettai Cooperative from 1952 to 1971. The Ammapettai Handloom Weavers' Cooperative Production and Sales Society, Ltd., was founded in 1938, and since then has grown to a membership of nearly 6,000 weavers. This makes it the largest primary society in Tamilnadu as well as one of the oldest.

Prior to A. Mariyappan's presidency, the position was held by six men for a period of about two years each. These men were Congress Party supporters and followers of Rajaji, who in 1937 had become the chief minister of Madras Presidency. During the 1940s, Kaikkoolar community leadership in Ammapettai still centered on the officers of the area's paavaDi council. The most prominent of these was P. Mariyappan, a lieutenant of the council and a member of the administrative board of the Sengunthar Subramaniyam Temple. This temple, built by Kaikkoolars in Ammapettai, is the focal Murugan temple of the locality's large Kaikkoolar community. In the mid-1940s, the power struggle referred to in Chapter 4 between Rajaji and Kamaraj over control of the Congress Party in Madras State was reflected locally in a municipal election held in 1946-1947, according to my informants. This election led to a confrontation between A. Mariyappan,

Kamaraj's supporter, and P. Mariyappan, who supported Rajaji, when the two men backed opposing candidates in the local municipal elections. In the dispute that led to the dissolution of the local naaDu council, P. Mariyappan tried to use his influence as a naaDu officer to force A. Mariyappan and his backers to withdraw their candidates. A. Mariyappan refused and was outcasted by the Trichengode thisai-naaDu; subsequently, the candidates supported by P. Mariyappan won the election.

However, the victory was short-lived. Rumors spread that P. Mariyappan had misappropriated 20,000 rupees in temple funds to finance the election, and A. Mariyappan's support in Ammapettai grew. Soon forty to fifty families were sharing his outcasted state because they continued to interact socially with him. Defiance of the naaDu's orders was so blatant that P. Mariyappan and other naaDu officers realized that the naaDu's authority within the community had been so weakened by the factional split that the council was no longer effective. P. Mariyappan then dissolved the naaDu and it has not functioned since. In the next election, A. Mariyappan nominated a new council candidate, A. Natesan, who won. Finally, in 1952, A. Mariyappan won control of the Ammapettai Cooperative.

There are several features of this dispute that deserve attention. First, it involved a confrontation between traditional and new leaders. The former were naaDu officers as well as locally prominent men. The latter were part of the new leadership associated with the caste Sangam. Second, this was to some extent a generational dispute. P. Mariyappan and his cohorts were a generation older than A. Mariyappan. In fact, the two men were kinsmen (*sambandam*, relatives related through female ties): A. Mariyappan's father's sister was P. Mariyappan's wife, and A. Natesan, A. Mariyappan's candidate, was the latter's son-in-law. Third, P. Mariyappan was a wealthy conservative. He attempted to base his popular appeal on his established traditional authority associated with the naaDu system. This was a risky tactic; his position as an officer of the caste council did not give him the authority to command political compliance from his community. If my present-day informants are to be believed, this was because P. Mariyappan and his followers supported the status quo that gave them authority. By contrast, advocating change, A. Mariyappan and his supporters, who were excluded from naaDu council leadership, sought to build their political base on the popular appeal of improving the standard of living of the common man. The caste Sangam advocated this social change, and the cooperative system was seen as the means of bringing it about.

When A. Mariyappan took over the Ammapettai Cooperative in 1952, its membership dropped from 579 to 522, undoubtedly due to a withdrawal of P. Mariyappan's supporters. But by 1953 membership had climbed to 703, almost tripling to 2,004 by 1956.

Kamaraj did not forget his supporters. In 1958 the Ammapettai Society built the Kamaraj Weavers' Colony with government funds. It consisted of 200 houses on 24.41 acres of land purchased by the colony. The state government funded the entire scheme at a cost of approximately 6,000 rupees per house (4,800 rupees as a loan and 1,200 rupees as a grant). The total cost of the project was approximately 1,039,350 rupees, the loan portion of which was to be paid back by the house purchasers at 4.5 percent interest per annum over a twenty-five-year period. In addition, amenities including roads, street lighting, a market and shop, park, school, a playground, and water were provided. Simultaneously, a house repair scheme was funded by the government in the amount of 37,309 rupees on a one-third subsidy, two-thirds loan basis.

Investigators of weaver welfare in Tamilnadu have long recognized the inferior standard of their housing. Housing projects, therefore, have been designed to alleviate this problem. These projects, however, are far beyond the financial means of primary societies. As with other government funding associated with the cooperatives, the societies have distributed social welfare to a particular sector of the economy. It is clear that Kaikkoolars, by controlling Ammapettai's cooperative, have been able to channel housing benefits to their community, as they have in Trichengode and Chennimalai, by controlling weavers' societies there. This is not to say that they have actively excluded other communities, but because the societies are located in Kaikkoolar neighborhoods, Kaikkoolar leaders have used the societies to benefit their own community. Thus, according to the Indian Census (Census of India 1961, vol. 9, XI-A:39, 46), in 1960-1961 there were 1,064 operative weavers' cooperatives in Tamilnadu and 15 housing colonies that would consist of 2,850 houses when completed. Ammapettai and Chennimalai, representing two societies with a combined membership of a little over 2,600, had 300 of these houses. Thus approximately 11 percent of the houses went to 1 percent of the societies. If the Trichengode housing project built under Kasiviswanathan's leadership is added, the percentage of houses for the three societies would be an estimated 14 percent.

It is clear that A. Mariyappan, as president of the state's largest society, and Nachumuttu and Kasiviswanathan, as society presidents and as president and vice-president of Cooptex, and all three men as close supporters of the ruling Congress Party, were able to deliver a disproportionately large share of government-funded housing to their membership. In return, the Congress Party and Kamaraj won strong support from society members. Society leaders who benefited have largely remained strong Congress supporters. Nonetheless, the housing available through these projects was limited, and there were many society members who did not benefit. In such inequities lie the seeds of future political change.

The Ammapettai society has provided another benefit to its members: an unusually extensive marketing system. Merchants and master-weavers perform this function in the private sector, where the weavers' total dependency on these persons makes them particularly vulnerable to exploitation. When yarn prices are high, the procurers try to pay weavers less for their products in order to keep textile prices down. When the market is glutted with cloth, the larger merchants pay less and store the cloth for later sale at higher prices. Weavers as producers are too poor to store their products. They must sell on a piece goods basis in order to meet their living expenses. Poor market conditions and the seasonality of sales generate periodic unemployment among weavers, making them susceptible to indebtedness and to the exploitation that observers of the handloom industry believe these conditions create.

Marketing is therefore one of the main functions of the cooperatives. In addition to sales to Cooptex – the largest single purchaser of society textiles – Ammapettai's cooperative operates thirteen outlets in Tamilnadu and Karnatica, and has thirty-eight agents who sell the society's cloth on a commission basis. The Ammapettai society also participates regularly in textile fairs and takes advantage of the government-subsidized sales of handloom textiles.

In conjunction with spinning mills, production societies such as that in Ammapettai also help to neutralize other market problems. The purpose of the cooperative spinning mills is to lessen the volatility of the yarn market, which is highly speculative and affected by the world market. These conditions have produced devastating consequences for petty weavers in the past. For example, Kaikkoolars say that during World War II, weavers in Pondicherry were impoverished by their inability to procure yarn, and most Kaikkoolars in the area at that time were forced to leave weaving for other professions. To avoid this uncertainty, yarn is advanced by the primary society directly to weavers, so that they do not have to purchase their own. They are paid a wage when they return the finished cloth to the cooperative. If they fail to return the finished goods, no further yarn is advanced. Cooperative dye factories have also been built to produce high-quality colored yarn.

In 1961 the Salem Cooperative Spinning Mills, Ltd., was founded a short distance from the Ammapettai Weavers' Society and across the road from the society's Kamaraj Housing Project. This mill cost nearly

12 million rupees in government funding ("Short Notes of the Working of the Mills" 1979:4). A dye factory was later built nearby and is operated by the mill. A. Mariyappan was president of the mill cooperative's governing board from its inception until his death.

Among the advantages the mill brings to Ammapettai is employment. The mill employs about 650 persons, approximately 60 percent of whom have weaver backgrounds. These workers are predominantly Kaikkoolars, although there are a few Thevanga Chettys. Office workers and persons who do not work directly with yarn production make up the bulk of the remaining 40 percent and come from a variety of castes, including *Naidus, Udaiyaars,* Gounders, *Pillais, Iyengar, Kanikkars,* and *Vanni Chettys,* as well as Muslims and Christians. Similarly, approximately 70 percent of the Ammapettai weavers' cooperative is composed of Kaikkoolars. Nearly 30 percent are Thevangars and a smattering come from other castes, including Naidus, Udaiyaars, and Gounders. Weavers earn, on average, between 250 and 350 rupees per month as members of the society.

In Ammapettai, A. Mariyappan was in charge of a cooperative complex that by the mid-1960s consisted of the primary society; its offices, warehouses, and marketing showrooms; a housing colony with associated amenities; the spinning mill; and a dye house. The whole complex was worth between 20 and 30 million rupees, possibly more. In turn, A. Mariyappan led his followers as supporters of the Congress Party. He and his vice-president played other leadership roles in the community as well. They founded and led a Mahatma Gandhi Society devoted to adult education. They participated in the building and administration of the Kaikkoolars' community marriage hall and in the administration of the caste's Subramaniyam temple. They also participated in religious societies. With the naaDu leadership unseated, they became involved in the leadership of nearly every major social institution in Ammapettai. Among these, the cooperative society was the premier association. The president of its board stood at the apex of the local leadership structure.

In 1971 A. Mariyappan died suddenly, and a struggle ensued among three Kaikkoolar leaders for the control of the Ammapettai Weavers' Cooperative. In the final years of A. Mariyappan's life, the Congress Party had lost control of Tamilnadu State to the non-Brahman party, the DMK. All three of the contending leaders of the Ammapettai Society were members of this party.

There are two explanations for this change in political allegiance among Kaikkoolar leaders. First, because of the importance of cooperatives to local leadership structures, the controlling political party wanted cooperative leaders to be party supporters. Subsequent history shows that society leaders were considered a part of the state political machine. Thus, it was difficult for a cooperative society leader to oppose the party in power without being attacked continuously by opponents. Further, effective leadership required society leaders to be able to draw on their ties within the government, which was the main source of funds for programs. A. Mariyappan used this affiliation to develop the cooperative complex in Ammapettai; after his death, the new leaders intended to draw on their ties with the DMK.

Second, DMK support among society members grew while A. Mariyappan was president. Part of this growth may be attributed to the general appeal of the DMK, a son-of-the-soil party, for Tamilians. But two other factors are indirectly mentioned by Kaikkoolars. There was the identification of DMK leaders with the Sengunthar caste, mentioned before, which was especially significant to Salemites because the wife of one important party leader, Nedunchurian, was from Shevapet in Salem City. Consequently, many Salemites saw the DMK as having their special interests at heart, a view encouraged by the DMK through policies designed to appeal to the working classes. Another factor explaining the emergence of DMK leadership in the Ammapettai cooperative was that A. Mariyappan and his followers had controlled the society's leadership for twenty years. Other aspiring leaders saw the DMK as offering them a chance to gain power, and the better their ties with the DMK leadership, the greater were their chances.

The first president after A. Mariyappan was E. A. R. Mariyappan, a Kaikkoolar pawnbroker elected to office in 1971. He was followed by two other Kaikkoolars in rapid succession in 1972 and 1973. They are rumored to have held the presidency through influence rather than by election. In 1974, when the DMK government was disbanded, the Ammapettai cooperative's governing board was also dissolved, and a special officer (SO) was appointed as administrator by the state government. Subsequently, when the ADMK came to power, it lacked a support base among society members, and chose to continue the SO administration.

But if infighting plagued the cooperative leadership in the 1970s, the situation among Kaikkoolars in Ammapettai was even worse. The population was crisscrossed by political and economic diversity. Those who had benefited under A. Mariyappan still tended to support Congress (now Congress I), But others supported the DMK and Nedunchurian's splinter party, the Purattaasi ADMK. In economic terms, the population was split into three segments: poor, nonsociety handloom weavers, society weavers who were somewhat better off, and relatively rich masterweavers and powerloom owners. The last group advocated the relaxation of legal restrictions on powerlooms, which were designed to protect the handloom industry and were advocated by the cooperative leadership. In addition, there were merchants and moneylenders, house owners and renters, government employees and the employees of cooperative and private enterprises, bus owners, teachers, and professionals, to name the main occupational divisions, all with their special interests. Ammapettai had become economically and politically diverse. The varied economic success of Kaikkoolar subgroups had led to diversity and to the loss of any sense of common interest among caste members.

Cooperative leadership and Kaikkoolar ties with the state

The cases of A. Mariyappan, Kasiviswanathan, and Nachumuttu are notably similar in ways that explain the importance of the weavers' cooperatives to local leadership. The caste Sangam never formed a strong economic base for leadership. The Sangam was an alliance of caste leaders. They sought to direct the aspirations of their caste fellows along particular lines in order to improve the caste's social standing and its economic and political involvement. But the Sangam never directly managed an economic program designed to bring about the caste's economic development. Its economic and social goals were indirectly achieved largely by applying political pressure, by advocating with the government policies that would aid and protect handloom weaving, and by supporting Western-style education. Although weavers benefited from the Congress Party and many local Kaikkoolar leaders were politically involved, politics and economics were ultimately divisive forces among Kaikkoolars. As political change occurred in Tamilnadu, the leaders of the Sangam remained politically conservative, so that by the 1960s they were out of touch with the diversity of Kaikkoolar interests. Many rank-and-file Kaikkoolars felt that if the Sangam were to be representative, it would have to stay out of politics. This outcome was the precise reversal of the Sangam's original purpose: Instead of creating a united Kaikkoolar caste that rejected local diversity, the Sangam today must represent the united caste in all of its diversity.

In the late 1930s, when some Kaikkoolars became active leaders in the Congress Party, the formation of the weavers' cooperatives had given local leaders an institutionalized economic basis for power positioned between a government that encouraged them and the common Kaikkoolar weaver who stood to benefit from them. These leaders, especially Nachumuttu, Kasiviswanathan, and A. Mariyappan, are remembered in the Salem-Erode region as having benefited weavers. But the extent of their influence is much greater than one might expect. They were not only important local leaders, but also played significant roles in developing the cooperative system in the state. They stood as political brokers between the weavers and the state and national governments. They developed the cooperative system with government funding, and by the benefits they brought to their communities created a loyal following for their political parties.

The political value of the cooperatives is evident in at least three ways. Local Kaikkoolar leaders in the three towns, whatever their economic interests, seek to gain control of the cooperative boards, which are central to their influence and power. The histories of the three cooperatives show that the state political party in power seeks to control the cooperatives' governing boards as an aspect of its control of local politics. Politically, the cooperatives are too involved and important to be left on their own. Finally, the weavers' cooperatives could not survive without the support of the ruling political parties that underwrite them. Cooperatives make political sense because they create a channel for funneling benefits to the local caste community in exchange for political support, but they do not make economic sense. This is apparent in the high cost of cooperative handloom production, the sluggish market in cooperatively produced handloom goods, and the necessity for large government subsidies to support cooperative production. Their uneconomic character is also evident in another, if less apparent, manner. Cooperatives have been very slow to respond to the rapidly growing export market in handloom textiles. This is in direct contrast to the response of private companies and is associated with the cooperatives' inefficient management structure.

In 1978 there were 946 primary handloom weavers' production and sales cooperatives in the state, nearly 80 percent of which were active (Government of Tamilnadu 1978:5). They exist because they provide an important way of dispersing social welfare benefits to weavers, and because political parties gain popularity by supporting them. Indeed, the 1961 Census (Census of India 1961, vol. 9, XI-A:36) indicates that the cooperative movement "was started primarily to relieve rural indebtedness." Weavers, wishing to avoid the uncertainties of the open market, join the cooperatives, often with government subsidies to pay their share capital requirements (Census of India 1961, vol. 9, XI-A:38). Many use the cooperatives as a safeguard. They produce for the private sector when sales are good and when more money can be had by doing so. Only in the off-seasons do they produce for the cooperatives. It is common, therefore, for cooperatives to find it difficult to maintain production during periods of high handloom demand.

There is no question that weavers have benefited from cooperatives. Cooperatives provide steady employment, limited lending facilities, and yarn. As a result, cooperative weavers earn enough to keep body and soul together. As a method of distributing social welfare, the cooperatives have the advantage of paying part of their cost while employing a major labor population. Private entrepreneurs who profit from their own innovative and cost-efficient handloom production do not consider the cooperatives a threat.

Kaikkoolar leaders feel that they have lost their power within the cooperative system since the mid-1970s. This has occurred at a time when the ADMK has made renewed efforts to develop weaver cooperative production. For the first time in this century, Kaikkoolars are without an institutional base for organizing a significant proportion of the caste around community leaders. NaaDus, the caste Sangam, and the cooperatives coexist, but the importance of the first two has been greatly reduced. They no longer have important political or economic functions. Cooperatives continue to be politically important, but Kaikkoolars no longer dominate the system. A shift away from caste as a means of organizing political and economic interests is occurring, and is being compounded by the Kaikkoolars' economic and political diversification. Perhaps realizing this, the ADMK has attempted to limit Kaikkoolar control of the cooperative system. Thus, it can use the system to make a more generalized appeal to handloom weavers while avoiding the factionalism created by diverse interests.

8 Interpreting the Kaikkoolars today: models of caste, weaving, and the state

The Kaikkoolars are a product of their history. Viewed ahistorically, their Kaikkoolars' customs and status are confusing and ambiguous. If the Kaikkoolars are to be characterized only by their present behavior, they may be ranked relatively high among non-Brahman castes. Beck (1972:159-167) places them seventh among eighteen castes in her study in KonkunaaDu. Moffatt (1979:72) describes their status as "relatively high" and places them fourth in his village of nineteen castes (1979:90). Each finds that in the study area in question, Kaikkoolars rank just below the dominant agricultural caste (Beck 1972:161ff; Moffatt 1979:90). This ranking also corresponds to the status Kaikkoolars are accorded in the Seven-City Territory. However, many of the Kaikkoolars' customs are decidedly low. And although Kaikkoolars are one of the higher non-Brahman castes, they are nondominant and nonagrarian, so that the ambiguity of their status is apparent from their inability to command services from other castes', a circumstance Kaikkoolars sometimes lament.

The Kaikkoolar residential pattern is also confusing. They live in homogeneous communities separated from those of other castes. This pattern suggests low status as we understand the use of social separation of non-Brahmans today. The Kaikkoolars' maintenance of separate temples in their residential areas, even when comparable temples used by other castes are nearby, also suggests low status. Another anomalous feature of the Kaikkoolar community is the relative insignificance of kinship to their social organization. Beck (1972) considers this a reflection of their nonagrarian occupation, but it is also typical of low-ranking and untouchable castes. In contrast, the Kaikkoolars' extensive naaDu organization suggests high status, as does their worship of vegetarian high gods. However, some features of Kaikkoolar ritual

143

practice are characteristically low. They make chicken, goat, and pig sacrifices to their family gods, kuladeevam, and many may eat a portion of these sacrifices. Usually only untouchables will eat pork. The caste hero-poet, OTTakkuutar, similarly is a mixture of high and low qualities. He is acknowledged to be one of the greatest Tamil poets, but his cruelty is widely recognized. Kaikkoolars are thus anomalous and ambiguous in many of their characteristics, neither purely high nor unambiguously low. They seem to hold no quality in a pure and homogeneous form.

An explanation for this confusion of status may be found in the Kaikkoolars' history as a caste formerly of the left-hand section and organized on a regional basis to facilitate interlocality trade. Viewed synchronically, the left-hand/right-hand distinction once mediated by Brahmans, the naaDu system of organization, and the division of the Kaikkoolars' cosmos into an interior, kin-oriented realm (associated with small-god temples, presided over by non-Brahman priests, and characterized by blood sacrifices) and an exterior, kingly oriented realm (associated with Saivite temples and presided over by Brahman priests and vegetarian values) form the social contexts that enable us to resolve the apparent ambiguity and inconsistency of Kaikkoolar behavior. These features and the special role of temples and Brahmans characterized Tamil society for a thousand years, and formed a base point from which twentieth-century social process has diverged. Our task is to understand the Kaikkoolars today as a community that has evolved from the pre-twentieth-century social order, and to interpret the historical data in light of what we know about Kaikkoolars today. Looking at both the present and the past allows a better understanding of both kinds of data.

Kaikkoolars and models of caste

Over the past two decades, discussions of Indian caste ranking have been dominated by two models: Marriott's (1959, 1968; Marriott and Inden 1973, 1977) argument that caste ranking is based on food and service transactions and on an Indian ideology that each caste has a distinctive "coded-substance,"[1] and Dumont's (1970b) dual model of

---

[1] By "coded-substance" Marriott means that Indians believe that castes differ from one another in their biological substance. This substance is affected by pedigree – each caste is said to have its separate origins maintained by endogamy – and by its distinctive behavior. Accordingly, each caste has its own distinctive code of behavior. If a caste followed the code of a different caste, its members' substance could be altered and it would become a different caste. Similarly, if persons of different castes married, the substance of both would be altered by their divergence from the endogamy code. The substance of their children would differ from that of their parents because of their mixed pedigree.

caste stratification (Kolenda 1978:62-85). Both models depict integrated unitary hierarchies of interdependent castes; caste ranking is seen as an essentially homogeneous system in which all castes from top to bottom participate. Even at the level of the excluded bottom – the untouchables – Moffatt (1979) demonstrates replication of the system.

There are Hindu castes, however, that do not fit this integrated image of caste ranking. Heesterman (1973:99-100) notes that although castes formerly of the right-hand section fit the hierarchical integrated model of jati stratification, castes of the left-hand section do not. Giving Dumont his own twist, Heesterman argues that castes formerly of the right-hand section are characterized by what Dumont calls the kingly model of behavior, in which land-based power and economic and ritual interdependence articulate the hierarchy. Castes once belonging to the left-hand section are characterized by the priestly model of behavior, which stresses independence among jatis and purity. Heesterman (1973:98-100) feels that this dichotomy represents an inner conflict of tradition and indicates that not all castes can be ranked by transactional interdependence or by a homogeneous and integrating ideology of purity and impurity.

Heesterman is one of several scholars who have called attention to castes that are outside the integrated hierarchy of interdependent castes. Mayer (1960:44-47), Pocock (1962:85-87), and David (1974: 52-63), for example, all describe groups of such marginal castes. The left-hand castes of south India seem to be an elaborated and institutionalized example of a common structural dichotomy among castes, distinguishing those that are politically and economically interdependent from those that are not.

Heesterman's hypothesis that left-hand castes follow a priestly or Brahmanical model of behavior, however, is a simplification. Only the Aachaari artisans actually claim to be Brahmans, a claim they have been making – at times with considerable success – since at least A.D. 1128 (Arokiaswami 1959:277). The other left-hand castes mirror the full range of statuses found among the right-hand castes. Beck (1970, 1972) also supports the idea that the left-hand castes are followers of the Brahmanical model of caste behavior. She believes that there are only two models for caste ranking. First, there is the politico-economic (kingly) model, which depicts castes as integrated by land-based power. Kin organization plays a key role in the local organization of these castes. Second, there is the religio-ideological (Brahmanical) model, in which castes are ranked by concepts of ritual purity and impurity. Castes following this model lack important kin-based local organizations. Since the landed castes are clearly followers of the kingly mode of behavior, and because the left-hand castes share some attributes with Brahmans, Beck concludes that the latter must follow the Brahmanical model (Mines 1982:478). Nonetheless, she recognizes that Kaikkoolars are an exception to the dichotomy and do not fit the Brahmanical model; she describes them as vacillating between Brahmanical and kingly modes of behavior (1972:266). In fact, the mirroring of the right-hand system by the left-hand system demonstrates that left-hand castes do not follow a Brahmanical model.

David (1974:50) has correctly observed that there are not two models of caste interaction but three: the kingly and priestly schemes, each of which incorporates bound mode castes, and the mercantile scheme that incorporates nonbound mode castes. The latter, he argues, emphasizes egalitarian transactions. Whereas aristocratic and priestly castes are based on transactional schemes of interaction that differentiate castes as subordinate and superordinate, merchants must be able to interact with anyone and bargain heatedly with them. Accordingly, the "mercantile scheme prescribes a code of equivalence and instrumentality, the opposite of hierarchical amity" (1974:52). The Kaikkoolars fit this third category of caste behavior, but only imperfectly.

The limitation of David's interpretation is that it focuses on the actual character of the interaction between merchants and their customers. It is restricted to the characterization of this particular type of local interaction. However, merchants are not the only members of this caste category, if castes formerly of the left-hand section are considered to conform to David's third category of caste behavior. Rather, the category incorporates a variety of castes that are economically independent of the dominant agriculturists of a locality. These may include petty agriculturists such as the Padaiyaachis in KonkunnaDu, and artisan castes such as the Aachaaris (Kammalars) and Kaikkoolars. The left-hand caste section also includes untouchables and moieties of castes such as barbers and washermen, who perform services for higher-ranking members of the division.

Unlike the agrarian life style, which determines kingly caste modes, mercantilism alone is insufficient to explain the nature of the left-hand caste division. Two factors are important for a complete explanation. The first is the economic independence of the left-hand castes from the control of dominant agriculturists, whatever the caste occupation may be. Artisans, petty agriculturists, and merchants fit this condition. The second is the claim of castes that are neither dominant agriculturists nor Brahmans – castes such as the Aachaaris, Kaikkoolars, and Beri Chettys – to statuses equivalent to those occupied by the dominant castes that are not of their section. The Aachaaris' centuries-long claim to Brahman status, and the Kaikkoolars' claim to a status equivalent to that of the VeLLaaLas, pit these paired but rival castes against each other and keep them separated. Economic autonomy, status competition with paired castes of the agricultural sector, and social separation together characterize the third caste category. It is misleading, therefore, to describe this category as defined exclusively by mercantile behavior, because such a generalization accurately characterizes only some of the castes in this scheme. The generalization is further weakened because it is derived from local interaction only.

For centuries, the Kaikkoolars and apparently other high-ranking left-hand castes have formed locality-segmented but regionally administered caste sodalities, or naaDus. Although at the sublocality level the Kaikkoolars have often been dominated by the more powerful VeLLaaLas in KonkunaaDu, they have exhibited at the locality and supralocality levels an autonomy that ultimately stems from their naaDu organization and their special relationship with the kingly states in south India. In historic times the Kaikkoolars, as a naaDu-organized caste, were defined as much by their relationship to the state as by their preexistence as artisan-merchants. In the twentieth century, this interrelationship with the state has weakened the caste's naaDu organizations and has impelled the Kaikkoolars to reorganize themselves on several occasions. The caste Sangam, the weavers' cooperatives, and the formation of special interest associations have resulted. However, the relationship of the Kaikkoolars to state organizations prior to the twentieth century is less clear and must be inferred.

The social and economic separation of weavers in the south Indian agrarian states

Stein (1980:25) characterizes the left-hand castes as the "outer core" of society in medieval times, as opposed to the "inner core" formed by the agrarian castes. But this distinction obscures the importance of the left-hand castes to south Indian society. Stein's depiction of these two sections is nonetheless understandable. Even today, Tamilnadu is predominantly a rural society; three-fourths of its population resides in villages. In the twentieth century, this agriculturally based rural society represents the largest sector of the economy, and the larger agricultural castes and their dependents are politically dominant in the countryside. However, the next largest sector of the economy is handloom weaving. Today in Tamilnadu, the weaving industry ranks second to agriculture as the largest employer.

When handloom textiles were a major export under the British prior to the 1830s, the weaving sector of the economy must have been significantly larger (Dutt 1903:126). Before British rule, northern Konku-naaDu was laced by a network of urban fairs and markets centered on the textile trade, connecting the administrative towns of the area's districts (Map 2). These districts had been created by Karnatic and Muslim rulers (Murton 1979:22-24). Through this network, textiles passed upward through the hierarchy of centers and out beyond the Konku area, whereas wealth passed down. Weavers also supplied the area's agriculturists with cloth. The concentration of weavers and markets in the administrative towns and the desire of administrators to have them point to the importance of this industry to the rulers during this and earlier times (Murton 1979:22-25). In many cities and villages, weaving and textile trade still represent the major industry. This is true of all the towns of the Seven-City Territory, including Salem, Trichengode, Rasipuram, Mallesamutram, Paramuttu, Taramangalam, and Edapadi, as well as other localities such as the village of Akkamapettai and its adjacent town, Sankagiridrug. These weaving centers were the administrative towns of the precolonial period (Murton 1979:23-24). Consequently, when speaking of the outer core, care must be taken to emphasize the economic and social importance of this other sector of society.

The importance of the two economic sectors of society is underscored by the symbolic uses of their products in south India. Agriculture and animal husbandry occupy a central place in ritual and philosophy. Agricultural products and animals are given as ritual offerings and as sacrifices at temples, and are used as markers of honor and status among castes. In similar fashion, textiles are given as endowments to temples and are central offerings in ritual gift giving. They are given at life-crisis ceremonies, and are used to mark statuses and to bind men in reciprocal and redistributive relationships. Every important life-crisis ceremony involves the exchange of textiles; every important temple requires their ritual use. On the one hand, food is offered to the gods, as are flowers and leaves, milk, ghee, and water. On the other hand, textiles are offered to clothe the gods, to shade them under umbrellas, and to decorate their carts and palanquins. In the past, cloth was also given to the deeva-daasis; when they died, their temples provided new clothes for their funerals. The giving of textiles was an important part of their dedication to and their role in temples.

I suggest that these two important categories of ritual offerings to the gods – the products of agriculture and the cow, and the products of the loom – are given these central symbolic roles because historically they formed the society's two main sources of productive wealth. But this wealth has two distinctive bases: the products of two differently organized sectors of society. The importance and the separate nature of these sources of wealth are clearly marked in ritual by the place the products of both have in worship and in ceremonies.

The British recognized the symbolic importance of both textiles and good harvests and their close association with administrative power. The activities of Lionel Place, a British collector during the 1790s, illustrate the central ceremonial use of textiles and the British recognition of their importance:

[Place] adopted the role of an indigenous king, acting as a mediator for important religious ceremonies. In the admittedly hostile words of a missionary, Alexander Duff, who was seeking to eliminate the connection of the [British] East India Company with such ceremonies, Place would call for "all the dancing girls, musicians . . . elephants and horses" attached to the temple at Conjeevaram, a temple city in Chingleput District. "Attending in person, his habit was to distribute cloths to the dancing girls, suitable offerings to the officiating Brahmins, and a lace garment of considerable value of the god." He also used Company troops and sanctioned the prayers of Brahmans "to propitiate the deity for a good harvest or for good trade." (Irschick, mimeo: 18).

At this time in history, textiles formed a major component of trade. The preceding quotation, therefore, illustrates not only the central symbolic use of textiles by a "kingly" power, but also the parallel symbolic significance of harvest and trade to economic well-being.

In the Indian scheme of caste ranking, accepting food or taking part in feasts are transactions that symbolically mark the interrelationships and relative ranks of the participants. To accept gifts of food is widely recognized as implying that the acceptor will provide services to the giver. In this manner, castes are ranked by the giving and receiving of food and services. Service recipients rank above service givers. By contrast, the textiles given at life-crisis ceremonies or at important festivals such as at Deepavali (festival of lights) and Pongal (harvest festival) are gifts that either demarcate relations that are meant to be equal or establish patronage in asymmetrical relationships. Reciprocal relations are usually those among relatives; asymmetrical relations are those between elder and younger kin, between the king and his subjects, among employers and servants, or among worshipers and the temples they endow.

Beyond the sphere of symbolic exchange, textiles have been an important trade item, establishing primary interrelationships among localities. If a local leader gathered weavers around his administrative centers, as in northern KonkunaaDu in the eighteenth century, he controlled an important trade resource. Similarly, if weavers could gain the protection of local rulers and administrators, their trade would be facilitated. In northern KonkunaaDu, the cities of the Seven-City Territory were all administrative towns, with concentrations of weavers located in or near them. The weavers were interconnected by a cycle of fairs, trade, and the Kaikkoolars' naaDu system.

The special significance of textiles and weavers, therefore, stems in part from the political-economic importance of textiles in south Indian society. Indian textiles were for centuries an important trade item (Bean 1981; Gittinger 1982) and a major source of wealth, sought not only by West Asian and European consumers but also by Southeast Asians, Chinese, and the south Indians themselves. In Tamilnadu the Kaikkoolars wove cloth and acted as merchants, trading cloth locally and over great distances, or acted as intermediaries in this trade (Arasaratnam 1980:266-267). These features of textile production and trade created the conditions for the Kaikkoolars' status rivalry with and residential separation from castes that were once members of the right-hand moiety. This separation and rivalry have a long history.

In medieval times, merchants and itinerant artisans such as the Kaikkoolars occupied positions of high status and power (Stein 1980:252). Stein writes:

We have substantial evidence that mercantile groups maintained [in Chola times] a formidable military capability which was required by the extensive itinerant trade network of the age. Ayyavole inscriptions bear this out, as does the famous Polonnaruva inscription of Sri Lanka . . . (ca. [A.D.] 1120) in which the Tamil *iDangkai veelaikkaarar* [left-hand caste warriors] are referred to in association with the trade organization of the *Valangkaiyar* [right-hand people]. References to *Kaikkoolar veelaikkaarar* [warriors] have suggested that artisans too were capable of maintaining armed units. (Stein 1975:75)

Later, from the fourteenth through the seventeenth centuries, a period following the decline of the Cholas, when trade was endangered by the autonomy of warrior chiefs, large trade associations such as the Manigraamam and the Ayyavole 500 were maintained and "always had armed escorts to protect them while passing through the dangerous territories lying between the [settled] nuclear areas" (Stein 1965:58). Both of these confederacies of merchants and artisans were engaged in trade in northern KonkunaaDu during this period, and textiles were among their commodities (Murton 1979:21-22). Stein notes that inscriptions reflect the great military pretensions of these trade organizations (recall the Kaikkoolars' claim to a brave military heritage). They also record the desire of agrarian-based warriors (the VeLLaaLas and Vijayanagara chiefs) to reduce the trade groups' military and political power. By the seventeenth century, the trade groups disappeared.

Undoubtedly, the power and wealth of weavers fluctuated greatly over time, and varied considerably among weavers, even as they do today among simple weavers, their masters, and the cloth merchants of their caste. But it is also clear that at times Kaikkoolars rivaled the agrarian-based castes in status and power. Perhaps this is in part the source of the title "Mudaliyar." Arokiaswami (1956:271) translates the term as meaning they who are first in society. But two quite separate communities carry the title: VeLLaaLa agriculturists and the Kaikkoolars. Both could be first because the society was divided into right-hand and left-hand sections, the positions of castes being validated by temple worship. Since the two castes belonged to different moieties, they worshiped separately and occupied separate social spaces. Accordingly, each could be considered first in its respective sphere. The castes' different sources of wealth and power facilitated this separation. The separation seems to have been emphasized by the weavers' nearly complete dissociation from agriculture and by the special desire of rulers to gather artisans around their administrative towns, where their manufactures could be encouraged and taxed.

When, in October 1800, Buchanan (1807, vol. II:199) passed through Ammapettai, then a town of about forty houses surrounded by untilled land, he remarked that it was occupied by weavers and merchants, who engaged in no agriculture at all. He noted the same pattern in Coimbatore (1807, vol. II:265). Akkamapettai is such a village even today. Since Chola times, many weavers have lived in commercial towns rather than agrarian villages. Buchanan (1807, vol. II:264-265) also commented favorably on the Mysore sultans' system of taxation of weavers in the late eighteenth century. He noted that the tax on looms decreased with the number owned by the weaver, a method designed to encourage production. Elsewhere he noted the effects of excessive taxation on Kaikkoolars (Buchanan 1807, vol. II:240), and in another reference showed interest in assessing the extent and taxation of inter-locality trade. The weavers' relationship with south Indian states, therefore, was based on their occupation. They produced valuable trade commodities, and as a result of their trade were taxed distinctively. The weavers' caste organization also reflects their distinctive place in society.

The pattern of weavers living separately from agriculturists in homogeneous communities as we find today is a tradition of some antiquity in south India. Bean (1981:8) notes that at the end of the eighteenth century in Mysore, "cloth makers usually lived apart from the agriculturists and their service castes, either in separate hamlets or in distinct villages." She says that the nature of weaving, with its need for space for warp processing and disposal of dye wastes, which spoil water, explain the need for separation. Weavers in Salem offer similar explanations (Mines 1982). After all, they are willing to live with the inconvenience that using the streets for sizing warps creates, but other communities are less tolerant.

This, however, is not the only explanation for their separation. Another is found in the left-hand/right-hand division of society. Frykenberg (1977) and Appadurai (1974) provide evidence on the nature of this moiety system, suggesting that Kaikkoolars lived separately because castes of the right and left sections were territorially segregated by decree when disputes arose. The cause of these disputes, when Kaikkoolars were involved, appears to have been the caste's desire to administer separately its own naaDus. Since naaDu territories were defined by temple worship, disputes often centered on the control of temples. Disputes also arose over the ritual rights and temple honors that defined the relative statuses of castes. Spatial separation, residential separation, the duplication of temples, the maintenance of caste-exclusive temples, the caste's economic independence, and its interlocality trade made it desirable and possible for Kaikkoolars to rule their own affairs. The importance of the naaDu structure as a system for administering interlocality trade provided a strong practical motive for maintaining the system. The residential separation of Kaikkoolars, therefore, is a result of their historic predominance in the towns of northern Konku and of the old patterns of trade in this area; the local organization of these Kaikkoolar communities is a product of their system of administration.

The nature of textile trade and Kaikkoolar relations with polities

The Kaikkoolars' independent administrative organization and social separation is centuries old. Hall (1980) has argued that in early Chola times the marketplaces of artisan-merchants (nagarams) were incorporated into naaDus, which were dominated by the agrarian elite. There was only one nagaram to a naaDu (Hall 1980:187). However, by the late eleventh century, as artisan-merchants became wealthier and more powerful, they broke away from agriculturist control to deal directly with state officials, and maintained armies to protect their trade as well as to plunder when the occasion arose (Hall 1982:202ff.). They were a political force of their own. In later Chola times under King Kulottungaa III (thirteenth century), Kaikkoolars, VeLLaaLas, and *Valangaiyars* – the last a caste not known today – were organized under caste leaders. Some Kaikkoolars believe that their present naaDu system is a later outgrowth of Vijayanagar (A.D. 1350-1650) policy that used the naaDus to organize localities under warrior chiefs who were principally agriculturists. In this way, Kaikkoolar naaDus may have been used to organize the weavers. In KonkunaaDu, some Vijayanagar naaDu chiefs are known to have been Kaikkoolars (Murton 1979:25).

Arasaratnam (1980:276) supplies some evidence that during the early colonial period, the heads of local naaDus, called naaTTavars in what is now Andhra Pradesh, were initially viewed as guild heads by the British. The British thought that the weaver naaTTavars controlled the weavers in their areas and that they could be used as economic brokers, along with masterweavers and merchants, to negotiate contracts for textile production. In fact, naaTTavars did not control weaver production other than their own. However, when the British tried to circumvent these social leaders and deal directly with weavers through agents chosen by the British, the naaTTavars and masterweavers organized a weavers' strike. Consequently, the British came to view the naaTTavars as a threat and resolved to weaken them (Arasaratnam 1980:276). NaaTTavars, who were the heads of local naaDus, therefore clearly had an important leadership role among village weavers in the mid-eighteenth century, and considered themselves the rightful representatives of weavers when dealing with outsiders, even if they did not in fact have the control over production that the British thought they did.

This certainly fits what we know about naaDu administration today. NaaDu leaders can order boycotts, tax local families to sponsor joint pujas, mediate disputes, and regulate interlocal relations among Kaikkoolars, but the naaDu is not a guild and does not control textile production. NaaTTavars were political and ritual heads but not guild masters. A few years later, Buchanan (1807, vol. II:265) described the head of the Kaikkoolars in what was then known as Northern Coimbatore, the KonkunaaDu area, as Natami Carun (NaaTTaaNmaikkaarar), presiding officer of the naaDu, and said, in the proverbial way of the colonial British, that he was the hereditary chief of the community. The Kaikkoolars' supralocal caste organization, therefore, dates from medieval times and certainly had multiple functions, including identity, ritual, political organization, trade, and the establishment of the caste's domain.

What role did the naaTTavars and the naaDus actually play in the textile trade? Unfortunately, we may never know directly, since no one in the early eighteenth century appears to have been concerned with the circumstances of weaving in outlying localities (Arasaratnam 1980:258-259). We can only infer what the situation was like by piecing together bits of information from the few extant historical accounts and from modern ethnographic data.

The commercialization of cloth production is old in south India, certainly dating from the early centuries of the first millennium. In medieval times, trade grew in volume and mercantilism became elaborated. Local merchants who supplied their own localities were distinguished from itinerant merchants who linked settled areas with their trade networks. It was these traders who formed the famous trading

associations and maintained armies for protection and for plundering.
It was they who developed ambiguous reputations as merchants and as
wandering brigands who, as one epigraph alleges, "demand taxes or
tolls by threatening people with drawn swords or by capturing them"
(Hall 1980:193).

In this age, trade centers already formed a hierarchy. There were
local markets (nagarams), and above them a few major entrepots
(*maanagarams*). In the centuries that followed (1350-1650), Vijayanagar chiefs sought to destroy the armies of both agrarian elites and
artisan-merchants. By the seventeenth century the great itinerant associations had disappeared, but among artisan-merchants, such as the
Aachaaris and Kaikkoolars, the pyramidal naaDu hierarchy remained.

The geography of the Kaikkoolars' naaDu system suggests its use.
The paavaDi naaDus are located at the level of primary production.
As we have seen, weavers outproduce local demand. In addition, localities specialize in the kinds of cloth they produce. Consequently, a
variety of mercantile specialties have developed to meet various marketing needs. Head-load, bullock-cart load, and shop merchants distribute cloth locally. A variety of weavers, masterweavers, and wholesale
buyers handle marketing supralocally and internationally, and a large
number of enterprises handle financing and ancillary aspects of the
weaving industry. The naaDu councils are located at marketplace
points in this geographic network of trade. Undoubtedly, they are
involved in regulating relationships among this multiplicity of specialties in textile production and marketing.

Map 2 illustrates how, in the Seven-City Territory, weaver naaDu
councils were located at urban administrative and marketing centers. It
also illustrates that the weavers of the Seven-City Territory maintained
relationships with each other when they met to worship at the annual
Ardhanaariisvarar festival held in Trichengode, renewing their membership in the territory and jointly sponsoring a puja in their name,
which was financed by the taxes gathered from their member naaDus.
This formation of a Kaikkoolar confederacy provided the forum (the
naaDu council) and the organization to regulate their affairs. If member naaDus or members of a naaDu refused to comply with council
decisions, they were outcaste. If outcaste, they had no community to
which to appeal in times of need and, when disputes arose, no means
of attaining settlement. For commercial textile producers and traders,
these were important needs.

NaaDu councils at all levels of the system's hierarchy met near their
Saivite temples to settle disputes that arose among Kaikkoolars within
their territories. Issues of price and trade, disputes about agreements,
and issues of precedence, we can speculate, were handled by the

naaDu councils within the stately context established by the kingly temples. Disputes that arose beyond the jurisdiction of the territory could be appealed to the Conjeepuran MahaanaaDu.

In Chola and Vijayanagar times, the Kaikkoolar associations clearly were a source of power with which the states had to contend. States taxed thoroughly the various aspects of production (Hall 1980:53); they tolled the movement of goods, and commerce itself was taxed. Artisan-merchants attempted to regulate their relationships with states. If taxed or abused too much, they escaped by leaving or by organizing strikes. In the late eighteenth century, judging by naaDu officer titles (Murton 1973:167-169), it is likely that Salem's Kaikkoolars collected taxes from among their number for their state rulers.

NaaDu councils, Kaikkoolars say, have the right to tax members of their communities. Today these taxes are used only for sponsoring the joint pujas that establish membership in caste territories. This right to tax is vested in the officers of the naaDus at all levels of the system. Community councils (paavaDi naaDus) collect locally; subregional locality councils (thisainaaDus) collect from subordinate naaDus; and presumably the regional council (MahaanaaDu), before its demise, could collect from the four subregional councils. In the recent past, Kaikkoolar naaDus could also collect taxes and represent subordinate allied castes at temple pujas. In the Erode-Akkamapettai region, the Padaiyaachi and the VeeTTuva Gounders were such allied agriculturist castes. The naaDus, therefore, can be seen as having the bureaucracy for territorially organizing an important segment of society. Since the Vijayanagar Empire ruled through naaDus, turned naaDu leaders into chiefs (Stein 1980:443), and later rulers in the seventeenth and eighteenth centuries located weaver centers at administrative towns, it is likely that the weaver naaDus were used to administer locality-segmented weavers and their allies, regulate their textile trade, and perhaps tax them as well.

This interpretation of the Kaikkoolar naaDus conforms to Stein's characterization of south Indian states as locality-based, segmented states rather than centralized, unitary bureaucratic states (1980, especially pp. 21, 45, 265, 266, 270). The Kaikkoolar naaDu system even today has the appearance of such segmentation and incorporates the dual sense of territoriality that characterizes the medieval segmented state. To quote Stein (1980:266-267):

The dual sense of territorial sovereignty as, on the one hand, an essentially ritual sort exercised by a king in a segmentary state and, on the other hand, as an essentially political or controlling sort which the king exercises in his own domain, but which is appropriately exercised by subordinate rulers in their domain, is seen as appropriate in the medieval Indian situation.

In a parallel manner, the Kaikkoolars' naaDu system combines these two senses of territoriality, being on the one hand a pyramidal hierarchy of locality leaders – described as chiefs by Britons at the end of the eighteenth century – and on the other hand a territorial hierarchy of kingly temple localities with Conjeepuram at the apex ritually defining the social domain of the caste as a unit. Even at the apex of the system, the limited political power of the aaNDavar (the head of the regional council, the Mahaanaadu) was evident, but he united the caste with his ritual status. Thus, the naaDu system was politically segmented by locality, but ritually unified through the pyramid of interlinked and increasingly important temples and caste offices.

The status of eighteenth-century weavers in northern KonkunaaDu, therefore, may be seen in part as an aspect of their place as semi-autonomous administrative segments in the south Indian states. These administrative segments were urban equivalents of the rural-based agriculturists' naaDu territories. Their equivalence ultimately stemmed from their economic importance to the regional polities. Accordingly, organized by their own chiefly naaDu system, the Kaikkoolar sodality administered their own supralocal caste affairs and relations with the state, and maintained and publicly proclaimed in naaDu temples their own social status and domains. Through the naaDu organization, the Kaikkoolars formed an elemental part of the segmented state as a caste sodality administering the domain of weavers and their dependents.

The existing remnants of the naaDu system clearly reflect this heritage of a segmented caste administration. If the area of the Seven-City Territory is demarcated by drawing a line encompassing the seven main centers of the confederacy (Map 2), Trichengode occupies the southern extreme of the area and Taramangalam, its counterpart in status, occupies the northern extreme. Even today, this is the area of densest weaver population in Salem District, which in turn has the largest weaving population in Tamilnadu State (Narayanaswami Naidu 1948:5-6; Census of India vol. 9, Part XI-A:63-67). Thus, the Seven-City Territory, the EeRuurunaaDu, integrates one of the main weaving subregions of Tamilnadu, reflecting the old administrative organization of the area when it was part of the native states controlling northern KonkunaaDu.

The pomp of naaDu pageantry also reflects a ritualized royal or chiefly mode that suggests the mirroring of the agriculturists' pageantry and a persistence of the ritual character of Kaikkoolar naaDus; the Kaikkoolars' locality councils, such as the Seven-City Territory Council, are like chiefdoms. The council officers preside over a segmented community united by common worship at the Ardhanaariisvarar

Temple. But they unite within their territory only members of their community and a few allies; they do not administer to the agriculturists nor, with a few local exceptions, do the latter administer to them. This ritualized political-economic separation of the territories of right-hand and left-hand castes is replicated in their ritual separation. They worship separately to avoid confusing the borders their worship creates. Under these circumstances, the rights of caste leaders to display ritual signs of office are expressions of the caste's chiefly status within the state. Indian Independence has made this kind of ritualized political integration unnecessary, and displays of emblems of office have become less pronounced, as have the left-hand/right-hand distinctions that reflected this ritualized territoriality.

The dual political nature of the naaDu system, a combination of ritual unity and segmented domain, continues to have some importance today. It is easily supposed, if the naaDus are thought of primarily as dispute settlement panchayats, that the naaDus would be displaced by India's contemporary court system. But naaDus have been used both to define the caste as a segment of the state and as courts to mediate disputes and establish custom. Contemporary naaDu leaders have continued to use the system to effect political ends. Both Ammapettai's and Salem's naaDus have been used by leaders to organize support for local and national political candidates. The Trichengode locality council, the Seven-City Territory thisai-naaDu, has also attempted to use its influence to support political candidates such as Rajaji and to force caste members to support favored candidates on threat of outcasting. As we have seen in the case of the Ammapettai dispute described in Chapter 4, naaDu leaders also controlled temple funds to which they had access through their administration of naaDu temples. In Ammapettai these funds were allegedly used on occasion to support the political candidates favored by naaDu leaders. In recent years, the Tamilnadu government has appointed special government officers to administer the Ammapettai Murugan temple and scores of others to prevent the use of temple funds in this manner.

It is little wonder that the Kaikkoolars have maintained their naaDus in the face of changes that appear to displace the system's political-administrative functions. The naaDus still symbolically define the caste's place in the land, are still used to organized political action, and continue to provide a sense of ritual integrity. When naaDus finally cease functioning, the heritage of the Kaikkoolars' system will remain a prominent part of their sense of identity, just as this sense, more than the fragmented persistence of the system, is central to their identity today.

Interpreting the Kaikkoolars today

The paradoxes of Kaikkoolar behavior and the ambivalence of their customs are explained by the caste's historic position as weavers in the segmented states of south India. NaaDus seem to have been the primary social institution defining the Kaikkoolars' social position within states; naaDu temples demarcated their territories and ritual unity, and were the contexts for ritual displays of status. Weaving provided the economic basis of their separation from agriculturists, establishing a foundation for social autonomy without political-economic dominance based on interdependent ties.

Like the secular and ritual supremacy of Brahmans and the left-hand/right-hand moiety division, caste naaDu systems are part of the segmentary order of south Indian society that persisted into the twentieth century. This happened because colonial policy was designed to avoid disrupting what Britons perceived to be the indigenous social order unless a custom was thought harmful to British rule, British trade, or on occasion British sensibilities. The result was a colonial state superimposed on a feudal, segmented social system. The beginning of administrative centralization in the last quarter of the nineteenth century initiated the process that ended this feudal system. It disrupted the old order among castes and the relationships of castes with the state, and ultimately brought about the revolutionary social transformation of south Indian society. Brahman dominance in politics, education, administration, and ritual all came under attack as the numerically superior non-Brahmans fought to gain control of their society. The implications of these attacks were far reaching. Swept up in these changes, Kaikkoolars in the late 1920s replaced Brahmans with their own priests (teesikars) in their Subramaniyan (Murugan) temples and in life-crisis ceremonies. They sought higher education and formed their caste Sangam. Simultaneously, Brahmans lost their priestly value as mediators of the social status of non-Brahman castes in the left-hand/right-hand moieties.

Both the supremacy of Brahmans and the left-hand/right-hand moiety distinction were eroded by the promise of the political democratization of local administration. In the 1920s and 1930s, non-Brahmans wanted a dominant role in the emerging government and felt that their demands were warranted by their numbers. They created the fear that they would be unsuccessful unless Brahmans were displaced from the positions that gave them social and ritual superiority. Non-Brahmans recognized the advantages of unity in a representative government, and non-Brahman leaders advocated minimizing differences among the ritually clean non-Brahman castes to create this unity. Already weakened by British centralization, the left-hand/right-hand distinction rapidly deteriorated in this environment.

Non-Brahmans could no longer compete for dominance of the separate social-ritual domains once provided by the left-hand/right-hand division. They competed instead for representation and benefits in a unified political-economic field. Consequently, the moiety distinction was disrupted in two ways simultaneously: structurally by the society's political unification, and ritually by the displacement of Brahmans from their position as the symbolic validators and arbiters of the social order. Within a decade, the moiety division ceased to be a vital social distinction. The deeva-daasi tradition was outlawed, and the maintenance of separate moiety rest houses at major temples was stopped. Disputes between rival castes of the two divisions diminished and disappeared in northern KonkunaaDu, and the meaning of the distinction began to fade. Today, only the shadowy legacy of this moiety system remains, fossillike, embedded in residence patterns, in the occasional use of caste emblems and signs, and in the contrasting models of caste behavior followed by the castes that once belonged to the two divisions.

In the twentieth century, the naaDu system's segmented organization and its lack of an executive body to represent the caste's interests spurred the Kaikkoolars to form a Sangam after dyarchy was introduced. The British had paid attention to lobbying couched in the language of caste. Kaikkoolar leaders saw that the caste needed to be united as a single body that could express a common set of needs in order to obtain the advantages the new form of government appeared to promise. This reorganization meant redefining the caste as a homogeneous social unit, a structure alien to the segmented naaDu framework. In addition, Sangam members had to accept executive rule in order to unify caste codes and represent caste interests to the government.

It is commonly stated by students of south Asia that social change in the twentieth century represents a new order of metamorphosis because it involves the formation of caste associations that link caste segments beyond the limits of village society. Because agriculturists showed little interest in these kinds of associations prior to moving to towns (Hardgrave 1970:48), supralocal caste organization is depicted as having little to do with the indigenous social order. This is a peculiar viewpoint for two reasons: First, the constant social development of south Indian society and its political economy brought about by changes in regional governments (Stein 1975; Murton 1979) belies the image of a static, traditional caste society. Second, this view seems to be prefaced by the judgment that the locus of society – its real center – is found only in villages. This viewpoint ignores the important caste networks that once tied the countryside to states and organized regions, including the agriculturists' naaDus and the trade networks of the Kaikkoolars. Further, the Kaikkoolars' Sangam, although structurally distinctive from earlier corporate forms, was a renewed effort to administer supralocal relationships with the state within the context of yet another change in government. It was not the Kaikkoolars' first attempt, and in this case motivation for reorganization stemmed from their self-interests associated with the handloom industry and their textile trade, just as such efforts had in the past. This manipulation of the relationship between local economic and social interests and the regionwide political order characterized Kaikkoolar caste organization before and during the twentieth century.

The Sangams of the Kaikkoolars and other castes experienced their greatest success during the period from about 1930 to 1960. The Kaikkoolars' Sangam, however, lacked the natural ties to the political economy that the naaDus once had. The Kaikkoolars' Sangam acted mainly as a political pressure group that advocated benefits for weavers, but it lacked any direct institutional ties with weaving. Consequently, when the handloom weavers' cooperative system began in earnest in the late 1930s and early 1940s, Sangam leaders were among its strong supporters. By the 1960s, the cooperative system had grown greatly in size, and political power in the caste had passed to men who held positions in the system's administration. Once again, local Kaikkoolar leaders held positions that placed them pivotally between the local needs and interests of weavers and the state's political economy. The cooperatives provided a ready conduit through which the government could pass welfare benefits to weavers and in return receive from weavers their political loyalty and support.

Kaikkoolar dominance of the system, however, has proved temporary. Political and economic differentiation has crisscrossed the caste with opposing self-interests, and in the early 1970s caste leaders lost control of the system's administration. The present state government seems to be interested in using the cooperative structure to appeal to weavers irrespective of caste. It certainly does not want to allow the cooperative structure to benefit the political opposition.

Now, at a time when caste identity is no longer an acceptable basis for incentive, the Kaikkoolars have no other appeal for unity. This separation of the Kaikkoolars' caste organization from Tamilnadu's political economy represents the most recent step in the caste's participation in the transformation of south Indian society.

Conclusions

As a result of centuries of change, Kaikkoolar caste organization today is a potpourri of forms acquired through history. Its lower-level naaDus and warrior heritage come from the late Chola period, and perhaps from the caste's involvement in the great trade organizations of the eleventh to sixteenth centuries. The organization of the Seven-City Territory, with its linked urban weaving centers and associated major temple complexes, seems to derive from the seventeenth- to eighteenth-century organization of northern KonkunaaDu. During that period, the karnatic rulers divided the region into districts, each of which had an administrative trading center (kasba). Seven of these towns today form the Seven-City Territory, the EeRuurunaaDu. In the twentieth century, the caste Sangam and the handloom weavers' cooperative system have been added to the castes' collection of organizational forms. The caste uses all of these institutions to structure its identity and manipulate its relationship with other castes and the state.

Looked at in this historical manner, the durability of caste identity is undeniable. The Kaikkoolars are mentioned in epigraphs throughout nearly a thousand years of history. But the dynamic flexibility of the caste's identity is also apparent. If the Kaikkoolars are taken as an example, then caste must be seen as neither a rigid, unchanging identity nor as a system without structural identity beyond the bounds of small localities incorporating a few villages at most and limited by the extent of kinship organization (Kolenda 1978:40-41). The Kaikkoolars have a regionwide organization that they have manipulated and redefined over the centuries in response to changes in state organization, in order to administer their interrelationships between locality and region.

The Kaikkoolars' relatively high status among non-Brahmans stems from the economic and ritual importance of textiles in south India. Always an important sector of the political economy and trade, textiles are also a central item in temple worship, festival gift giving, and all life-crisis rituals. Although the average weaver is poor, he is independent of the control of agriculturists and cannot be commanded to perform services for them. But many Kaikkoolars have also been able to acquire considerable wealth as masterweavers and as participants in trade. At times, the average weaver has even been in better circumstances than many agriculturists (Bean 1981). In precolonial KonkunaaDu, regional political powers sought weavers to reside in or near their administrative cities (Murton 1979), because the textile trade not only brought wealth but also linked localities in a network of exchange relationships forming one level of the state's sodality. Consequently, the Kaikkoolars' central importance to trade, their relative autonomy in the context of the agriculturists' localized political dominance, the weavers' occasional wealth, and the ritual importance of textiles all contribute to the caste's relatively high status among non-Brahmans.

The Kaikkoolars' status is also symbolically buttressed by their heritage as warriors and by their use of major temples to define their caste membership. It is at jointly sponsored pujas that the caste's hierarchical order is legitimized and its status and signs of rank are publicly displayed.

The caste's supralocal naaDu organization and judicial separation from the locality's dominant agriculturists juxtapose the social status of Kaikkoolars and Gounder VeLLaaLas in the Seven-City Territory. Kaikkoolars and Gounders are rivals in mythical and historical heritage, in economic independence, and in their naaDu organizations. In addition, both claim a comparable status in temples; both use Saivite temples to integrate their caste's naaDu organizations; both formerly dedicated women as deeva-daasis; and each maintains its ritual separation from the other as a legacy of the left-hand/right-hand division of society and the castes' social rivalry. This separation and duplication of statuses characterize the left-hand/right-hand moiety system and indicate that, in addition to the rural-based kingly and priestly caste categories, the left-hand castes formed a third category that mirrored aspects of the other two. The third category, however, also contrasted to the priestly and kingly castes because its members were economically independent of the dominant agriculturists. A few of its castes were also predominantly urban rather than rural, and all of them were nondominant. They could neither command services of other castes nor, with the exception of untouchables, could they be commanded. This gave them an appearance of autonomy and separation from the agriculturists' caste scheme.

The legacy of this moiety division of society lasted for hundreds of years and largely explains the continuing tendency for residential separation of the two castes. The intensity of these castes' status rivalry dictated the need for this spatial separation. The legacy of the division also explains some of the appearance of low status that today may be mistakenly attributed to the Kaikkoolars. The legacy explains why Kaikkoolars frequently maintained separate temples or separate rest homes at shared temples, and in the past prevented VeLLaaLa Gounders from taking their celebrations and ritual processions through Kaikkoolar areas. Reciprocally, the legacy also explains why, when the Kaikkoolars took their processions through the Gounders' residential areas in nineteenth-century Tinnevelly, the result was social tension and conflict.

The mistaken conception of low Kaikkoolar status is also a result of the south Indian non-Brahmans' division of their social cosmos into two realms. Family gods and small gods require blood sacrifices to ensure the well-being of self and kin; they form the interior realm. The high Saivite gods, however, are kingly and require Brahmanical worship. They define the caste's identity, status, and supralocal organization, and form the exterior realm. The Kaikkoolars identify with both types of gods; they use both to order and explain their social world. The small gods' world is the world of parochial locality and local concerns. The high gods' world is the world of the state and region. Kaikkoolars are involved in both, and this involvement is the source of their caste's structure. Belief and caste structure, therefore, complement one another.

The contemporary ambiguity about Kaikkoolar status disappears when the legacy of the left-hand/right-hand division is recognized, their naaDu organization is understood, and the symbolic importance of their divided cosmos for ordering their social world is accepted. Like their cosmos, this world consists of two contrasting realms, that of kin and locality and that of the region and state. The problems that arise with the integration of locality and region have spurred the Kaikkoolars' social change when governments have reorganized their region. In the twentieth century, the Kaikkoolars have moved from the left-hand section of a divided political economy to central involvement in the economy of the contemporary unified democratic state. The shift has taken them from a segmented feudal organization to the polyethnic organization of modern India.

References

Ames, Michael M. 1973. Structural dimensions of family life in the steel city of Jamshedpur, India. In *Entrepreneurship and Modernization of Occupational Cultures in South Asia,* Milton Singer, ed. Program in Comparative Studies on Southern Asia, Monograph 12. Durham, N.C.: Duke University Press.

Appadurai, Arjun. 1974. Right and left-hand castes in south India. *Indian Economic and Social History Review* 2:216-259.

1981. *Worship and Conflict Under Colonial Rule: A South Indian Case.* Cambridge: Cambridge University Press.

Appadurai, Arjun, and Carol Appadurai Breckenridge. 1976. The south Indian temple: authority, honor and redistribution. *Contributions to Indian Sociology* n.s. 10, 2:187-211.

Arasaratnam, S. 1980. Weavers, merchants and company: the handloom industry in south-eastern India 1750-1790. *The Indian Economic and Social History Review* 17:257-281.

Arokiaswami, M. 1956. *The Kongu Country.* Madras: The University of Madras Press.

Baker, Christopher. 1976. *The Politics of South India, 1920-1937.* Cambridge: Cambridge University Press.

Barnett, Steven Alan. 1973. The process of withdrawal in a south Indian caste. In *Entrepreneurship and Modernization of Occupational Cultures in South Asia,* Milton Singer, ed. Program in Comparative Studies on Southern Asia, Monograph 12. Durham, N.C.: Duke University Press.

Bean, Susan. 1981. The fabric of social life in pre-British Mysore. Paper presented at the Western Conference of the Association for Asian Studies, Berkeley, California.

Beck, Brenda E. F. 1970. The right-left division of south Indian society. *Journal of Asian Studies* 29:779-798.

1972. *Peasant Society in Konku.* Vancouver: University of British Columbia Press.

Beck, Brenda E. F., ed. 1979. *Perspectives on a Regional Culture: Essays About the Coimbatore Area of South India.* New Delhi: Vikas.

Beck, Brenda E. F., and Annama Joy. 1979. Coimbatore City – the spatial distribution of thirteen major castes in the urban area today. In *Perspectives on a Regional Culture*, Brenda E.F. Beck, ed. New Delhi: Vikas.

Beteille, André. 1965. *Caste, Class and Power: Changing Patterns of Stratification in a Tanjore Village*. Berkeley: University of California Press.

Brunner, Edward M. 1974. The expression of ethnicity in Indonesia. In *Urban Ethnicity*, Abner Cohen, ed. Association of Social Anthropologists, Monograph 12. London: Tavistock.

Buchanan, Francis. 1807. *A Journey from Madras through the Countries of Mysore, Canara, and Malabar*. 3 vols. London: Bulmer.

Census of India. 1961. *Handlooms in Madras State*, vol. 9, Part XI-A. Government Publications.

Clothey, Fred W. 1978. *The Many Faces of Murukan: The History and Meaning of a South Indian God*. New York: Mouton.

David, Kenneth. 1974. And never the twain shall meet? Mediating the structural approaches to caste ranking. In *Structural Approaches to South Indian Studies*, Harry M. Buck and Glenn E. Yocum, eds. Chambersburg: Wilson Books.

Directorate of Handlooms and Textiles, Tamilnadu. 1978. *Development of the Handloom Industry in Tamilnadu, Sixth Five Year Plan*. Madras: Department of Handlooms and Textiles.

Dubois, Abbe J. A. 1906. *Hindu Manners, Customs and Ceremonies*. 3rd ed. Trans. by Henry K. Beauchamp. Oxford: Clarendon Press.

Dumont, Louis. 1970a. A structural definition of a folk deity of Tamil Nad: Aiyanaar, the lord. In *Religion, Politics and History in India*, Louis Dumont, ed. The Hague: Mouton.

1970b. *Homo Hierarchicus: An Essay on the Caste System*. Chicago: University of Chicago Press.

Dutt, Romesh. 1903. *The Economic History of India in the Victorian Age*. London: Routledge & Kegan Paul.

Epstein, T. Scarlett. 1962. *Economic Development and Social Change in South India*. New York: Humanities Press.

Fox, Richard. 1970. Rajput "clans" and rurban settlements in northern India. In *Urban India: Society, Space and Image*, Richard Fox, ed. Program in Comparative Studies on Southern Asia, Monograph 10. Durham, N.C.: Duke University Press.

1971. *Kin, Clan, Raja, and Rule*. Berkeley: University of California Press.

Fox, Richard G., and Allen Zagarell. 1982. The political economy of Mesopotamian and south Indian temples: the formation and reproduction of urban society. *Comparative Urban Research* 9:8-27.

Frykenberg, R. E. 1977. Perspectives on social transformation in south India. Thirty-ninth annual meeting of the Association for Asian Studies, New York City. Mimeo.

Gittinger, Mattiebelle. 1982. *Master Dyers to the World: Technique and Trade in Early Dyed Cotton Textiles*. Washington, D.C.: Textile Museum.

Gough, E. Kathleen. 1955. The social structure of a Tanjore village. In *Village India*, McKim Marriott, ed. Chicago: University of Chicago Press.

1956. Brahmin kinship in a Tamil village. *American Anthropologist* 58:826-853.

1960. Caste in a Tanjore village. In *Aspects of Caste in South India, Ceylon, and North-West Pakistan*, E. R. Leach, ed. Cambridge Papers in Social Anthropology, No. 2. Cambridge: Cambridge University Press.

Government of Tamilnadu. 1978. *Development of the Handloom Industry in Tamilnadu, VI Five Year Plan.* Madras: Department of Handlooms and Textiles.

Hall, Kenneth R. 1980. *Trade and Statecraft in the Age of the Coolas.* New Delhi: Abhinav Publications.

1981. Peasant state and society in Chola times: a view from the Tiruvidai-marudur urban complex. *The Indian Economic and Social History Review* 18:393-410.

Hardgrave, Robert L., Jr. 1969. *The Nadars of Tamilnad: The Political Culture of a Community in Change.* Berkeley: University of California Press.

1970. Urbanization and the structure of caste. In *Urban India: Society, Space and Image,* Richard G. Fox, ed. Program in Comparative Studies on Southern Asia, Monograph 10. Durham, N.C.: Duke University Press.

Harper, Edward B. 1964. Ritual pollution as an integrator of caste and religion. In *Religion in South Asia,* Edward B. Harper, ed. Seattle: University of Washington Press.

Hart, George L., III. 1975a. Ancient Tamil literature: its scholarly past and future. In *Essays on South India.* Asian Studies at Hawaii, No. 15. Burton Stein, ed. Honolulu: University Press of Hawaii.

1975b. *The Poems of Ancient Tamil: Their Milieu and Their Sanskrit Counterparts.* Berkeley: University of California Press.

Heesterman, J. C. 1973. India and the inner conflict of tradition. *Daedalus* 102:97-113.

Indian Standard December 10, 1967.

Irschick, Eugene F. 1969. *Politics and Social Conflict in South India: The Non-Brahman Movement and Tamil Separation 1916-1929.* Berkeley: University of California Press.

1982. Bureaucracy and Society: Selective Perception and Political Choices in Twentieth-Century South India. Mimeo. Book manuscript.

Joy, Annama, and Brenda E. F. Beck. 1979. Coimbatore City—the historical background to its social composition at present. In *Perspectives on a Regional Culture,* Brenda E. F. Beck, ed. New Delhi: Vikas.

Khare, R. S. 1973. One hundred years of occupational modernization among Kanya–Kubja Brahmans. In *Entrepreneurship and Modernization of Occupational Cultures in South Asia.* Milton Singer, ed. Program in Comparative Studies on Southern Asia, Monograph 12. Durham, N.C.: Duke University Press.

Kolenda, Pauline M. 1968. Region, caste, and family structure: a comparative study of the Indian "joint" family. In *Structure and Change in Indian Society,* Milton Singer and Bernard S. Cohn, eds. Chicago: Aldine.

1978. *Caste in Contemporary India: Beyond Organic Solidarity.* Menlo Park, Calif.: Benjamin/Cummings.

Lynch, Owen M. 1967. Rural cities in India: continuities and discontinuities. In *India and Ceylon: Unity and Diversity,* Philip Mason, ed. New York: Oxford University Press.

Mackenzie, J. S. F., Capt. 1875. Caste insignia. *The Indian Antiquary* 4:344-346.

Mandelbaum, David G. 1970. *Society in India.* 2 vols. Berkeley: University of California Press.

Marriott, McKim. 1955. Little communities in an indigenous civilization. In *Village India,* McKim Marriott, ed. Chicago: University of Chicago Press.

1959. Interactional and attributional theories of caste ranking. *Man in India* 39:92-107.

1968. Caste ranking and food transactions: a matrix analysis. In *Structure and Change in Indian Society*, Milton Singer and Bernard S. Cohn, eds. Chicago: Aldine.

Marriott, McKim, and R. Inden. 1973. Caste systems. In *Encyclopaedia Britannica* 3:982-991.

1977. Toward an ethnosociology of south Asian caste systems. In *The New Wind*, Kenneth A. David, ed. The Hague: Mouton.

Mayer, Adrian C. 1960. *Caste and Kinship in Central India: A Village and Its Region*. Berkeley: University of California Press.

Meillasoux, Claude. 1973. Are there castes in India? *Economy and Society* 2:89-111.

Mencher, Joan P., and Helen Goldberg. 1967. Kinship and marriage regulations among the Namboodiri Brahmins of Kerala. *Man* n.s. 2:87-106.

Miller, Eric J. 1954. Caste and territory in Malabar. *American Anthropologist* 56:410-420.

Mines, Mattison. 1972. *Muslim Merchants: The Economic Behaviour of an Indian Muslim Community*. New Delhi: Sri Ram Centre for Industrial Relations and Human Resources.

1975. Islamisation and Muslim ethnicity in south India. *Man* n.s. 10:404-419.

1977. Kin centers and ethnicity among Muslim Tamilians. In *Papers in Anthropology* 18, 2:259-274. Norman: University of Oklahoma Press.

1982. Models of caste and the left-hand division in south India. *American Ethnologist* 9:467-484.

Moffatt, Michael. 1979. *An Untouchable Community in South India: Structure and Consensus*. Princeton, N.J.: Princeton University Press.

Murton, Brian J. 1973. Key people in the countryside: decision-makers in interior Tamilnadu in the late eighteenth century. *The Indian Economic and Social History Review* 10:157-180.

1979. The evolution of the settlement structure in northern Konku to 1800 A.D. In *Perspectives on a Regional Culture: Essays About the Coimbatore Area of South India*, Brenda E. F. Beck, ed. New Delhi: Vikas.

Nagata, Judith A. 1974. What is a Malay? Situational selection of ethnic identity in a plural society. *American Ethnologist* 1:331-350.

Naidu, B. V. Narayanaswami. 1948. *Report to the Court of Enquiry into Labour Conditions in the Handloom Industry*. Madras: Government Press.

Nilakanta Shastri, K. A. 1966. *A History of South India from Prehistoric Times to the Fall of Vijayanagar*, 3rd ed. Madras: Oxford University Press.

Obeyesekere, G. 1974. A village in Sri Lanka: Madagama. In *South Asia: Seven Community Profiles*, Clarence Maloney, ed. New York: Holt, Rinehart and Winston.

Opler, Morris E., and Rudra Datt Singh. 1948. The division of labor in an Indian village. In *A Reader in General Anthropology*, C. S. Coon, ed. New York: Henry Holt.

1956. The extensions of an Indian village. *The Journal of Asian Studies* 16:5-10.

Pfaffenberger, Bryan. 1980. Social communication in Dravidian ritual. *Journal of Anthropological Research* 36:196-219.

1982. *Caste in Tamil Culture: The Religious Foundations of Sudra Domina-*

tion in Tamil Sri Lanka. Foreign and Comparative Studies South Asian Series, No. 7. Syracuse, N.Y.: Syracuse University Press.

Pocock, D. F. 1960. Sociologies: urban and rural. *Contributions to Indian Sociology* 4:63-81.

———. 1962. Notes on Jajmani relationships. *Contributions to Indian Sociology* 6:78-95.

Raghavaiyanger, S. Srinivas. 1893. *Progress in the Madras Presidency During the Last Forty Years of British Administration.* Madras: Government Press.

Rowe, W. L. 1973. Caste, kinship and association in urban India. In *Cross-Cultural Studies of Urbanization,* A. Southall, ed. London: Oxford University Press.

Rudolph, Lloyd I., and Susanne Hoeber Rudolph. 1967. *The Modernity of Tradition: Political Development in India.* Chicago: University of Chicago Press.

Saberwal, Satish. 1971. Regions and their social structures. *Contributions to Indian Sociology* n.s. 5:82-98.

Salem Cooperative Spinning Mills. 1979. Short notes on the working of the mills. Typescript.

Schwartzberg, Joseph. 1967. Prolegomena to the study of south Asian regions and regionalism. In *Regions and Regionalism in South Asian Studies: An Exploratory Study,* Robert I. Crane, ed. Program in Comparative Studies on Southern Asia, Monograph 5. Durham, N.C.: Duke University Press.

Schwartzberg, Joseph, ed. 1978. *A Historical Atlas of South Asia.* Chicago: University of Chicago Press.

Senguntha Mittiran. 1930. Bavani real Sengunthars deserved success: again defeat for the Moolakkaarar. Vol. 4:132.

———. 1930. *Chittrai* issue. Vol. 4.

———. 1930. Decisions of Salem Ammapet Sengunthar Mahaajana Sangam. Vol. 4:138-139.

———. 1930. *MaarkaRi* issue. Vol. 4:439.

———. 1931-32. Resolutions of the Second MahaanaaDu. Vols. 5-6:131.

Senguntha Samuuha Kaittari, Maatar, Maanila MaanaaDu. 1976. Erode: Koovai MaavaDDa Sengunthar Mahaajana Sangam.

Stein, Burton. 1965. Coromandel trade in medieval India. In *Merchants and Scholars: Essays in the History of Exploration and Trade,* John Parker, ed. Minneapolis: University of Minnesota Press.

———. 1968. Social mobility and medieval south Indian Hindu sects. In *Social Mobility in the Caste System in India. Comparative Studies in Society and History, Supplement III,* James Silverberg, ed. The Hague: Mouton.

———. 1975. The state and the agrarian order in medieval south India: a historiographical critique. In *Essays on South India. Asian Studies at Hawaii, No. 15,* Burton Stein, ed. Honolulu: The University Press of Hawaii Press.

———. 1980. *Peasant State and Society in Medieval South India.* New Delhi: Oxford University Press.

Thurston, E. 1909. *Castes and Tribes of Southern India,* 7 vols. Madras: Government Press.

Turner, Victor. 1974. *Dramas, Fields, and Metaphors: Symbolic Action in Human Society.* Ithaca, N.Y.: Cornell University Press.

Washbrook, D. A. 1976. *The Emergence of Provincial Politics: The Madras Presidency, 1870-1920.* Cambridge: Cambridge University Press.

Glossary

Aachaari: artisan caste specializing in working gold, brass, iron, stone, and wood; they claim Brahman status and are the highest ranking of the former left-hand division of castes; also called Kammalar.

aaNDavar: head officer of the Kaikkoolar's highest territorial council, the MahaanaaDu; office and council now defunct.

ADMK: political party in Tamilnadu. Anna Dravida Munnetra Kazhagam.

Aiyanaar: important small god in Tamilnadu.

AkkarainaaDu: "other side of the river council territory"; a term sometimes used to refer to the council territory to which the Kaikkoolars of Erode belong, more accurately called PoondurainaaDu.

AngaaLammaa: a common Kaikkoolar family goddess.

annakaavaDi: a pole with bowls at both ends used by worshipers to carry offerings to God.

Ardhanaariisvarar: a manifestation of the god, Shiva, whose body is divided into male and female halves.

Ayyavole 500: medieval supralocal corporation of merchants.

Balija: Telugu merchant caste, often found in Tamilnadu.

bhakta: devotee.

brahmadeya: medieval Brahman settlements.

Brahman: a priestly and scholarly varna; also used to refer to any of a variety of jatis claiming Brahman status; often important landowners in Tamilnadu.

Chettiar: name of several Tamil and Teluga merchant castes, also used by the Teluga weaving caste, the Thevanga.

Chetty: variant of Chettiar.

CholamaNDalam: one of the five microregions of medieval south India.

cinnataali: "small tali," a subgroup of the Kaikkoolar caste; predominates in the EeRuurunaaDu.

Deepavali: fall festival of lights.

deeva-daasi: woman dedicated to a temple principally by VeLLaaLas (right-hand section) and Kaikkoolars (left-hand section), a practice now outlawed.

169

DMK: Dravida Munnetra Kazhagam, a political party in Tamilnadu.

drishti: supernatural force, e.g., *kaaN* drishti, evil eye.

EeRuurunaaDu: the seven-city council territory of the Kaikkoolars; corresponds to VaTa Konku, northern KonkumaNDalam, one of the five microregions of Tamilnadu, headquartered in Trichengode.

Ganapathi: the elephant god, also called Pillaiyaar and Vinayakar.

Gounder: VeLLaaLa caste of cultivators in western Tamilnadu, sometimes called VeLLaaLa Gounders or Konku VeLLaaLas; former rivals of the Kaikkoolars in right-hand/left-hand caste disputes in the Konku region.

gurupuja: worship of dead religious leaders.

iDangkai jati: left-hand caste, a category of castes of the left division.

IiTTiyeRabathu: title of collection of poems praising the Kaikkoolars, composed by the medieval Tamil poet, OTTakkuutar.

Iyengar: category of Brahmans, followers of Vishnu.

Iyer: category of Brahmans, followers of Shiva.

jajmani system: a customary, nonmarket division of labor involving inheritable service and ritual relations joining families of different castes.

jati: caste.

jatka: horse-drawn taxi.

kaariyakkaarar: officer of a naaDu council, next in rank to the presiding officer.

Kaarttikai: the Tamil month of November-December.

Kaikkoolar: a Tamil weaving caste, also known as Sengunthar Mudaliyar.

Kammalar: see Aachaari.

kasba: a market town.

Kavisakkravarttin: title given to Ottakkuutar, meaning king among poets.

KavuNTar: see Gounder.

khaadi: handspun, handloom cloth.

kiiRuur: east village, a subunit of a naaDu territory; location of a council one level higher than a village council in the Kaikkoolar's 72 naaDu system; also kiiRgraamam; meeLuur is its counterpart.

kiraamam: a revenue village and subunit of the VeLLaaLa's naaDu system; same as graamam.

KonkumaNDalam: one of the five traditional microregions of Tamilnadu, also KonkunaaDu.

KoorainaaDu: location of the TalaikooDa Kaikkoolars, the section of Kaikkoolars who refused to sacrifice sons for the medieval poet OTTakkuutar.

kooyil: temple.

Kshatriya: warrior varna.

kuDi: house.

kuDumpam: family.

kuladeevam: family god.

kumbaabisheekam: purification ritual of icons, temples, or other holy images.

kuuTTam: Kaikkoolar term for clan.

maaDa viiti: streets marking a temple's perimeter.

Maadeeri: leather worker caste, untouchables once of the left-hand section.

maanagaram: supralocal merchant organization in medieval Tamilnadu.

maapiLLai siir: wealth given to son-in-law by bride's parents during first years of marriage; custom abandoned by Kaikkoolars.

Maariyammaa: goddess who gives and protects people against smallpox.

MahaanaaDu: the highest council of the Kaikkoolar 72 naaDu system, now defunct.

maNDapam: rest hall often associated with a temple.

maNigraamam: confederacy of merchants in medieval south India.

mantiravaadi: black magician.

meeLuur: west village, a subunit of a naaDu territory, location of a council one level higher than a village council; kiiRuur, east village, is its counterpart in the Kaikkoolar's 72 naaDu system; also meeLgraamam.

moohini: female ghost.

Moolakkaaran: caste formed by the descendents of deeva-daasis, which claims Sengunthar Mudaliyar identity.

Mudaliyar: a caste title claimed by both VeLLaaLas and Kaikkoolars; it means "he who is first" and is given honors and respect.

munsif: native judge under British rule.

muppaaTTukkaarar: subcaste leader among Gounders at the kiraamam level.

naaDu: a council territory corresponding in the Kaikkoolar's 72 naaDu system to a confederacy of 30 or more villages; the third level in the Kaikkoolar system immediately above the kiiRuur and meeLuur councils; also, a general term meaning council territory, or council.

naaTTaaNmaikkaarar: head officer of a Kaikkoolar territorial council, or naaDu, also called periyathaanakaarar, "generous man"; occasionally naaTTar or naaTTavar.

naaTTar: head officer of a naaDu.

Naattukottai Chetty: wealthy mercantile caste in Tamilnadu.

naaTTavar: head officer of a naaDu.

Nadar: middle-ranked caste in Tamilnadu, formerly called Shanars, toddy tappers, an occupation they now disavow.

nagaram: the local organization of merchants in medieval Tamilnadu, which came to rival the cultivators' naaDus.

nagaswaram: an auspicious double reed woodwind musical instrument.

NavaviirarhaL: title of the nine original Kaikkoolars described in myths as the sons of Shiva.

OTTakkuutar: medieval Tamil poet and member of Kaikkoolar caste; considered a kavisakkravarttin, a king among poets.

paavaDi: grounds used by Kaikkoolars on which to stretch their warps.

paavu: warp.

Padaiyaachi: in KonkunaaDu a nondominant cultivator caste, which aspires to be identified as "Vannikula Kshatriya."

panchayat: village council.

pangaaLi: lineage coparcener.

Paraiyan: untouchable, commonly agricultural laborers, formerly of the right-hand section of castes.

parisam: bride wealth, wealth given by groom to his bride's family.

periyanaaDu: supralocal council territory, in the Kaikkoolar's 72 naaDu system; corresponds to the thisainaaDu, one of four council territories next in jurisdiction to the MahaanaaDu, the highest council territory.

Periyataali: "big tali," a section of Kaikkoolars also known as the Konku Kaikkoolars.

periyathaanakaarar: head officer of a Kaikkoolar naaDu council, also known as naaTTaaNmaikkaarar.

Pillaiyar: the elephant god, also Ganapathi and Vinayakar.

Pongal: Tamil harvest festival.

Prasaadam: food given to worshipers at temple, symbolic left-over food from the god's meal.

puja: worship.

Rattukaarar: a subgroup of Kaikkoolar weavers, rugweavers.

Rendukkaarar: a subgroup of Kaikkoolars who weave with a double-threaded warp.

Saliars: a caste of Tamil weavers.

Sambandam: men related through an affinal link.

SaamikaTTi Kaikkoolars: a subgroup of Kaikkoolars also called Cinnataali Kaikkoolars; characterized by a lingam tied to their arm, a custom now defunct.

sangam: association.

santhai: bazaar

Sengotuveelar: a form of the god Murugan found at Trichengode.

Sengunthar Mudaliyar: ritual name for the Tamil weaving caste, the Kaikkoolars.

Sowraashtraas: a caste of north Indian silk weavers who reside in Tamilnadu and claim to be Brahmans.

sannyaasi: individual in the final stage of his life; a wandering religious mendicant.

Taipuusam: festival to Murugan in the Tamil month of Tai (January-February).

teesikar: non-Brahman priest.

Udaiyaar: cultivator caste of Tamilnadu.

vaikasi: Tamil month of May-June.

Vaishnava: worshipers of the god, Vishnu.

vakaiyaraa: kindred, or kinsmen, whose relationship is ill-defined.

valangkai jati: right-hand caste, a category of castes centered around dominant cultivators, now defunct; castes of the right-hand divison.

VaTa Konku: northern Konku, roughly the area of the Kaikkoolar's EeRuurunaaDu.

VeeTTuva: a term distinguishing certain castes of KondunaaDu who were formerly of the left-hand section.

VeLLaaLas: group of cultivator castes in Tamilnadu.

VeLLaikkaikkoolar: a subgroup of the Kaikkoolar caste, also called Periyataalikaikkoolars or Konku Kaikkoolars; widows of this group wear white saris, hence the name.

vibuuti: ash marks worn on forehead by worshippers of Shiva after prayer.

Vinayakar: the elephant god, also called Ganapathi and Pillaiyar.

Index

Aachaari, *see* Kammalar
aaNDavar, 17, 88, 89, 90, 91, 95, 99
agriculturists, *see* right-hand castes
akam, 52
AkkarainaaDu, 24
All-India Handloom Board, 131
All-India Handloom Fabrics Marketing
  Cooperative Society, Ltd., 131
Ames, Michael M., 6
Ammapettai Handloom Weavers' Cooper-
  ative Society, 92-4, 129, 131-9, 134,
  135; leadership in, 135-6 and political
  power, 93, 138-9
Andhra Pradesh, 153
AngaaLammaa, 80
Anjuviittu NaaTTaaNmaikkaarar, 95
Anna Dravida Munnetra Kazhagam
  (ADMK), 118, 119, 123, 128, 129, 133,
  134, 139, 142
Annadurai, C., 133
annakaavadi, 58, 63
Appadurai, Arjun, 7, 28, 33, 34, 36, 37,
  38, 44, 45, 53, 100
Arasaratnam, S., 19, 133, 150, 152, 153
Ardhanaariisvarar temple, 52, 86, 87,
  154, 156
armies, *see* Kaikkoolar, armies
Arokiaswami, M., 13, 14, 16, 33, 43, 47,
  75, 76, 85, 151
association, *see* Sangam
Ayyavole 500, 13, 14, 43, 76, 150

Baker, Christopher, 21, 30, 34, 100-3, 106
Balasubramaniyam, C., x, 106, 110
Balija, 45
Barnett, Steven Alan, 7
Bean, Susan, 150, 151, 161

Beck, Brenda E. F., 5, 6, 7, 8, 9, 30, 32,
  36, 37, 38, 47, 48, 49, 68, 76, 77-81, 85,
  95-97, 143, 145
Beri Chettiar, 44, 68, 146
Beteille, André, 7
bhakta, 58
bound mode/nonbound mode, *see* caste
brahmadeyas, 74
Brahmans and caste models (*see also*
  caste), 67-70; and government service,
  101; and non-Brahman movement,
  101-2, 114-15, 158-9; and power, 74-5,
  76; as priests, 34, 35, 41, 53-4, 74, 75,
  86, 87, 100, 115, 144, 145, 159; and social order, 73-5, 104, 147, 160
Breckenridge, Carol, 7, 28, 34, 53
Brunner, Edward M., 31
Buchanan, Francis, 13, 16, 19, 28, 41, 45,
  48, 76, 95, 151, 153

caste (*see also* social change) bound
  mode/nonbound mode, 14, 33, 146; and
  class, 118-19; models of (*see also* kingly
  vs. priestly caste models), 67-71, 144-7,
  149, 162; organization of, 3-4, 30; political interests and, 102, 107-8, 123-4,
  159; right-hand/left-hand castes, *see*
  right-hand (*valangkai*)/left-hand
  (*iDangkai*) castes
caste association, *see* Sangam
casteism, 107-8
Census of India, 1961, 121, 123, 128, 136,
  141, 156
Chennimalai Weavers' Cooperative Production and Sales Society, Ltd. ("Chentex"), 130, 131

173

Chentex, *see* Chennimalai Weavers' Co-operative Production and Sales Society, Ltd.
Chola, 30, 36, 43, 44, 55, 56, 70, 150, 151, 152, 155, 161
cittirameeli periyanaaDu, 30
class, 118-19
Clothey, Fred W., 54
Congress Party, 93, 106, 117, 118, 122, 124, 125, 126, 128, 129, 131, 133, 134, 136-7, 140; Congress (I, Indira), 106, 107, 118
cooperative spinning mills, 125, 127, 128, 131, 137
Cooperative Union, Tamilnadu, 125
cooperatives, *see* handloom production cooperatives
Cooptex, 122, 123, 126, 127, 128, 129, 131, 133; development of, 131; govern-ment support of, 131-2, 133-4
cosmic realms and Kaikkoolar belief, 72; and *naaDu* system, 96; exterior cosmic realm, 52-61; interior cosmic realm, 61-7; interior (kin based) and exterior (state based) realms contrasted, 51, 52, 61, 63-4, 144, 163

David, Kenneth, 14, 32, 37, 68, 145, 146
deeva-daasi, 13, 15, 17, 27-9, 31, 34, 41, 46, 60-1, 67, 89, 95, 96, 100, 104, 149, 159, 162
Department of Handloom and Textiles, 133
Directorate of Handlooms and Textiles, 121
Dravida Munnetra Kazhagam (DMK), 106, 117, 123, 129, 132, 133, 138, 139
drishti, 65
Dumont, Louis, 4-5, 6, 7, 9, 70-1, 144, 145
Dutt, Romesh, 148
dyarchy, 35, 91, 93, 98, 99, 101, 104, 159

EeRuurunaaDu (Seven-City Territory), 8, 24, 25, 27, 52-4, 69, 81-90, 91, 97, 114, 115, 124, 126, 128, 132, 143, 148, 154, 156, 161, 162
entrepot: defined, 8
Epstein, T. Scarlett, 7

Fox, Richard G., 5, 6, 51n
Frykenberg, R. E., 16, 40, 45

Gandhi, Indira, 106, 107, 129, 133
Gandhi, M. K., 92, 93, 107, 110, 117, 124, 127, Mahatma Gandhi Society, 138

Gittinger, Mattiebelle, 12, 150
gods: as kings, 52, 55; small gods, 61-5, 78, 80
Goldberg, Helen, 7
gotram, 77
Gough, E. Kathleen, 7
Gounders, *see* VeLLaaLa
Government of Tamilnadu, 141
Govindar, Polivar, 133
gurupuja, 59

Hall, Kenneth R., 4, 9, 12, 26, 30, 36, 37, 42, 49, 76, 85, 89, 152, 155
handloom, *see* textile production
Handloom Export Promotion Council, 131
handloom production cooperatives, 22-4, 31, 69, 92-4, 110, 111, 119-20, 121-42, 147, 160; benefits from, 122, 126-7, 129, 130, 136, 137, 141; capital financ-ing, 131-2, 136, 138; and caste, 123; dyeing, 130; growth of, 121-2, 125-6, 133-4; housing, 126, 130, 131, 132, 136; and Kaikkoolar political decline, 123, 128-9, 132-3, 139, 142; leadership, 122, 125-9, 135-6, 140-2; loans, 126; and marketing, 111, 126, 130-1, 132, 134, 137, 141; and politics, 93, 122, 123, 127-9, 132, 133, 136-7, 138-9, 140-2; and *Senguntha Mahaajana Sangam*, 117; and state, 140-2, 160, 161; and yarn (*see also* cooperative spinning mills), 111, 127, 137; as social welfare, 111, 122, 134, 136, 138, 141; structure of, 122, 128
Hardgrave, Robert L., Jr., 30, 103, 108, 159
Harper, Edward B., 7
Hart, George L., III, 11, 12, 28, 52
Heesterman, J. C., 16, 32, 37, 67, 68, 70-1, 145
Hinduism, inner conflict, 70-1
Home Rule, 101

Inden, R., 144
Indian Standard, 12
Irschick Eugene F., 35, 99, 101, 102, 106, 110, 149

Jagadeesan, Subbalakshmi, 119
jajmani, 73
Joy, Annama, 6

kaariyakkaarar, 82, 86
Kaikkoolar (Sengunthar Mudaliyar), 7, 9-10, 11-32; armies, 12, 13, 16, 73, 76, 150; Beck, Brenda E. F. and, 80; be-liefs (*see also* cosmic realms), 51-72,

143-4, 163; caste subdivisions, 24-30, 96; and class, 118-119; and Congress Party, 122, 129; contrasted with kingly and priestly castes, 11-12, 67-70, 113-15, 146; cooperatives (*see also* handloom production cooperatives), 121-42; education, 90, 93, 94, 97, 98, 99, 102, 103, 105, 109-10, 113; and ethnicity, 31; identity (*see also naaDu;* regional organization, below) 11-12, 38, 40, 43, 54-5, 56-61, 72, 88, 90, 104, 105, 108, 157, 161-3; *IiTTiyeRabathu,* 56; kinship and marriage, 31, 62, 90-1, 94, 103, 104, 109, 115; local organization (*see also* residence pattern, below), 19-21, 66, 70, 81, 151-2, 162; meaning of names, 55; and Murugan/Shiva, 54, 57-60; occupational diversity, 118; origin myth, 54-5; parochialism and, 105; political interests of, 106, 117-19, 124, 157, 159; political structure of, 93, 117, 123, 129, 138-9; regional organization (*see also naaDu*), 14, 16-18, 24-32, 44, 48, 52-4, 65, 69, 72, 81-95, 143, 147, 152-4, 157, 161-2, 163; residence pattern (*see also* local organization, above), 46, 143, 151, 152; right-hand/left hand moiety (*see also* right-hand/left-hand castes), 13-15, 28, 70-1, 144, 146, 147, 151-2, 158, 162, 163; ritual sacrifice, 16, 52, 56-9, 61-2, 114, 144; rivalry and disputes, 14, 15, 16, 28, 39-40, 41-2, 43, 45-6, 65, 66, 88, 97, 105, 139-40, 147, 150-1, 162; *Sangam* (*see also Senguntha Mahaajana Sangam*), 21-2, 161; significance to anthropology, 32; size of weaving community, 123; social change, 23, 93, 99-103, 105, 109, 110-20, 123, 147, 158-60, 163; social status, 15-16, 74, 104, 115, 143-144, 147, 150-1, 161-3; as sodality, 70, 72; and states, 31, 63, 69-72, 98, 123-4, 147-52, 155-6, 158, 160, 163; and Tamil literature, 56-7; as temple builders and controllers, 35, 65-7; trade (*see also* textile trade), 13, 18-21, 26, 76-7, 154, 160, 162; Vishnavites, 16, 27; warriors (*see also* armies, above), 55, 57, 69, 73, 88, 98, 161-2; weaving (*see also* textile trade; textile production), 18-21, 121, 148, 158
Kallar, 71
kalyaaNam maNDapam (*see also maNDapam*), 81
Kamaraj Nadar, 125, 128, 129, 134, 136, 137; Kamaraj Weavers' Colony, 136
Kambar, 56

Kammalar (Aachaari), 42, 43, 45, 46, 47, 69, 76, 81, 95, 145, 146, 154
Karappan Aiyanaar, 60
Karappanasami, 57-9, 63, 64
Kasiviswanathan Mudaliar, *xii,* 124-9, 132, 136, 140
Kavisakkravarttin, 56
khaadi, 99, 110, 127
Khare, R. S., 6
kiiRuur naaDu, 17, 83, 95
King Kulottungaa III, 152
kingly vs. priestly caste models (*see also* caste; right-hand/left-hand castes), 67-71, 162
kiraamam, 77, 79
Kolenda, Pauline, 5, 6, 30, 145, 161
Konku, *see* KonkunaaDu
Konku barbers, 46
KonkunaaDu (*see also* VaTa Konku), 7, 8, 16, 19, 24, 44, 46, 47, 48, 54, 57, 71, 75, 76, 77, 79, 81-90, 96, 97, 114, 146, 147, 148, 149, 150, 152, 156, 159, 161
kooyil kanakkan: defined, 16
Kshatriya raj, 7, 73
kuDumpam, 77
kuladeevam, 26-7, 52, 61-4, 71, 78; defined, 15
kumbaabisheekam, 59, 63

land: and *naaDu* systems, 80, 86; as source of power, 4-5, 74
left-hand caste, 9; characterized, 3-4, 14; contrasted with right-hand castes, 4, 9, 80-1; *naaDus,* 81-95
left-hand/right-hand castes, *see* right-hand/left-hand castes
Lynch, Owen M., 4

maaDa viiti, 39, 55, 81
Maadeeri, 47
maanagarams, 154
maapiLLai siir, 115, 116
Maariyammaa, 38-9, 49, 64, 65, 83; *puundaarikaarar,* 65; *saambaveesam,* 65
Mackenzie, J. S. F., Capt., 89, 95
Madras Handloom Board, 125
Madras Provincial Handloom Weavers' Cooperative Society (Tamilnadu Handloom Weavers' Cooperative Society, Ltd.), *see* Cooptex
Madurai Viiran (*see also* gods), 63, 64
mahaanaaDu, 17, 89, 90, 91, 94, 95, 99, 155, 156
maNDapam: defined, 34; *kalyaaNam* (marriage halls), 81, 128, 130, 138; and *naaDus,* 95, 96; and right-hand/left-hand castes, 100

Mandelbaum, David G., 4, 5, 67
maNigraamam, 14, 43
mantiravaadi, 65
Mariyappan, A., 92, 130, 134-40
Mariyappan, E. A. R., 139
Mariyappan, P., 92, 134-6
marketing, *see* textile trade
Marriott, McKim, 4, 5, 43, 68, 144
masterweavers, *see* textile production
Mayer, Adrian C., 32, 37, 145
meeLuur naaDu, 17, 83, 95
Meillasoux, Claude, 36, 38
Mencher, Joan P., 7
merchants (*see also* textile trade), armed,
    89
Miller, Eric J., 7
Mines, Mattison, 16, 31, 37, 42, 62, 69,
    146, 151
Moffatt, Michael, 15, 39, 143, 144
Montagu-Chelmsford Report, 101
moohini, 64, 65
Moolakkaaran, 27-9, 31, 65, 66, 103-5
Mudaliyar, M. Shanmugam, 91
Mudaliyar, Nachumuttu, 110
Muniyappa (*see also* gods), 64
muppaaTTukkaarar, 78, 79
Murton, Brian J., 7, 19, 75, 76, 77, 78,
    97, 148, 150, 155, 159, 161
Murugan, 12, 15, 16, 38, 49, 52-5, 58-60,
    66, 71, 81, 83, 95, 158

naaDu: characterized and defined, 7, 8,
    75-7; characterized by Beck, Brenda E.
    F., 77-81; decline of, 23, 79-80, 88,
    90-4, 100, 105, 154, 159; development
    of, 89; and disputes, 79, 82, 83, 86, 88,
    97, 138, 155; dual territorial nature of,
    156-7; functions of, 82, 83, 87-8;
    Gounder officer (also *naaTTu* Gounder
    or *naaTTar*), 79; Kaikkoolar officer (or
    naaTTavar or *periyathaanakaarar),* 82,
    86, 95; Kaikkoolar system (72 *naaDus;*
    see also* Kaikkolar, regional organiza-
    tion), 16-18, 19, 26-31, 44, 48, 61, 62,
    69, 81-95, 143, 147, 152, 154, 155, 166,
    161, 163; Kaikkoolar/VeLLaaLa sys-
    tems contrasted, 77, 85-6, 95-8, 162;
    Kasiviswanathan, 126, 128; kinship ba-
    sis of, 77-81, 86, 96; and land owner-
    ship, 76, 79; and left-hand/right-hand
    castes, 34, 37, 38, 40, 42, 48, 76, 80-1,
    85, 95, 147; *naTTaaNmaikkaarar,* 126,
    153; officers of, 78-9, 82, 86, 95, 153,
    156; political use of, 134-6, 157; size of,
    77-8; and small and high gods, 79, 80;
    and social order, 73-75; and states, 74,
    78, 89, 97, 98, 147, 152-6; structure of,

17, 29, 77-81, 81-90, 95-8, 154, 159;
    taxation, 76, 78, 82, 83, 153, 155;
    temples, 76-9, 86, 95, 96, 152, 154-6,
    158, 162; and territorial domain, 87-8;
    trade, 75, 76, 89-90, 97, 98, 150, 152-6,
    160; VeLLaaLa system, 77-81
naaTTar, see naaDu
NaaTTavar, see naaDu
Naattukottai Chetty, 102, 103
Nachumuttu Mudaliyar, 125-6, 130-4,
    136, 140
Nadar, 48, 103
Nadavadikkai, 88
nagaram, 14, 42, 89, 152, 154
nagaswaram, 87, 89
Nagata, Judith A., 31
Naidu, B. V. Narayanaswami, 19, 103, 156
Nairs, 102
Natesan, A. 135
Natesan, C., *xii*
Nattuvan, 29
NavaviirarhaL, 54-5
Nilakanta Shastri, K. A., 57
nonbound mode, *see* caste
non-Brahman movement, 93, 100-2,
    114-15

Obeyesekere, G., 6
Opler, Morris E., *x,* 5, 73
OTTakkuutar, 11, 27, 56-7, 59, 144

paalaiyams, 78
PaavaDi grounds, 40, 66, 81
paavaDi naaDu, 17, 81-3, 89, 91, 94, 155
paavu, defined, 17
Padaiyaachi, 41, 47, 71, 82, 109, 146
panchayat, 73
pangaaLi, 63
Paraiyan, 47
parisam, 115
pattakkaarar, 77, 79, 80, 95
Periyar, *see* Ramaswami Naicker, E. V.
periyathaanakaarar, 86
Pfaffenberger, Bryan, 7, 42, 47
Place, Lionel, 149
Pocock, David F., 4, 6, 32, 37, 145
powerlooms, *see* textile production
puja, 47, 49, 52-4, 64, 68, 76, 82; defined,
    2
puram, 52
Purattaasi ADMK (Purattaasi Anna Dra-
    vida Munnetra Kazhagam), 139; Ne-
    dunchurian, 139

Raghavaiyanger, S. Srinivas, 103
Rajagopalachariya, C. ("Rajaji"), 92,
    124, 125, 129, 134-5, 137

Ramaswami Naicker, E. V. (Periyar), 93, 102
residence patterns, 66
right-hand caste, 3-4, 8; and states, 68; "bound-mode," 14
right-hand (*valangkai*)/left-hand (*iDangkai*) castes (*see also* caste), 14, 28, 33-50, 80-1, 100, 104, 133, 152, 158-9, 162; caste status, 34, 100; characterized, 34, 41, 70-1, 80-1, 145-147; cities, divided by, 45-6, 152, 162; disputes, 34, 38-40, 45, 105, 159, 162; origins of, 36-7; replication of 46-7, 49; separation of, 45, 46, 66-7; and social order, 73, 151, 157, 160; taxation and, 47, 71
Rowe, W. L., 6
Rudolph, Lloyd I., 108
Rudolph, Susanne Hoeber, 108

Saberwal, Satish, 8
sabhaa raj, 74
sacrifice, 56-9, 61, 63, 65
sakti, 58
Salem Cooperative Spinning Mills, Ltd., 118, 127, 131-2, 137-8; caste composition of, 138
Saliars, 122
Sambandam, S. K. 132
sambandam, 135
Sangam, see Senguntha Mahaajana Sangam
Sastri, Lal Bahadur, 128
Schwartzberg, Joseph, 8, 12
Seela naaDu, 83
Senapur, 73
Sengotuveelar (*see also* Murugan), 52
Senguntha Mahaajana Sangam (*Sangam*), 22, 23, 29, 31, 69, 91, 94, 99-120, 130, 147, 158, 160; accomplishments, 108-20; and caste behavior, 105, 109, 113, 159; and community, 115-116; decline of 106-8, 140, 160; and education, 113, 117, 140; formation of, 103-5, 108; and handloom industry, 105, 117, 140, 160; and marriage rules, 109; and *naaDu* system, 100, 105, 108; and non-Brahmanism, 105; and political interests, 106, 107-8, 117-18, 119, 121, 122, 140, 159, 160, 161; and social welfare, 111, 126; and weaving, 110, 121, 140
Senguntha Mittiran, 66, 102, 104, 105, 106, 109, 114, 115, 116, 118
Sengunthar Mudaliyar, *see* Kaikkoolar
Senguntha Samuuha Kaittari, Maatar, Maanila MaanaaDu, 81
Seven-City Territory, *see EeRuurunaaDu*
Shiva (Saivism), 15, 16, 49, 52-4, 57-60, 79, 95, 96

silai, 59
Singh, Rudra Datt, 73
sittan, 59
social change, 6, 10, 30-2, 35-6, 75, 80, 99-103, 105, 109, 111-20, 158-60, 163
South India (*see also* social change; Kaikkoolar); characterized, 7, 43, 73-5, 151, 158-60; contrasted with north India, 6-7, 73
Sowraashtraas, 122
states, 31, 63, 69-72, 89, 98, 155-156; dual territorial sense of, 155-7
Stein, Burton, 7, 12, 13, 14, 16, 17, 19, 30, 33, 36, 37, 38, 42, 43, 44, 46, 73, 74, 75, 76, 77, 78, 85, 147, 150, 155, 159
Subramaniyam, C., 107
Sudra, 74
Suurabatman, 11, 54-5

TalaikooDa Mudaliyars, 27, 57
talamai naaDu, 85
taali: defined, 24
tallivaittal, 92
Tamil-speaking Muslims, 62-3
taNDalkaaran, 82, 87
taxation, 47, 71, 76, 89
teesikar, 66, 158; defined, 15
temples, 6-7, 28, 78, 158; as definers of caste domains (*naaDus*), 52-54, 61, 65, 70, 77, 95, 96, 100, 158; and honors, 42, 45, 47, 49, 52, 61, 67, 68, 104; and kin and kingly cosmic domains, 78; as kingly palace, 28, 55, 98; and *kuladeevam,* 62; and left-hand/right-hand castes, 34, 38, 40, 48, 49, 66-7, 162; as political-economic institutions, 35, 37, 42, 51, 77, 135; and trade, 75
territory, *see naaDu*
textile production (*see also* textile trade; weaving), 107, 110, 111, 117, 147; and cooperatives, 118, 119, and export, 111-2, 123; governmental support of, 117, 119-20, 127, 131, 133, 134; handlooms vs. powerlooms, 107, 112, 113, 119, 131; masterweavers, 126, 130; policy, 122; powerlooms, 110, 111, 112, 113, 118, 127, 131; size of, 111, 121; weavers, 110-11, 112, 118, 119, 131, 137, 151
textiles, 18-19, 147-50, 161; ritual exchange of, 148-9, 161
textile trade (*see also* weaving), 4, 12, 18-21, 25-6, 31, 77, 99, 107, 110, 111, 148, 149-52; *entrepots,* 26; export, 112;

marketing, 127, 130-131; master-weavers, 19, 20, 110; merchants, 20, 29, 107, 112, 150, 153; and *naaDus*, 98, 148, 150, 152-6, 158, 160, 161; and state, 31, 37, 76-7, 149-56; and temples, 37; taxation, 151, 155
Thevanga Chettiar, 7, 122, 138
thisainaaDu, 17, 26, 85-7, 95, 155
Thurston, E., 28, 44, 46, 49, 81, 95, 100
tiruvoodu, 58
trade, (*see also* textile trade), 42, 44
Turner, Victor W., 44

Udaiyaar, 48
Urumaa Kattaradu (*see also* Kammalar), 44
uur, 77
Uur Gounder, 49, 78, 79, 80, 95

Vaikasi Teer festival, 82, 86
vakaiyaraa, 27
Valangkaiyars, 152
Vanniyar Kulashattriya, 56
VaTa Konku, *see* konkunaaDu, 7, 24
VeeTTuva barbers, 46

VeeTTuva Gounders, 47, 71, 82, 155
vegetarianism, 15
VeLLaaLas (including Gounders and Konku VeLLaaLas), 13, 15, 16, 27, 28, 39, 40, 41, 42, 43, 44, 45, 46, 47, 48, 49, 65, 67, 74, 75, 76, 77, 79, 85, 95-7, 105, 112, 114, 133, 147, 150, 151, 152, 162; *naaDu* system and descent, 76, 77-81; as priests, 78
vibuuti, 59
Vijayanagar; state, 44, 78, 150, 152, 154; times, 76, 89, 155
Viirabaahu, 54

warriors, *see* Kaikkoolar, armies
Washbrook, D. A., 21, 30, 34, 101
weavers (*see also* textile production; textile trade); and cooperatives, 122, 138
weaving (*see also* textile trade) 7, 8; importance in Tamilnadu, 121; weaving communities in Tamilnadu, 122
worship, *see puja*

Zagarell, Allen, 51n